NO MORE

God Bless America!

Dr. Ron Mast

KatEisenman
1.20.2017

NO MORE

TAKING BACK AMERICA

IF I WERE PRESIDENT
THE FIRST 100 DAYS

Dr. Thomas Masters

WE THE PEOPLE of the United States, in Order to form a more perfect Union, establish Justice, insure domestic Tranquility, provide for the common defense, promote the general Welfare, and secure the Blessings of Liberty to ourselves and our Posterity, do ordain and establish this Constitution for the United States of America (September 17, 1787).

The Constitution is not an instrument for the government to restrain the people, it is an instrument for the people to restrain the government.

—Patrick Henry

In this present crisis, government is not the solution to our problem; government is the problem.

—Ronald Reagan

CONTENTS

APPENDIX:

ACKNOWLEDGMENTS

Most authors place this part of the book at the end of the book along with whatever voluminous notes and bibliographies that corroborate their work. This book, while rooted in the practical aspects of the subject matter, is still a work of fantasy—my fantasy on what would happen if someone who is a true patriot and conservative were to be elected president. In writing this book I relied mostly on my own knowledge and experience, but I also used the guidance provided by many conservative authors and their works on our country and our destiny. This section is devoted to these authors, their works, and their thoughts. Without their guidance, albeit unintentional, this book could not have been written. Words cannot express my gratitude for all those listed in this section and others who I may have unintentionally forgotten to mention. I ask pardon in advance for any forgetfulness on my part; it was not on purpose. I would encourage any readers of this book to read any or all of the following works by these listed authors. Their gifts of the written word are far superior to mine.

AUTHORS AND WORKS:
1. Mark Levin, *The Liberty Amendments*, *Plunder and Deceit*, and *Liberty and Tyranny*
2. Ann Coulter, *Adios, America* and *Mugged*
3. Dennis Prager, *The Ten Commandments*
4. Mark Steyn, *America Alone* and *After America*
5. Bret Stephens, *America in Retreat*
6. James Rickards, *The Death of Money*
7. Michelle Malkin, *Who Built That*
8. George Gilder, *Wealth and Poverty*

9. Serge Trifkovic, *The Sword of the Prophet*
10. Robert Spencer, *Arab Winter Comes to America*
11. *New American Bible: St. Joseph Edition*
12. The US Constitution

SECTION 1

THE JOURNEY BEGINS

Introduction (September 11, 2014)

227 Years Later . . .

I have always been a patriot. My grandparents came to America from Poland and Russia over one hundred years ago, enduring the rigors of Ellis Island and settling in New Jersey. All were hardworking immigrants working to the day they died, providing for their families. My grandmother told the story of how during the Depression, in order to save their house from foreclosure, she moved her family and my disabled grandfather into the basement and rented out the rooms in the house to factory workers. The workers each paid five dollars a week for complete room and board including laundry. My mother tells of how during this period, she and her sisters would walk along the railroad tracks and pick up pieces of coal for cooking and heating the house. My grandparents endured the rigors of world wars, the Great Depression, and the beginnings of the Great Society, of which the progressives are so proud. I represent three generations of military service: my father served during World War II and Korea, my service was during the Vietnam War, and my son served in Iraq.

My father was a great man; what more can I say? He retired after twenty-five years of service in both the navy and the army. He was at Pearl Harbor on December 7, 1941. My mother tells the story that because of the news blackout, she did not know if he was alive or dead for almost three months after the attack. With God's help, he survived the wars and was able to have a bountiful life, raising five children in this great country of ours.

The above is my heritage, and this book may be my legacy. It is a work of fantasy, dreaming of a world that was and a country that was and what has happened to that country since the tumultuous days of the 1960s. America was founded on God-ordained principles not seen in the past. God blessed our young nation with people like George Washington, Thomas Jefferson, James Madison, John Adams, and Benjamin Franklin, individuals totally unique in the course of history in the fact they came together to form the USA and devise a form of government, a republic, destined to shine above all others. Others followed—Abraham Lincoln, Theodore Roosevelt, Ronald Reagan—taking up the continuing fight to uphold America and the Constitution that forms the basis of our laws. These were not perfect men—no one is—and this is not a perfect country—no country is—but compared to all others in the history of man on earth, nothing comes close.

However, in the last fifty years our country has fallen off the path. We live in a sort of "Twilight Zone," a popular TV show in the '60s in which what was real becomes something else. As the caption used to say, "You have entered the Twilight Zone." These last ten years have seen the ever-hastening decline of our country. We are not being conquered from the outside, we are succumbing from within.

I will attempt to break out of the Twilight Zone in which the country has been ensconced for the last fifty years and endeavor to steer the ship of state back to headings envisioned by forefathers. I suppose many of you have thought about the phrase, "If I were president . . ." I would do this and that and stop the insanity that has become our country. I would right the wrongs and stop its socialization. We are becoming the United Socialist States of America, and not the United States of America. As Harry Truman once said, "The buck stops here!" This book will point the way toward stopping the insanity. Many of the following pages will offend many in this country and around the world. So be it! I was born in a different country than the one that exists now, and I will fight to get it back.

"GOD BLESS AMERICA!"

INAUGURATION DAY

"I DO SOLEMNLY SWEAR THAT I WILL SUPPORT AND DEFEND THE CONSTITUTION OF THE UNITED STATES OF AMERICA AGAINST ALL ENEMIES, FOREIGN AND DOMESTIC; THAT I WILL BEAR TRUE FAITH AND ALLEGIANCE TO THE SAME; THAT I TAKE THIS OBLIGATION FREELY WITHOUT ANY MENTAL RESERVATION OR PURPOSE OF EVASION; AND THAT I WILL WELL AND FAITHFULLY DISCHARGE THE DUTIES OF THE OFFICE WHICH I AM ABOUT TO ENTER. SO HELP ME GOD."

"Mister President, Mister President."

My mother looks at me and says quietly, "Tommy, I think he is talking to you."

I look around and a marine is standing before me. He says, "Mister President, it is time for you on the stage." I smile and follow him to the balustrade.

Looking out at all the thousands of people standing out in this cold day of January 2017, I think back on my journey to this place and time. All the people who supported me these past fifteen months, the volunteers, the myriad people believing in me and my mission. I quietly shake my head. I look at the vice president, who is standing there with her family. She was so taken aback when I asked her to join my campaign. I even advised her against running with me. She chose the adventure even though there have been many who have vilified her and her beliefs. I look at the former president askance. The contempt on his face is barely concealable. He knows what is coming down; he knows that I will use all my resources to reverse or nullify as many of his presidential dictums as possible. His legacy will be that of a failed president, just like Carter.

Now it is time, and I head to the justice who will perform the oath of office. I put my hand on the Bible, which is actually my father's Bible. I can imagine him looking at me from above and smiling—that is, if saints smile. The oath starts, "I do . . ."

I walk to the podium and wait for the applause to stop. This is the time, this is the place; here history will be made. I hold my notes in my hand but probably will not use them. The teleprompter is vacant; my speechwriters offered to write the speech, but what they wrote was not me, so I said, "Thanks, but no thanks." I look out at the audience and say silently, "Dear Lord, guide me in this endeavor. Help me do Your will." I feel better.

"My fellow Americans, before I start on my speech, I ask your indulgence. If you will all stand wherever you are, face our flag or imagine our flag and repeat with me:

'I pledge allegiance to the Flag of the United States of America, and to the Republic for which it stands, one Nation under God, indivisible, with liberty and justice for all.'

"Now if you will indulge me again while the band plays one of my favorite songs ever, a song by George M. Cohan, 'It's a Grand Old Flag.' For those of you who know the words, feel free to sing along." (Appendix D)

As the band plays, I smile and start to relax. My heart is beating a little more slowly. I take a sip of water and look out at the vastness of the throngs and the city. Washington, DC, has been a symbol of our country's greatness, but it has, like our country, grown small. The vast majority of Americans do not trust the government or any of its governmental institutions. Congress is held in contempt and the justice system abounds in radicalism. The last eight years have been a total Obamanation, pardon my sarcasm. The song ends and now it is my turn again. I see many smiling faces and many not-so-smiling. God bless them all!

"Thank you all for coming here today and listening to my oration. I am totally humbled to be standing here. I have had a chance to read some of the inaugurals from prior presidents and know that my talents are not nearly as bountiful as theirs. I will try to do my best.

"I am a very pragmatic man. Others may have the flowery words and catchphrases and the rhetoric that goes with the speeches. Mine will focus on the here and now and outlining to you all that will be coming down the road. All presidents have advisors, and I do also, so I should take the time to introduce my two main advisors." I hold up my Bible in my right hand.

"The first is my family Bible, from which I read something every day. I am a Christian, plain and simple. I do not apologize for my faith and am very proud to be Catholic. Without God, I, you all, and this nation will not survive. So this is my guide. The next advisor is this little booklet, only thirty pages long, but it is the foundation of our country." Here I hold up the Constitution in my left hand. "Hard to believe that the foundation of our whole republic is written in thirty small pages. The Affordable Care Act was over two thousand pages. How far we have come!

"As you all are aware, I am not a professional politician. My profession is that of a physician. I believe that God has called me to this task of being president in order to start the healing of America. Since I am not a professional statesman, you may ask, then just what are my priorities in career and life? Many years ago, while I was in medical school, I attended a class taught by an elderly doctor, whose name unfortunately escapes me. He was lecturing on the hardships of medicine as a career and how many doctors ended their marriages in divorce and had drinking and drug abuse problems. He gave the class his dictum. 'We all need priorities, and if we keep our priorities, we can navigate very difficult waters.' The priorities were one, God; two, family; three, country; four, career; five, self. As long as one kept those priorities in that order, one was safe. I have always kept those priorities as much as possible.

"Because I am a faithful man, I have made arrangements to attend Mass each morning here in the White House. Sundays I will attend Mass in the Immaculate Conception Church in Washington. I would encourage you for whatever religion to attend services each and every Sunday. I would also encourage you to devote a little time each day in prayer to God. Believe me, it is time well spent. We all need sustenance and guidance throughout our lives, and daily prayer goes a long way to achieving peace of mind and soul. Those of you who are blessed with families and children hopefully incorporate God into your daily lives. Our children look to parents for love and guidance. As I said above, the Bible is a beautiful book to be read as much as possible for answers in life.

"After church services, my routine will be to have breakfast with my family. Many days there will be two breakfasts, one personal and the other professional. I plan on meeting regularly with my cabinet; the top members of Congress, both House and the Senate; the joint chiefs of staff; members of various churches in the USA; business leaders; foreign dignitaries; and the like. I intend to stay in touch and listen attentively to the beating of America's heart from as many sources as possible. Polls are not the answer, personal contact is the answer.

"Now, let us look at my daily routine over at least the next hundred days. As a representative of you, the people, my job and my actions should be an open book. To that end, the presidency will again become a full-time job. Each Monday the media and you, the people, will get my time card from the prior week. The private sector accounts for hours worked and so should I. I promise that there will be a full week's work done each and every week. Time on the golf course is not working. My vacation should be limited to what the private sector has, two weeks a year. I urge members of Congress to follow my actions and start working full-time also, and not campaigning or taking extended breaks. Congress works an average of one hundred and thirty days a year, less than half the time of those in the private sector. But they still get paid for full-time. This must end.

"My daily routine will be of paramount importance to you, the citizens of the USA and the world at large. In the last fifty years America has lost much of its greatness, not from being conquered but from a loss of heart. We have been infected and, like all infections, if not checked, we the host can and will be destroyed. This disease, progressivism, liberalism, socialism, Marxism, whatever you may like to call it, is a cancer destroying us and our way of life. This cancer has spread slowly over the last fifty years, infecting all our hallowed institutions, our schools, our government, our military, and much of our private sector. I hear talks of secession and I can sympathize with the fears that provoke this response. Sadly, we have regressed from a God-fearing nation to a fearful, increasingly godless nation. We have become afraid of our own shadow both in our private and public lives. Political correctness has taken over everywhere. Every time someone says something controversial, that person is immediately lambasted as racist, homophobic, anti-women, anti-Hispanic, anti-everything. I ask you, America, what happened to free speech guaranteed by the Constitution?" Here I read the First Amendment. "Does anyone remember the quote from Evelyn Hall from her biography *The Life of Voltaire* where she states, 'I may not agree with what you say, but I will defend to the death your right to say it'?

"With this in mind, every day for the next hundred days, I will address the nation with a particular problem and our solution to that problem. These problems will cover the broad spectrum of our society, border issues and immigration, social issues like race, culture, and language, Big Brother issues of our government and how to remedy them, economic issues and how to jumpstart the engine of our country, capitalism, foreign affairs, and our military. The only break in the routine will be that each Sunday will be a day of rest, for me and those of you who believe in the Sabbath—a day to worship in the church of your choice.

"My remedies will encompass not only actions by my executive branch, but actions by Congress, and, most importantly, actions by a Constitutional Convention of the States to address possible new amendments to our Constitution to regain control over what has been lost these fifty years.

"I know many of you are now leery of what will be coming down the road. I can assure you that each day's problem and solution will be significant to our future as a nation and as a people. Much of what I will address will be welcomed by many, much will be scoffed at, and much will be resented. I can promise you this: the two advisors I mentioned earlier, the Bible and the Constitution, will be my guides over the next hundred days.

"To give you a taste of the difficult topics that will be addressed, I will outline just two:

"Since the pilgrims landed in what is now the state of Massachusetts in 1620, the language of our country has been English. All our official documents are in this language; the two most important documents of our society, the Declaration of Independence and the Constitution, are in English. This language is taught in our schools and is the main language of commerce throughout the world. Our heritage is the English language, not

German, not Russian, not Spanish, not Chinese, not Arabic. However, there is a repugnant movement to replace English with multilingualism. Official documents are printed in various languages. Even voting documents are printed in numerous languages. NO MORE! To be a citizen of the USA, you must speak English. I will propose that Congress pass a law, which I will immediately sign, to make English the official language of the USA. If Congress fails to act, I will propose a constitutional amendment to make it so. In the interim, I will issue an executive order making all government documents used in our country to be in English only, including all voting documents.

"Theodore Roosevelt addressed the next problem over a hundred years ago. He stated in a speech that 'hyphenated Americans' are not true Americans because their allegiance is often to the hyphenation rather than to the word 'American.'[1] However, in the past hundred years, we have become a hyphenated nation with emphasis not on being an American, but on whatever the hyphenation is. Much of this was done in the name of the mantra, diversity. NO MORE! I will issue an executive order eliminating in government documents all references to cultural, ethnic, biological, and religious distinctions where possible. Americans will be stated as Americans. If there is a qualifier, such as race, ethnicity, religious affiliations, these will come after the word 'American,' not before. Those of you who attach more importance to the hyphenation than to the word 'American' should think about where your loyalties are.

"Other major areas of discussion these coming days will be the state of our economy and how to jumpstart this magnificent engine called capitalism. In the words of a famous president, 'Government

---

[1] Roosevelt, Theodore. "Hyphenated American." Speech, Carnegie Hall, New York City, October 13, 1915.

is not the answer to the economy, government is the problem.' I think it is time for the government to stand aside and let the private sector do what it does best—run the engine!

"Now what does any engine need to run? It is simple: fuel, and the fuel for our engine is energy, namely, petroleum! All the monies poured into alternative fuels have largely failed. I do not see any airplanes, for example, running on solar power. The trucking and railroad industry upon which our country relies for moving goods and services around the nation will not be running on solar power, or electricity, or wind power in the foreseeable future. So it is petroleum that has and will continue to fuel our economy. Seventy years ago, our country was the largest exporter of petroleum-based products in the world.[2] We went from that scenario to the largest importer! How sad! And even sadder is that we have had to import oil and be reliant on countries who are not our friends and in many cases despise us. NO MORE! The soothsayers have been predicting the end of oil for the last hundred years, and they have been wrong, wrong, wrong. We have proven reserves of oil and gas to last from five hundred to a thousand year,[3] and more reserves are discovered every day. The oil shale in the western states has not even been tapped. We built the Alaskan pipeline over forty years ago over the objections of the environmentalists, who predicted disaster to the animal life and plant life in Alaska. All predictions were proven

---

[2] "Oil - The Origins of U.S. Foreign Oil Policy." Encyclopedia of the New American Nation. Accessed June 14, 2016.
http://www.americanforeignrelations.com/O-W/Oil-The-origins-of-u-s-foreign-oil-policy.html.
[3] Clemente, Jude. "U.S. Oil Reserves, Resources, and Unlimited Future Supply." Forbes. April 2, 2015.
http://www.forbes.com/sites/judeclemente/2015/04/02/u-s-oil-reserves-resources-and-unlimited-future-supply/#12d896585dab.

false.[4] The sad aspect of this venture is that the natural gas reserves in Prudhoe Bay are still there, waiting to be extracted. These gas reserves in Alaska vastly outweigh the oil reserves. NO MORE. This office will be working with the State of Alaska to start the gas pipeline ASAP. Forty years is enough of a stalemate. My goal is to have the gas pipeline be completed before the end of my term. Think of the jobs that will be created with this pipeline. I lived in Alaska during the oil pipeline construction. The economy boomed not only in Alaska, but the whole Pacific Northwest. Let's do it again!

"Congress and the prior president have stalled the Keystone Pipeline for years. NO MORE! I am issuing an executive order to immediately start working on the pipeline. Not only will it provide thousands of needed jobs, it will help reduce our dependency on foreign oil.

"Speaking of dependency, it is often an ugly word whether speaking about personal relationships or institutions. We have been dependent far too long on foreign sources for our energy. NO MORE! I am setting a goal for our nation that in five years, we will be totally energy independent and will be a major exporter of petroleum products, both oil and natural gas.

"I will be working with Congress to pass a number of measures. One will be to increase the number of oil refineries in the US threefold in the next five years. We will erect at least five natural gas refineries in the US for refining and distillation of natural gas for usage in vehicles and also for export to other nations. I will

---

[4] Anderson, R. Warren. "Alaska Pipeline Doomsayings Revisited." Media Research Center. April 19, 2006. http://www.mrc.org/news/alaska-pipeline-doomsayings-revisited.

ensure that the government agencies that have been hampering building refineries will be curtailed in the future.

"T. Boone Pickens, the oil entrepreneur, a number of years ago had a plan to create an infrastructure of natural gas outlets around the nation and convert cars and trucks to run on natural gas. The expense at that time was around five hundred dollars per vehicle. But the savings, folks, are immense. The natural gas equivalent to regular gas is one-third. Yes, think of gas prices at the pump for less than two dollars a gallon. The savings for our nation would be colossal. Transportation costs would drop by over fifty percent. The cost of moving goods will drop. I have asked Mr. Pickens to help my administration in this project. The fueling stations are already in place, we just need to expand them to include natural gas pumps. I am directing that all vehicles in the executive branch be converted to natural gas by the end of the year where feasible.

"Speaking of alternative energy sources, the one proven alternative which has been lambasted in the past twenty years but is the most sustainable, the most economical, and has the ability to meet the electrical needs of vast numbers of our cities and population, is nuclear power plants.[5] Here again the government has served mainly to stymie the startup of any and all nuclear power plants. This is insane and must stop. This presidency is committed to tripling the number of nuclear power plants in the USA in the next ten years. I long for the day when there is at least one nuclear power plant in each state of the USA.

"The next alternative power source which has been around for ages is, of course, solar power. I think it ironic that in the last fifty

---

[5] "Quick Facts: Nuclear Energy in America." Nuclear Energy Institute. July 2015. http://www.nei.org/Master-Document-Folder/Backgrounders/Fact-Sheets/Quick-Facts-Nuclear-Energy-in-America.

years of technological marvels, the technology behind solar power has not progressed. As usual, I think the government is the problem. I urge the private sector to expand research into this area and take the lead in developing more efficient and cheaper solar convertors for the consumer. I urge the utility companies, who I suspect have not been pushing this source of power, to step up to the plate and increase the solar industry. Folks, we get up every morning and there is the one constant in our lives, the sun. Not harnessing this in increasing amounts is downright foolish.

"There are many other aspects of our economy that I will address in the coming days. Our government now consumes over twenty-five percent of GDP. [6] That is absurd and must be addressed. The tax structure, both corporate and personal, is debilitating to the economy. We as a people get taxed in almost every aspect of our lives, from buying gas to buying groceries. Between federal, state, local, property, and sales taxes, there is precious little left for our own use. NO MORE! We fought a revolution to stop taxation without representation and here it is two hundred forty years later, and we are still fighting the same battle, only it is not England who is the villain; it is WASHINGTON.

"The subject of government waste and corruption is a constant theme in our lives. Much of my talks over these next few months will address the leviathan called the federal government. My talks will identify specific areas in our government wasteland where cuts will start to be made. Balancing the budget will be one of my highest priorities. Every family in the US has to live within their budgets or they will go bankrupt. The government should be

---

[6] "What Is the Total US Government Spending?" US Government Spending. Accessed June 14, 2016. http://www.usgovernmentspending.com/.

required to do the same. Again, all the soothsayers will say it can't be done. Well, one of the big keys to healing our economy and our country is stopping the infection of big government.

"There are now over fifteen cabinet members and agencies that report to the president. I promise that by the end of my term, that number will be cut in half. Agencies that curtail the people will not be cut back, but eliminated entirely. Agencies that usurp the power of the states will be stripped of their power and also be eliminated. It seems that the only growth sector in the economy year after year is the growth of government. NO MORE! The Tenth Amendment was designed to give power to the states and not the federal government. However, in the last fifty years this has been stifled. One of the major goals of my presidency is to reverse that trend. It is time for the states to step up to the plate and resume their rightful place in governing the people of each state.

"Another part of the Big Brother problem is the runaway judiciary, something our forefathers never anticipated happening. How in the name of all that is good can one person in the judiciary overrule the will of the people by an often subjective view of the Constitution? This, I promise you, will all end. This office will be working with Congress to reverse this diabolical course. If it means impeaching these runaway judges, so be it. If it takes a constitutional amendment to limit the powers and terms of the judiciary, we will work to that end. I will also work to allow Congress to have veto power over judicial decisions. Much of this will also be addressed in the coming weeks.

"My fellow Americans, I have been a little long-winded and I promise you that I will be more succinct in my speeches in the future. Thank you all for your support and trust. I hope every day the actions of this office will justify your faith and trust. We are a God-fearing and faithful nation and will continue to be such. Those who demand a secular nation devoid of any aspect of God in our lives, our institutions, and our government will be profoundly disappointed in my administration. Every day will be a prayerful one from this office, and every speech will end with an invocation to God and thankfulness for His bounty. No longer will prayer in our schools be forbidden, no longer will the Pledge of Allegiance be something disdained, no longer will the cross be a sign of derision, no longer will our flag be desecrated.

"I go now to start much of what I have elected to do as your president. If you will indulge me one more time, I will ask you all to stand wherever you are for two songs both embedded into the fabric of our nation. Feel free to sing along."

"GOD BLESS AMERICA!"
and
"AMERICA THE BEAUTIFUL" (Appendix D)

SECTION 2

SECOND BILL OF RIGHTS

Day 1: The Constitutional Convention

Excerpt from the US Constitution, Article V: *"On the application of the legislatures of two-thirds of the several states, shall call a convention for proposing amendments, which, in either case, shall be valid to all Intents and purposes, as part of the Constitution, when ratified by the legislatures of three-fourths of the several states . . ."*

My fellow Americans, on this first day of my hundred-day agenda in speaking with you, the American public, I want to talk about our freedoms guaranteed by the Constitution, which have been steadily eroded by our government, all three branches, especially the judicial, for the past fifty years. Since the various civil rights laws that were passed in the 1960s, we Americans have seen much of what was in the Bill of Rights and the Constitution totally overruled, misinterpreted, or just plain ignored. Sad to say, all of this was in the name of new "rights" that were never included in the Constitution. It would have been one thing if these "rights" had been amended into the Constitution, but they became extraconstitutional with no basis for legality. The Supreme Court, of course, went along with this charade for the past fifty years, even promulgating more and more "rights" that also were, in fact, extraconstitutional. The court that was to protect the American public from tyranny has become the instrument of said tyranny. The end result—we stand as a nation with our Constitution in tatters and our federal government hell-bent not in curbing these abuses, but expanding them.

For example, discrimination has been expanded over the years to include virtually every special-interest group—witness the gay movement, every new and enhanced minority group, witness the illegal alien community, and even our enemies, the Muslim terrorists who have been killing our people every day at home and abroad. It seems like every special-interest group has more "rights" than we do as Americans. This insanity must end and, as I said above, our government is the cause, not the solution of our problems, as a great president once said.

Fortunately, the framers of our Constitution had the God-given foresight to put into the Constitution the ability of the states and we the people to bypass Congress, the president, and the judiciary to directly change our Constitution through the amendment process. I wish to thank the well-known scholar Mark Levin for his book *The Liberty Amendments*, in which he eloquently outlines how we can take back our country and change the carnage that has arisen. I have asked Mr. Levin to be my ambassador at large, traveling to all the fifty states to encourage the representatives to pass resolutions favoring the states' participation in a Constitutional Convention. I am hoping that within the next twelve months, enough states will pass their resolutions. Thirty-eight states are needed to pass. The convention then will be held in a city designated by the convention. I propose either Houston or San Antonio, Texas, as a site. Texas, as many Americans are aware, was an independent nation that decided to join our republic in the 1840s, and is unique in that respect. That is why they are the Lone Star State. They achieved independence after defeating Mexico. Texas should lead the nation now in achieving independence once again, not from Mexico, but from Washington.

This process over the next one to two years has the potential of radically changing the political, religious, and economic outlook of our nation. We the people have the ability to affect these changes. The White House has set up a website called WH2017.org. On this website, divided by each state, are the names, addresses, phone numbers, and email addresses of all state representatives for state and federal offices. I urge each and every citizen listening to the sound of my voice to contact many of your local representatives and voice your opinions on these issues. Whether you agree or disagree, your representatives need to hear your collective voices on these matters, especially on the convention.

Over the next thirty days, I will be proposing each day new amendments for your consideration. Some will be readily evident as needed. Many will be controversial. I expect many of you will have passionate feelings, pro and con, on these issues. Nevertheless, the dialogue must start and we the people need to take back our country.

I will begin the dialogue tomorrow by introducing a second Bill of Rights, each expanding the original Bill of Rights set to the Constitution in 1789. This second Bill of Rights will address much of what has been changed concerning "rights" in this country. The following days I will address each of the amendments proposed by Mr. Levin in his book. I will expand on his arguments for the amendments but will try not to detract from his treatise. As you will see in the coming days, these amendments can have profound ramifications on our republic. Our forefathers gave us the tools; it is up to us to now use those tools for the betterment of our nation.

"GOD BLESS AMERICA."

DAY 2: CHURCH AND STATE

Amendment 1: Separation of church and state rulings are declared void except for any instance of a state-sponsored religion, such as Sharia law and Muslim theology.

My fellow Americans, good morning. Today I will address the first in what I call the expanded Bill of Rights, namely the separation of church and state, or SOCAS, issue. The original First Amendment to the Constitution stated, "Congress shall make no law respecting an establishment of religion, or prohibiting the free exercise thereof . . ."

Our forefathers expressed the freedom of religion into our Constitution, but, unfortunately, along the way that freedom has been overturned. Aided by a judiciary that has brazenly misinterpreted the Constitution, America has been forced to adhere to a mythical separation of church in all affairs of government, federal, state, and local, including education. This separation is not and never was in the Constitution. As a historical fact the Supreme Court consistently ruled in favor of the freedom of religion until 1947.

In this year, the Supreme Court reversed over 150 years of precedence and ruled in the case of *Everson v. Board of Education* that "The First Amendment has erected a wall between church and state. That wall must be kept high and impregnable. We could not approve the slightest breech." This "separation" was based on letters from Thomas Jefferson and not even addressed in the *Federalist Papers* as legal basis for said rulings. Mr. Jefferson's letters addressed the proclamation of a state-sponsored religion, a special topic never espoused in the United States. The Supreme Court further ruled in 1962 in the case of *Engel v. Vitale* to continue this concept of "separation of church and state" by ordering that all prayers in schools were to be disallowed.

These two cases effectively set the precedence of "separation of church and state" as public policy and established the rationale for exclusion of any religious thought or action in the public arena.

Based on these erroneous Supreme Court decisions, virtually all Christian activities into the affairs of our country have been curtailed. Witness in 1973, *Roe v. Wade*, legalizing abortion nationwide. The Christian church's response was tepid at best; many Protestant sects even rolled over and accepted abortion as part of their religious orthodoxy, ignoring the biblical fifth commandment, "Thou shall not murder"! The Catholic Church, probably the staunchest opponent of abortion, was also virtually silent on the subject. Since religious activity has been tax-exempt from the inception of the federal income taxation, the federal government has used the tax-exempt status as a bludgeon to curtail religious thought and expression in the US.

In the last fifty years, the situation has gotten horribly worse: prayer is banned in all public schools; even the Pledge of Allegiance, which has the expression "under God," is also eradicated in schools because of the "God" phrase. Every time someone objects, the SOCAS is brought up to quell any and all religiosity. Daily, one can read in the media instances of religious abuse: sports teams cannot invoke God before a game; children cannot wear any religious items on their persons in school. However, if someone wears something obscene, that will be allowed. A tablet in the Arkansas Supreme Court building on which the Ten Commandments were displayed was taken down in the name of SOCAS, even though the Ten Commandments plaque is on the Supreme Court building in Washington. The progressives are trying to get the motto for the city of LA changed because it has religious figures in it. The cross over the Los Angeles National Cemetery, over two hundred years old, is being forced down in the name of this insanity.

I could go on ad nauseam. Perhaps the most egregious of the craziness is the attack on Christmas holiday celebrations everywhere in the US. Christians are lambasted, schools are forbidden to have Nativity scenes on display in schools, and mention of Christmas outside of churches is frowned upon. In the prior administration, Christmas was not even mentioned; rather, Muslim celebrations were espoused and celebrated.[7]

Speaking of which, the attack on Christianity in the US using this SOCAS as the focus of the attack has one notable exception, the Muslim theology. How can it be that the theology responsible for 9/11 be allowed freedoms not granted to any other churches in the US?[8] Aided by our Democratic Socialist Party (DSP), eager to bow down to the clerics, any mention of Muslim butchery, depravity, or murder is not only frowned upon[9] but also stopped,[10] except for certain conservative radio talk show hosts, and even they are pressured to parse their words.

NO MORE! This amendment will go a long way in stopping this insanity and reestablish our Christian churches to their rightful place in the US.

"GOD BLESS AMERICA."

---

[7] "Obama Cancels 'Christmas In Washington'… But Not This Muslim Holiday." Clash Daily. December 01, 2015. http://clashdaily.com/2015/12/obama-cancels-christmas-in-washington-but-not-this-muslim-holiday/.

[8] Kelso, Maria. "Does the American News Media Have an Anti-Christian Bias?" The Daily Signal. December 26, 2013. http://dailysignal.com/2013/12/26/media-anti-christian-bias/.

[9] Wright, John C. "Pro-Islam Bias in the News." John C Wright's Journal. May 17, 2016. http://www.scifiwright.com/2016/05/pro-islam-bias-in-the-news/.

[10] Brumfield, Ben, and Leone Lakhani. "Anti-Muslim Slant by American Media Giants Reaps Criticism." CNN. July 30, 2013. http://edition.cnn.com/2013/07/30/us/rel-muslims-newsmakers/index.html.

Day 3: English, the Official Language

Amendment 2: English is the official language of the US. NO other language will be used in federal, state, and local documents. Voting documents will be in English only. All citizens naturalized or born must speak English in order to vote.

My fellow Americans, good morning. This day, I will elaborate on a topic that was mentioned in my inaugural address—our language, which is English. Not to repeat my speech prior, English is our native language. It defines who and what type of people we are. It is an inherent part of the fabric of our country, and as such, if it is not honored, the fabric of the US will start to unravel. No matter what country one visits in this world—Russia, Spain, Germany, Japan, China—each country and their language is unique and treasured. Any attempt to destroy, degrade, or denigrate their language will be met with violent protest. Only in the US have we as a nation been trying to destroy one of our most valued treasures, the English language. At a recent nationally televised football game, an international company, Coca-Cola, had a commercial of a US patriotic song starting in English then regressing into a hodgepodge of other languages not related to the USA.[11]

As I stated before, English is the language of two of this country's most important documents, the Declaration of Independence and the Constitution. Our forefathers, unfortunately, overlooked the requirement to have an official language; that oversight will be remedied now.

---

[11] ListitudePolitics. "CONTROVERSIAL: 'America The Beautiful' Coca Cola 2014 Super Bowl Commercial | Political Topics." YouTube. February 03, 2014. https://www.youtube.com/watch?v=vUGDQo2Pb6g.

In the interim to the amendment, I will propose a law making the English language our official language. If Congress passes such legislation, I will immediately sign it into law. Given the current state of affairs both in Congress and the Supreme Court, I doubt such a law will be passed, let alone not be overruled by the Supreme Court. Therefore, the amendment as stated will probably be the best recourse in this matter. A simple amendment, it will have vast ramifications in both the public and private sectors. Government documents will no longer be printed in scads and scads of languages. Voting documents will be in English only. Registration to vote will be in English. Legal documents will be in English, save, of course, for those esoteric Latin phrases the attorneys like to use. Public schools will be taught in English. If special classes are required to get foreign-speaking individuals up to speed, those will be extracurricular. Bilingual signs in all public sectors will be taken down. All media used by our government will be in English only.

As to the private sector, I do not control the private sector, and if private companies want to conduct business in languages other than English, I wish them well. If private companies want to hire bilingual employees for translation purposes, again, I wish them well. Our public institutions, however, including schools, hospitals, and quasi-government facilities will revert to the English language. When I as a private individual am traveling abroad, I have to accommodate the languages of the country I visit; foreigners visiting here will have to do this also. Lastly, with respect to any work permits for the US, English will be a requirement for such a permit. Thank you for your attendance.

"GOD BLESS AMERICA."

Day 4: Sanctity of Life—Conception

Amendment 3: Life begins at CONCEPTION. Abortion in all forms, at any time during the pregnancy, is forbidden except to save the natural life of the mother. In all other circumstances abortion will be considered murder.

In 1973, a year that will go down in infamy, the Supreme Court ruled again erroneously and spuriously that a "woman's right to privacy" allows abortion. Privacy is not a topic anywhere in the Constitution. This ruling, *Roe v. Wade*, opened the doors to our nation's debasement. Since that year forty years ago, over fifty million babies have been murdered—yes, murdered—while we as a people, as a Christian nation, have sat idly by, making excuses, saying that these were not babies, only potential babies, not yet human. The obvious retort here is if the fetus it is not a human life, then what is the fetus?

Fifty million babies, folks—more than all the people killed in World War II, more than we have lost in all our wars since the Revolution, more than all who died in the plagues that wiped out most of Europe during the Middle Ages, more than the lives the communists purged in Russia. How many potential Einsteins were eliminated, how many Lincolns, how many Hemingways, how many Sinatras, how many Edisons, how many Shakespeares? Those souls are lost forever, and our nation has not even begun to pay the price. The Bible is quite clear. The fifth commandment is "Thou shalt not murder."

Folks, answer a simple question: "How does one destroy a nation, any nation?" Destroy the families. By killing our babies, we are destroying our families and thus our nation.

Science has long since proved that life begins at conception.[12] That is, when the sperm and the egg unite, the DNA is combined and life begins. There is a wonderful book, *A Child Is Born*, by Lennart Nilsson, which I used in my OB practice, that literally pictures each day in the life of the human fetus from conception to birth, a nine-month journey to a new human baby. I would suggest that copies of this book be put in all our schools to teach our children the lessons we as a Christian people have forgotten: that life is precious and to destroy it on a personal whim is obscene.

The progressives have been arguing for the last fifty years that bringing into the world damaged goods, so to speak, is a greater problem. Statistics show that the average abortion is done on a white, female, twenty- to twenty-five-year-old high-school graduate who is Christian in faith, working, and not married. Since *Roe* was signed, better than a million babies a year are being aborted. Over 90 percent have been for convenience, not to save the life of the mother or due to baby abnormalities. Nothing more than inconvenience. Ninety percent, folks, done because the baby was inconvenient. How sad! Especially sad is the fact that in my faith, Catholicism, over 25 percent of the abortions done in the US since 1973 have been done to Catholic women![13]

There are over three million couples in the US that cannot conceive for whatever reason.[14] The vast majority of these couples would give anything to have a baby. How sad it is that we promote

---

[12] Terzo, Sarah. "Life Begins at Conception, Science Teaches | Live Action News." Live Action News. January 13, 2013. http://liveactionnews.org/life-begins-at-conception-science-teaches/.

[13] "U.S. Abortion Statistics." Abort73. May 25, 2016. http://www.abort73.com/abortion_facts/us_abortion_statistics/.

[14] "Adoption Statistics." Child Welfare Information Gateway. https://www.childwelfare.gov/topics/systemwide/statistics/adoption/#gen.

abortion every day in the media and do not promote adoption at all. We make abortion easy, an outpatient procedure; pay five hundred dollars and the job is done. But when you try to adopt, the government obstacles are hideous. It takes months, sometimes years, to adopt. Again, our government is the problem, not the solution. Another hideous example here is that if you are gay, the adoption becomes easy; if you are a heterosexual couple, the opposite is true.[15]

Only one side of this story has been repeated throughout these last fifty years. The greatest abortion mill in the US, Planned Parenthood, is even subsidized by the federal government, even though laws have been passed forbidding the federal government from paying for abortions. The excuse is that the federal grants go somewhere else in the corporation and not for abortions. This is a total canard, made even worse by the recent scandals of Planned Parenthood selling baby parts on the open market.[16] Horrific! In my budget, all funding for Planned Parenthood will stop immediately.

I would like now to tell three stories on the other side of the coin—three couples who did not abort and stayed on God's pathway even though the sorrow was immense. All three stories will bring tears to your eyes as they did mine, but they remind us what it is to be a Christian in every sense of the word.

The first story is of a couple from Missouri; the mother was eighteen weeks pregnant, in for her first ultrasound of the baby. All

---

[15] "LGBT Adoption." Lifelong Adoptions.
http://www.lifelongadoptions.com/lgbt-adoption.
[16] Ertelt, Steven. "Planned Parenthood CEO Confirms It Will Not Stop Selling Body Parts From Aborted Babies." LifeNews.com. September 30, 2015.
http://www.lifenews.com/2015/09/30/planned-parenthood-ceo-confirms-it-will-not-stop-selling-body-parts-from-aborted-babies/.

was happiness and joy. The couple was astonished when the doctor looked at the ultrasound and discovered that the baby was anencephalic, that is, born without the brain except for the brainstem. The baby would survive in utero, but would die immediately after birth. The doctor advised an immediate abortion. The couple were devout Christians; they discussed the issue and decided on a different pathway. The mother would carry the baby to term. During the rest of the pregnancy the couple planned a "bucket list," various experiences they wanted to show their baby as if he would live. Trips were planned to the Grand Canyon, the ocean, the national parks, and zoos. During all the trips, the couple talked with their baby, explaining the sights and sounds that were going on.

Finally, the pregnancy came to term, the mother delivered, and the baby was baptized and wrapped in beautiful baby clothes. The couple took pictures and the baby died in a few hours. Instead of a sad experience, this family chose the God pathway. The mother and father said that they lived more in those few months than ever before. Their baby was buried in a Christian cemetery and, I am sure, is now with God.

The second story is also heartrending. A Christian couple was pregnant, the mother in her twentieth week. She noticed a lump in her left breast and notified her doctor; a biopsy was done, and the lump was found to be malignant. Moreover, the cancer had spread: third-stage metastasis. Chemotherapy was the only therapy that had a chance of stopping the spread. The doctor advised the mother to start the therapy. She asked, "What about my baby?" The doctor told her the therapy would kill the baby. Clear choices, yes? The mother looked at the father and at the doctor and said, "My baby deserves to live." She refused any therapy until the baby was born.

The pregnancy was continued until thirty-four weeks when the healthy baby was delivered by C-section. The mother then started the chemotherapy. Two years later now, the baby girl is alive and well. Yes, the mother's CA is in remission. Again, life was chosen, not death.

The last story deals with a famous lady known to you all, Sarah Palin. She too had to make life-and-death choices. During her last pregnancy, she and her husband found out that their baby had chromosomal abnormalities—a Down's baby. Again the doctors advised abortion as an expedient. Sarah and her husband took the life route. Their child is seven years old today, a thriving young boy, and he is the joy of their family! The sad part about this story is how during the 2008 presidential campaign, this courageous lady was continually vilified by the media and abortion advocates for not getting an abortion.[17] Tell me, folks, who are the Christians here? My fellow Americans, the decision for us as a Christian people is simple. Pro-choice is pro-death. Do we choose pro-life or pro-death? My choice is life!

"GOD BLESS AMERICA."

Day 5: Marriage

Amendment 4: Marriage shall be defined as being between one man and one woman; no other marriage combination will be legal and recognized in the US. Any other marriage contract in force currently will revert to a civil contract only.

---

[17] "Public Image of Sarah Palin." Wikipedia. https://en.wikipedia.org/wiki/Public_image_of_Sarah_Palin.

Good morning, my fellow Americans. The subject today, as usual, is another touchy one—namely, marriage and what I designate nontraditional marriage. First of all, marriage has been the bedrock for the Judeo-Christian peoples for thousands of years. Marriage has always been defined as being between one man and one woman. There have been attempts for polygamous marriages in the past, the last with the Mormon church, but they have been short-term at best. The current nontraditional marriage being espoused is, of course, gay marriage. It is interesting to note that that the wave of states allowing same-sex marriage is not a product of the peoples in each state voting for same-sex marriage, but of individual state and federal judges ruling in favor of same-sex marriage, overruling many times the express will of the people for the opposite. This insanity finally culminated in the Supreme Court of the United States, or SCOTUS, ruling in 2015 that same-sex marriage is to be the law of the land. This is not government of the people; it is government against the people!

Of course, because of these arbitrary rulings, now advocates of other nontraditional marriages want their "rights," namely incest marriage, animal marriage—human and pet—transsexual marriage, and pedophiliac marriage.[18] The list grows each day.

Marriage as an institution has enabled human civilization not only to survive but thrive these thousands of years. It is the essential fabric that enables nations, peoples, religions, and, yes, families to survive. Christian theology is based on the marriage

---

[18] "Gay 'Marriage' Ruling Opens Door to Polygamy and Religious Persecution: Dissenting Justices." LifeSite News. June 26, 2015. https://www.lifesitenews.com/news/gay-marriage-decision-opens-the-door-to-polygamy-and-religious-persecution.

contract between a man and a woman. The Bible is replete with references to traditional marriage and condemnation of homosexuality. I will mention only one passage, from Matthew 19, where Jesus Christ the Son of God stated simply:

Have you not read that from the beginning, the Creator made them male and female and said, "For this reason a man shall leave his father and mother and be joined to his wife, and the two shall become one flesh."

Nowhere in the Bible is gay marriage mentioned, because it was and still is an abomination in God's eyes. From the Old to the New Testament, all references to marriage and the family deal with a man and a woman united in marriage. Christianity elevated the institution into a holy sacrament over two thousand years ago.

Fast-forward to the twentieth century. The progressives are eager to totally rewrite over four thousand years of human history, ignoring the political, legal, economic, social, and religious consequences of their actions. Here again, the progressives do not care about order, about country; their agenda is simply to destroy what is and replace it with who-knows-what.

In order to understand the upheaval that is arising in the world, let us look realistically at the homosexual behavioral pattern. There are over 8 billion people on this earth and over 8 billion behavioral patterns, some general, many related to families, ethnicities, tribes, and nations. Not all behavioral patterns are beneficial; many are destructive, and many are horrible by nature.

Homosexuality is a behavioral pattern that affects less than 2 percent of any given population, not 10 or 20 or whatever the gays try to pretend.[19] That is right, folks, less than 2 percent of the population are exclusively gay; that is two people out of a hundred people. Now certain population centers—San Francisco, for example—have a higher percentage because in any society, groups with similar traits tend to flock together. I am sure many of you remember the gay bathhouses of San Francisco, where sexual antics could involve ten, twenty, or more partners in a single night.

Homosexuality as a behavior pattern has always centered on the sex act, not on any other form of human intimacy. A study by the University of Pennsylvania on young adult males twenty to thirty years old showed that the average straight male had a total of eight sexual experiences in his life and the gay male had an average of twenty sexual experiences a year.[20] Think of those statistics; no wonder AIDS is increasing in the US.

The gay advocates have tried for years to prove that there is a genetic component to the behavior, and they have, of course, failed in this proof. It is a purely learned behavior, heavily influenced by the individual's personality and especially the age of the person involved in the activity. The younger a person is introduced into the gay lifestyle, the more likely they will accept the lifestyle as "normal."[21] Notice how, nationwide, high schools now have gay and lesbian clubs in the schools. I guarantee the

---

[19] Volokh, Eugene. "What Percentage of the U.S. Population Is Gay, Lesbian or Bisexual?" *Washington Post*. July 15, 2014. https://www.washingtonpost.com/news/volokh-conspiracy/wp/2014/07/15/what-percentage-of-the-u-s-population-is-gay-lesbian-or-bisexual/.

[20] Slick, Matt. "Statistics on Sexual Promiscuity among Homosexuals." CARM. https://carm.org/statistics-homosexual-promiscuity.

[21] "What Causes Homosexual Desire and Can It Be Changed?" Family Research Institute. February 3, 2009. http://www.familyresearchinst.org/2009/02/.

clubs are more than social gathering places. It is ironic that these same high schools do not allow heterosexual clubs to form.

Sex education in elementary and high schools now emphasize the normalcy of gay relationships, especially sexual. Another horrible story is that in the last thirty years, sex education now prevails in all public schools, elementary and private, is government sponsored, and is totally secular in nature. Sexual intercourse is taught as normal in any form, man to man, woman to woman, incest, bestiality, nothing is left out. The family setting is now almost gone. Is it any wonder that more and more children are having gender-identification issues?

Fifty years ago, homosexuality was listed as a psychiatric disorder by the American Psychiatric Association (APA), part of the AMA. Suddenly it was dropped as a disorder. Why? Because a high-ranking doctor in the APA was gay and used his influence to drop the disorder.

Because it is a behavioral pattern, we can analyze it as such and make societal judgments as to the validity of allowing and encouraging said behavior. First of all, homosexuality is a product of a leisure society. Societies fighting for survival (third-world countries) will not have this behavior exhibited. Travel to Africa, the Middle East, China, or Indonesia; homosexuality is virtually nonexistent. A sad fact is that in all societies in the past that have condoned homosexuality, all have faded out of the human existence.

Pardon me now as I put on my doctor persona. Next, and also quite obvious, homosexuality is biologically in error. Humans were designed to reproduce, man and woman, not man and man or woman and woman. The equipment does not work. Some gay couples have used science to circumvent the process, e.g., surrogates. The fact still remains—the biology is wrong. With biology, of course, the anatomy is wrong also, and the innovative ways of circumventing this has led to increased incidence of STDs in the population. The gay advocates try to ignore the fact that HIV and its final stage, AIDS, are and always have been a gay disease, brought into this country by gays and spread primarily though the gay population. AIDS is extremely difficult to spread heterosexually. This virus has been with us for over fifty years, and, folks, there is still *no* cure. Science is not even close to a cure. Thanks to the left, the gays have been very successful in covering their tracks in the spread of the disease. I as a doctor have to report a patient with an STD. However, someone with AIDS, an STD, I have to get their permission to report. Millions of gays in the US have HIV and AIDS and the reporting is nonexistent. The government relies on computer models to deduce the infection in the population.

As a behavioral pattern, homosexuality is also sociologically and societally in error. Society exists by having its individuals reproduce and increase the society. Homosexuality does not help in this matter. It is a dead-end process. Economically, gays make up a very small part of society and as such do not improve the society economically. As a matter of fact, billions of dollars have been spent by private and mostly government agencies to combat AIDS and will continue to be spent in keeping AIDS patients alive. Think of this, folks. AIDS is an entirely elective disease; you don't get it from kissing, or sitting on a toilet seat, or shaking hands. One has to engage in specific abnormal behavior to get the virus.

Lastly, and vastly important to me, homosexuality is theologically in error. No major religion condones it. Our Bible, the bedrock of Christianity, specifically forbids the practice as an abomination. Pardon me while I quote again from the Bible, Old Testament, Leviticus 18:

I am the LORD. You shall not lie with a male as with a woman; that is an abomination.

We as a Christian nation cannot allow the visible expression of marriage to be suborned to include gay marriage, not to mention all the other forms of alternate marriage now coming out. This amendment will stop this insanity. We are a free nation; many forms of human intimacy are condoned as long as they are kept in private. Civil contracts are and always have been available for parties wishing to provide for certain rights and privileges. Same-sex marriage is wrong and will always be wrong, for our nation and for humanity.

"GOD BLESS AMERICA."

Day 6: Citizenship

Amendment 5: Citizenship is defined as (1) being born in the US and having at least one of the parents a legal citizen of the US, or (2) being born outside the US or in its territories and having both parents legal citizens of the US. The "anchor baby" phenomenon is abolished. All such births from the year 2000 to present shall be legal only if at least one of the parents is currently an American citizen. All other persons can apply for American citizenship through the normal channels. The Fourteenth Amendment is changed in part to reflect this new amendment, specifically the first sentence listed below. The sentence in question is the following:

All persons born or naturalized in the United States, and subject to the jurisdiction thereof, are citizens of the United States and of the state wherein they reside.

My fellow Americans, 150 years ago the Fourteenth Amendment was passed for the express purpose of defining the legal status of blacks brought to the US as slaves. It has been broadened way beyond its intent. Aided again by an active judiciary, citizenship in the US has been redefined to mean almost anything. NO MORE!

To be a citizen of the US is a privilege, not an absolute right. Every country in the world has very tight reins on who they allow as citizens. It is time that we in the US tighten the reins here. When I was a doctor in California, the pregnant illegals would stand outside the hospital until they went into labor. They then entered the hospital and could not be turned away. They delivered—gratis, of course—and left the next day with their magic birth certificate, another anchor baby. With this certificate, the parents could enter our country legally, and then their family could also enter. These illegals would then have more children to solidify their presence in the US. Having a legal citizen in their family allowed them to get on a multitude of governmental aid—welfare, housing, food stamps, medical care, legal care—the largesse of the government has no bounds. NO MORE!

In the coming days I will address this issue in greater detail, examining means to stop this illegal flow of personae into our country. Until then, this amendment will stop a main avenue by firming up the citizenship requirements. Other issues will also be addressed. Citizens must speak English to maintain their citizenship. To vote, proof of citizenship must be shown. I think it is highly ironic that to buy liquor in the US, one must show a picture ID to prove one's age. However, to vote, in many cases no ID is required. NO MORE! Photo ID, driver's license, passport, or a birth certificate with picture must be presented in order to vote. Any noncitizen attempting to vote will be guilty of a felony.

Speaking of driver's licenses, if states approve driver's licenses for noncitizens, any and all such licenses shall be embossed with the initials "NC" on both sides of the license designating that the individual is not a citizen of the US.

"GOD BLESS AMERICA."

DAY 7: REST

Our Father, Who art in heaven, hallowed be Thy name, Thy kingdom come, Thy will be done on earth as it is in heaven. Give us this day our daily bread and forgive us our trespasses as we forgive those who trespass against us. Lead us not into temptation but deliver us from evil. Amen.

"GOD BLESS AMERICA."

DAY 8: IMMIGRATION

Amendment 6: The Kennedy Immigration Act of 1965 is declared void. All immigration into the US is suspended for ten years in order to assimilate the immigrants into the US who have arrived over the last thirty years. After ten years, immigration will be limited to 500,000 individuals per annum. Congress can increase the quota by up to 10 percent of the prior year's quota. The annual quota system will be based on the population demographics present in the 1960 census.

All illegal aliens in the US will have one year to return to the country from whence they came. After the one-year grace period, all illegals remaining will be deported, and their assets in the US will be confiscated and sold to pay for their deportation.

All federal government benefits to illegals are hereby rescinded. This includes but is not limited to medical care, legal care, social security, Medicare, and educational benefits.

Visas to enter the US will be for a duration of ninety days only; work visas will be for a period of six months only. All student visas will expire in six months and will need to be renewed every six months.

My fellow Americans, we pride ourselves as a nation of immigrants. My own grandparents came to the US over one hundred years ago through Ellis Island. My grandmother almost was sent back to Europe because it was thought that she may have had TB. Unfortunately, beginning with the Kennedy Act in 1965, our immigration laws have been shattered and largely ignored. Up until 1965, immigration was based on population demographics existing then in the US at that time. As a historical sidenote, immigration into the US was suspended for forty years from 1920 to 1960 to assimilate the immigrants.

The last fifty years have changed all that in the name of "diversity," and it has wreaked havoc on the US. This country was founded by Europeans and settled by Europeans since the sixteenth century. The progressives, however, have changed the demographics dramatically over the last fifty years. Third-world countries are given priority in getting to enter, and Europeans are put at the back of the bus.[22] We open our borders and country not to the best and the brightest but to the misfits, unwashed, criminals, sick, and largely illiterate. It is claimed that unless checked within

---

[22] History.com Staff. "U.S. Immigration Since 1965." History.com. 2010. http://www.history.com/topics/us-immigration-since-1965.

thirty years, the demographics of our county will show a majority of third-world peoples in our country; the European populace will be the minority. No other country in the world allows this chaos. Canada, for example, has extremely strict immigrations rules involving education, wealth, and health status.

The last two Democratic Socialist Party, or DSP, presidents have allowed third-world immigrants with huge health issues—such as AIDS, Ebola virus, and TB—into our country. Millions of illegal children have been allowed in with no health checks. They have also enabled the so-called "Dream Act" for illegals to circumvent the immigration laws. NO MORE!

Since 1965, Congress has enacted several immigration laws to try and stem the tide; all have been to no avail and have been ignored by the executive branch. My predecessor is a prime example, setting his own personal criteria on whether or not to follow the laws enacted, a clear violation of his oath of office. To me, the only way to save our country from the tsunami of illegal immigration is by the amendment process, a pathway Washington cannot overrule.

Now many on the left will state that it is impossible to deport ten to twenty million illegals. Here again we ignore history. In 1955 our country had a crisis of illegals from Mexico and South America entering our country. President Eisenhower issued an executive order—yes, some executive orders are beneficial—deporting over three million illegals back to the country of origin. Within six months, the deportation was completed and the illegal invasion was stopped, at least for the next ten years until the Kennedy bill was passed. Notice the pattern here, folks—the 1965 bill was passed by a DSP congress and signed into law by a DSP president.

The left will also say that we will lose more than we gain. The Congressional Budget Office, or CBO, has estimated that the illegals cost the American taxpayer over $150 billion a year in government aid, subsidies, education, and other benefits. The illegals also send over $100 billion back to their home country each year. [23] No wonder Mexico encourages its citizens to come to America; monies received from the illegals are the second biggest source of revenue for Mexico after oil.[24]

Lastly, in the last ten years of a prolonged recession, when 100 million of our own citizens have left the workforce because of the inability to find a job,[25] how can we allow ten to twenty million illegals access to jobs that our citizens deserve? There was an illegal crackdown in Kansas City recently at a meat-packing plant where fifty illegals were rounded up and deported. When the company advertised to refill the jobs, over six hundred citizens applied![26]

NO MORE! This insanity must stop. Our borders will be secure and the illegal immigrants here will return to where they originated or will be deported. This country is responsible to its citizens, not to the citizens of other countries. This amendment will be the start of setting the record straight. Being from the southwestern part of the US, I see many cars every day with Mexican license plates. I hope they have legal visas, or they are gone.

---

[23] "The Fiscal Burden of Illegal Immigration on United States Taxpayers (2013)." Federation for American Immigration Reform. July 2010. http://www.fairus.org/publications/the-fiscal-burden-of-illegal-immigration-on-united-states-taxpayers.

[24] Associated Press. "Mexico Got More Money from Remittances Than from Oil Revenues in 2015." NBC News. February 3, 2016. http://www.nbcnews.com/news/latino/mexico-got-more-money-remittances-oil-revenues-2015-n510346.

[25] Meyer, Ali. "Americans Not in Labor Force Exceed 93 Million for First Time; 62.7% Labor Force Participation Matches 37-Year Low." CNS News. April 03, 2015. http://cnsnews.com/news/article/ali-meyer/americans-not-labor-force-exceed-93-million-first-time-627-labor-force.

[26] "Postville Raid." Wikipedia. https://en.wikipedia.org/wiki/Postville_Raid.

I will be addressing specific plans regarding the illegal question, border issues, employment issues, and "Dream" status in the coming days. Rest assured, the problem will be solved, much to the chagrin of the DSP and the illegal advocates. Until then,

"GOD BLESS AMERICA."

DAY 9: BORDER ISSUES

My fellow Americans, today's speech will be a continued examination of the problems presented by the massive influx of illegals into our country. The amendment proposed yesterday will go a long way to curbing the influx, but more action is needed. We cannot rely on Congress because laws passed by Congress are either negated by the Supreme Court or totally ignored by the executive branch.

Therefore, I, as your president, will take direct action to secure our borders and stop the tidal wave. As of today, I am ordering four divisions of armed forces to the southwestern states—Texas, New Mexico, Arizona, and California—bordering Mexico. These divisions will be comprised mainly of National Guard troops, supplemented by Army Reserves, and will be under the command of the joint chiefs of staff. This office will be working with the governors of the mentioned states in coordinating troop activities. These troops *will* secure the border by whatever means. These troops will be armed and dangerous, with full fighting complements of armor, planes, helicopters, and drones. Let me put this clearly so there is no misunderstanding—illegals crossing the border will be turned back immediately. All armed illegals will be treated as terrorists and our troops will interdict them and eliminate their presence. This is war, my fellow Americans; an invasion of the US will no longer be tolerated. These troops will remain on the border indefinitely until all threats have been eliminated.

While the military on the border will curtail most of the illegal crossing, emphasis will also be on completing the border fencing—double fencing, as seen in Israel, and very high-tech. This will be done in the next six to twelve months. This fencing will protect our borders from California through Texas.

Once the border issue is under control, the states bordering other countries will have responsibility for maintaining their respective borders. They will also have prime responsibility for addressing the illegal population in their state. The federal government will work closely with the states to insure not only border control but rapid deportation of illegals back to their respective countries.

The border patrol will have expanded duties. I am sure most of you have been stopped for a traffic violation in your life. The border patrol will do a variant of that. They will issue "fine" tickets and will give them out to public, private, companies, and individuals hiring or employing illegals. The initial fine per illegal will be one thousand dollars, the second violation will be five thousand, and the third violation will be ten thousand. The fines will be payable within thirty days; assets will be seized if the fines cannot be paid. We have instituted in the US E-Verify to check on the legal status of noncitizens. It is not being used; if it is used by individuals or companies, the fines can be circumvented. In all other cases the fines stand. No longer will there be illegals standing on each street corner begging for jobs. Any person found in that circumstance will be deported immediately if he or she is an illegal.

All federal government largesse will be rescinded immediately—food stamps, access to medical care, legal care, housing, and any other benefits they have been able to accumulate. Education is for our citizens and our citizens only. Illegals attending elementary, high school, and college will no longer be eligible for any aid by the government. If illegals want educational benefits, they will pay for those benefits.

Continuing on in this vein, any noncitizen in the US desiring goods and services in the US can pay cash and receive those items. Governmental aid of any sort will not be forthcoming and is reserved for citizens only.

Speaking of governmental aid, foreign countries who encourage their citizens to illegally come to the US will within thirty days see their foreign grants from the US dropped by 50 percent to pay for the deportation process. If the problem still exists in six months, all foreign aid to that country or countries will be stopped. If that does not stop the problem, tariffs and trade restrictions will be implemented ASAP.

Sadly, the problem extends to some our own cities and states. "Sanctuary cities" and some states now give aid and comfort to their illegal population. NO MORE! Cities and states that knowingly harbor illegals will have all federal aid suspended immediately for a period of five years. This aid includes but is not limited to grants for medical, education, welfare recipients, roads and transportation, housing, and hospitals. Unfortunately, this "sanctuary" concept has extended to other institutions, namely churches, hospitals, and private foundations. These institutions who support the illegal invasion will immediately have their tax-exempt status suspended indefinitely.

Until tomorrow,

"GOD BLESS AMERICA."

Day 10: Right to Bear Arms

Amendment 7: The Second Amendment is amended to read, the right of every American citizen to bear arms without interference from the federal, state, or local government shall not be infringed upon. Unless convicted of a felony crime, or judged mentally incompetent, or found to be a terrorist, no government agency shall interfere with said rights of the individual. Government-required reporting of any and all arms is repealed. Congress shall pass no laws limiting said rights except in a state of national emergency.

Said amendment applies only to American citizens. All noncitizens in the US must have a US permit to own any firearms. Any noncitizens found with illegal weapons will be guilty of a felony and subject to immediate deportation and confiscation of all weapons.

My fellow Americans, our government in the last fifty years has been trying through laws and the Supreme Court to restrict and even negate the Second Amendment. It is only through organizations such as the NRA that these efforts have not succeeded. Every crisis in the US that occurs with someone killed with a weapon, the cry goes out for more gun control. The Brady Bill, passed in the 1980s to curb gun violence by requiring gun registration in all public outlets except gun shows, has proven ineffective in either curbing gun violence or stopping violence in general. All it has accomplished is to give the federal government a giant database over the last twenty-five years of gun owners in the US.

The left has constantly railed against concealed-weapons permits granted to citizens in thirty-seven states now, even though all studies show decreased gun violence in those states that allow concealed weapons and increased gun violence in those states that have restricted gun access laws.[27] Chicago has one of the highest murder rates of cities in the nation and the most restrictive gun control laws. Every state that has restrictive gun laws—and by the way, these are "blue" states, heavily Democratic—has increased problems with crime and violence within their states. Other countries that restrict access to guns, like Mexico, where citizens cannot even own a gun unless it is with permission from the government, have extremely high murder rates.[28] Since the citizens do not have access to guns, the outlaws and cartels are loaded with weapons. In many cases the outlaws are better armed than the police. In England, to get access to a gun, one must join a gun club where the weapons are kept until used by the owner. Even the police are not armed in England. Again with the increased violence in England and Europe; only the bad guys get to be armed.[29]

We forget that as Americans one of the main reasons we won the Revolutionary War was that we the citizens were armed and used those arms in fighting for our freedom. Even before the Revolutionary War, our being armed helped stabilize the frontier areas from Indian and foreign attacks. The militia was an essential part of our social fabric.

---

[27] "Gun Facts | Gun Control Facts Concerning Concealed Carry." Gun Facts. August 17, 2013. http://www.gunfacts.info/gun-control-myths/concealed-carry/.

[28] J. D. Tuccille. "Mexico Shows That Tight Gun Control Laws Don't Guarantee Compliance." Reason.com. December 11, 2012. http://reason.com/blog/2012/12/11/mexico-as-an-example-that-tighter-gun-co.

[29] "Firearms-Control Legislation and Policy: Great Britain." Library of Congress. July 30, 2015. http://www.loc.gov/law/help/firearms-control/greatbritain.php.

Today we have the National Guard and the Reserves in each state. Both are needed to protect the safety and well-being of our citizens. As I mentioned yesterday, the expanded role for both the National Guard and the Reserves along our southern border will again aid in the defense of our country.

"GOD BLESS AMERICA."

DAY 11: FREE SPEECH

Amendment 8: The First Amendment is changed to include the following: Free speech is sacrosanct in the US whether in a public or private setting, with the exception of conscious libel or slander. The First Amendment in all media, phone, newspaper, and internet shall not be infringed upon. Civil rights issues are subordinate to the First Amendment.

Government monitoring media, public or private, will not be allowed except in a national emergency and authorized by a majority of both houses of Congress.

My fellow Americans, one of our basic freedoms since our country was founded has been the concept of free speech in both public and private settings. However, over the years, Congress and the Supreme Court have continued diminishing the concept of the First Amendment to the point where most people can no longer speak freely, except in their own homes, because of fear that they will be sued or arrested for saying something that is not politically correct, or PC. When I was in college, I was privileged to go on a study tour to Russia, which was then very much under communist control. Everyone there was scared to death of the KGB and someone listening to their conversations. When I was with some American officials, they showed me the "bugs" in their apartments.

For people to talk freely with you, it had to be outside, preferably with traffic around, to drown out anybody listening. It was horrible! Fast-forward forty years and it is now the same in our country. As I said in the beginning, remember the quote from Evelyn Hall from her biography *The Life of Voltaire* in which she stated, "I may not agree with what you say, but I will defend to the death your right to say it."

Look around you, folks. Everywhere is "political correctness"; the newspapers you read, talking with your friends in public—heck, talking on the cell phone, people will automatically look around to see if anyone can hear if they say something controversial. How many media personalities regularly get fired or upbraided if they say or utter an indelicate word? All speech has to be prefaced with a "politically correct" disclaimer that the person will be saying something controversial. Notice also that the people mostly affected by "political correctness" are the Caucasian majority population in the US. Minorities, blacks, Indians, Hispanics, Muslims, almost anyone else can say what they please no matter how indelicate or vindictive or obscene, and they are given a free ride. Witness the black Muslim movement: their leaders can espouse publicly the most vile, horrible, and obscene exclamations, and no one says a word. But if a white public figure, say, Sarah Palin, states something controversial, it is front-page news.

Sad to say, almost all institutions in the US, public and private, have succumbed to PC. Schools especially are intolerant of free speech. Name any public colleges that will have conservative personae at any of their functions. Virtually all TV stations are PC, except maybe for FOX TV, but even that station is succumbing rapidly. The Federal Communications Commission, or FCC, constantly monitors all media for PC, especially talk radio—probably the last bastion of free speech—but even those stations and personalities have to tone down what they say. Witness probably the most famous radio talk personality, Rush Limbaugh. How many times has he been lambasted in the media for his comments on the radio? It makes no difference if he is telling the truth. PC overrides all else. I have noticed that even this last bastion is slowly being subverted; almost half of the commercials are from the government proclaiming some form of PC the public has to adhere to, and because the stations are regulated by the FCC, these "commercials" must be allowed. NO MORE! One of my first duties this year will be to abolish government agencies that hamper free speech; the FCC will be one of the first.

Now any "right" can be abused, and that is for the courts to handle. But a situation where the progressive left in this country has all the free speech rights and the conservative right has none is intolerable and will be stopped.

Lastly, in the past eight years, government monitoring of media and individuals has expanded exponentially. This will cease! Whether it is the National Security Agency (NSA), the Internal Revenue Service (IRS), or the Environmental Protection Agency (EPA), all government agencies engaging in such activities will stop immediately and will be disbanded where appropriate. Databases accumulated by these agencies will be destroyed and monitored by an oversight organization appointed by Congress and reportable to the American public. The huge underground data-storage facilities that have been constructed over the past ten years will be deactivated and records accumulated not directly related to the safety of the US will be eradicated. The horrors of "Big Brother" are upon us, and we need to stop this train wreck.

Thank you for your attendance today.

"GOD BLESS AMERICA."

DAY 12: CIVIL RIGHTS

Amendment 9: All civil rights acts passed into law, starting with the 1964 Act, that are not supported by the Constitution or any of the constitutional amendments are hereby abolished.

Discrimination, for whatever reason, is abolished as a legal concept.

Reparations for whatever reason to repair "damages" done in the past is abolished as a legal concept. Affirmative action is abolished as a legal concept.

My fellow Americans, many of the issues we face as a nation started when the progressives rammed through Congress and signed by progressive presidents "civil rights" acts that were never included in the Constitution. It would have been another matter if Washington had passed constitutional amendments and were ratified by a majority of the states. These "civil rights" bypassed the Constitution and, aided by a radical Supreme Court, made extraconstitutional "rights" the law of the land. In the past fifty years, our country has been paying a horrible price for these extraconstitutional rights not only economically, but also sociologically, religiously, and personally. These rights have been used by our government to suborn the citizens of the US and force us all to accommodate concepts like political correctness, diversity, affirmative action, reparations, or whatever the new flavor of the month is. None of this was voted on by the citizens of the US, but came into being through government control. Who would have thought that animals would have more legal rights than humans, that noncitizens would have more "rights" than citizens, that a species of garter snail would have more legal rights than a person's private property rights?

For example, the Americans with Disabilities Act passed in 1992 by a DSP congress and a DSP president allows anyone to claim a disability and have a "service" animal. That person can then force all private and public institutions to accept this animal on the premises for whatever the reason. All private property rights of the business, practice, or institution, whether public or private, individual or corporate, is suborned to the "disabled" person and his service dog. Health hazards, sanitary conditions, and safety issues with the animals are not relevant.[30]

Compounding these extraconstitutional laws are the thousands of federal, state, and local regulations that have ballooned supporting these laws. Everywhere one turns, the government has a regulation controlling virtually all aspects of any activity. Whether starting a business or building an edifice or decorating one's property, there are "civil rights" laws that pertain to that activity. Look around your world, America. Handicapped stickers are everywhere, handicapped parking in every building site. Have you noticed how literally anyone can get a handicapped sticker for their vehicle? I have seen huge fifty-foot RVs with a handicapped sticker. The best one was a handicapped sticker on a Ferrari sports car in Sedona, Arizona. The latest outrage is in all public outlets, specifically retail outlets, where motorized transportation must be provided for anyone with a "disability." People will stand at the entrance of the store waiting on the next motorized cart.

As with any social agenda aided by federal law, the original purpose—to correct an "injustice"—rapidly falls by the wayside until the law is expanded to include the whole universe. Medicare,

---

[30] "Frequently Asked Questions about Service Animals and the ADA." Americans with Disabilities Act Questions and Answers: Service Animals. July 20, 2015. https://www.ada.gov/regs2010/service_animal_qa.html.

another "new" civil right passed in 1965, was to provide healthcare to the elderly at a reasonable cost. The cost estimates long-term were bypassed within ten years. When the law was passed in 1965, the estimated cost of Medicare in 1990 was to be $90 million. When 1990 hit the cost had risen to $90 billion a year. Currently it is $400 billion per annum and rising.[31] Medicare is expanded to include illegals, Social Security disability recipients, the indigent, and soon all the "dreamers."[32] All these additional groups, of course, have not paid into the system but will get the benefits. Who pays? The American taxpayer! The "right to healthcare," another "civil right," will be addressed in the coming days when I address the Obamacare Act of 2010.

Look at affirmative action, initially designed to give blacks an equal chance at jobs, the work environment, and education. Quickly it became an avenue for anyone not white to get ahead at the expense of the white person. Qualifications, test scores, and abilities no longer mattered—only race and color. Quotas became the norm, and race and color became the deciding factor in many walks of our political, economic, and educational institutions. The last president ran on his race and won. Ninety-five percent of the black voters in the US voted for him, not on his qualifications—he had none—but because he was black.[33]

Since the 1960s this country has spent over $15 trillion on "civil rights" issues,[34] which incidentally matches our current national

---

[31] Chantrill, Christopher. "Medicare Spending Analysis." US Government Spending.
http://www.usgovernmentspending.com/medicare_spending_by_year.
[32] Hayward, Steven, and Erik Peterson. "The Medicare Monster." Reason.com. January 1993. http://reason.com/archives/1993/01/01/The-medicare-monster.
[33] Kuhn, David Paul. "Exit Polls: How Obama Won." POLITICO. November 5, 2008. http://www.politico.com/story/2008/11/exit-polls-how-obama-won-015297.
[34] Chantrill, Christopher. "Budget of the United States Government." US Government Spending.
http://www.usgovernmentspending.com/federal_budget_pie.

debt.[35] What have we gained in these fifty years? The country is further divided, poverty has increased as a percentage of the population, and the racial strife is worse than ever. Washington continues blindly along, singing tunes of delirium and wondering why things are not better but thinking that things could be better if just more money is thrown at the problem. Of course, the monies thrown are our tax dollars, not theirs. Entitlement programs emanating from the civil rights laws take over 65 percent of the annual federal budget and are growing each year.

Even the word "entitlement" should be an obscene word to the American taxpayer. Why are some entitled to your monies without your say-so? It would be one thing if you gave your money away to charity or other organizations, but our government blatantly decides to take from the American taxpayer without compensation in the name of . . . what? For a while the process was covert; now the news is everywhere. Entitlement programs are the biggest part of our federal government's budget—not the defense of our country, not compensation to veterans, not roads, not transportation, not education of our young. Entitlements to the millions of "entitled," and more are added every year. The amnesty orders of my predecessor added millions onto the tax rolls as new "entitlements." When is the American taxpayer going to become "entitled"?

NO MORE! This country was founded and grown over two hundred years by people who stood up and fended for themselves. Many came here with little, but with hard work, diligence, and trusting in God, they carved out the wilderness and made a living and life for themselves and their following generations. They asked

---

[35] Chantrill, Christopher. "Government Debt in the United States." US Government Spending. http://www.usgovernmentdebt.us/.

not for entitlements but for a chance to prove themselves and make a life for themselves and their families. Think of all the industries formed in the US over the last two hundred years: railroad, automobile, oil, electrical, shipping. All were formed and grown by individuals pursuing their dreams and making things happen. This is the heart of America, not entitlement programs or government aid. It is ironic how the mantra for many seeking public office is that they claim to be from a poor family background and by hard work they carved out a handsome life. That used to be true; however, looking at many in the DSP, they all came from privileged backgrounds,[36] often under some "entitlement" program. Witness our last president—his whole life was based on "entitlements."[37]

In the coming weeks I will be addressing specific aspects of government that have grown over the last fifty years to provide and expand these various "civil rights" and "entitlement" programs. There will be, I promise you, drastic changes in these arenas. Agencies that have cropped up and grown into behemoths will be curtailed and in many cases dissolved. One such behemoth is the Department of Education, arisen in the DSP Carter years to address who knows what. Education always has been the responsibility of the local populace and supported by their tax dollars. Here again this department was created to resolve certain "civil rights" issues not dealt with on the local scale. NO MORE! This department will go the top of my hit list in the next months. The education of our young will revert back to the state and local

---

[36] Pollock, Richard. "Seven of the Top Ten Wealthiest Members of Congress Are Democrats." PJ Media. November 15, 2011. https://pjmedia.com/blog/seven-of-the-top-ten-wealthiest-members-of-congress-are-democrats/.
[37] "American President Barack Obama." Miller Center. http://millercenter.org/president/obama.

arenas. Parents will again get to control the education of their children, not some faraway bureaucrat in Washington.

Thank you for your attention today.

"GOD BLESS AMERICA."

Day 13: States' Rights (Part 1)

Amendment 10: The original Tenth Amendment is reinforced and reaffirmed regarding state versus federal powers. In any legal arena, powers not specific to the federal government will revert to state control. Powers arising in the last fifty years that suborn state control to federal control will be rescinded within ninety days of ratification of this amendment.

My fellow Americans, our federal government has grown into a leviathan, engulfing all in its insatiable appetite for growth and control. As can be seen in the amendments proposed in the past few days, control must be wrested away from this leviathan and given back to the people. Part of the problem probably stems from the Civil War over 150 years ago. A vacuum was created, and the federal government stepped in to fill the void. Aided again by various radical Supreme Court decisions, the federal government has assumed controlling interest in every aspect of our lives. NO MORE! I was elected, I think, to help stop this outrage and return control to the people. As I said prior, we fought a Revolutionary War to gain our freedoms; the war is now with Washington.

Important in this equation is that the states need to step up to the plate and take responsibility for their citizens and their welfare. If the people of a state pass amendments to stop, say, same-sex marriage, then it is the state's responsibility to uphold their citizens' desires. This idea that the people of a state pass a law and the state government refuses to enforce the law is an abomination. Government officials who fail to do the will of the people should be impeached and driven out of office. All this will not be easy, as will be seen in the coming days. With rights come responsibility, fiscal and otherwise. No longer will the states be able to shrug off duties and obligations to the federal government. No longer will the federal government be "Big Brother." Thank you all for your support!

"GOD BLESS AMERICA."

DAY 14: REST

Our Father, Who art in heaven, hallowed be Thy name, Thy kingdom come, Thy will be done on earth as it is in heaven. Give us this day our daily bread and forgive us our trespasses as we forgive those who trespass against us. Lead us not into temptation but deliver us from evil. Amen.

SECTION 3

LIBERTY AMENDMENTS

Day 15: Introduction to Liberty Amendments

My fellow Americans, good morning. These next few weeks I will continue our dialogue on how to protect our rights as citizens and how to protect and enhance our Constitution, which, as we have discussed, is being shredded each and every day, not only by congressional actions and inactions but also by a radical Supreme Court and federal judiciary that change the law at their whim and even promulgate new laws, which was not the intention in the Constitution.

I have already outlined ten amendments that will help correct some of these extraconstitutional efforts that have contributed to the current political, social, economic, and religious upheavals that this country has been experiencing these last fifty years.

In the coming days I will be proposing even more amendments to help set this nation back on a healthy pathway. As I stated days ago, I wish to thank the constitutional expert Mark Levin and his outstanding book, *The Liberty Amendments*, for his guidance in formulating these particular amendments. I will be examining each of his amendments and paraphrasing his rationale for each amendment. I, of course, will be adding my own thoughts on each amendment. In some areas I may modify an amendment or enhance it and will note that as the time comes. I encourage any citizen to read Mr. Levin's book for a more in-depth analysis of each amendment. As before, I also strongly encourage all citizens to contact your congressional and state representatives to voice your opinions on these measures. They need to hear very loudly the voice of the people on these matters.

Whereas the first ten amendments dealt with primary rights, the following amendments will propose broad, sweeping changes in our government spending, taxation, regulations, states' rights, private property rights, and a variety of economic issues. Some of the amendments are lengthy, and, where applicable, I will synthesize the amendment. Here again the full discussion is in the aforementioned book by Mr. Levin.

Again, I and this office are strongly behind the voting for and establishing of a constitutional convention, hopefully to be approved by the state legislatures. Thirty-four state approvals are needed to authorize the start of the convention within the next twelve months. This, my fellow Americans, is your moment in history to approve drastic changes in this ship of state and stop the headlong path into the iceberg dead ahead. All of you know the story of the *Titanic*, and how that "unsinkable" ship fared after hitting the iceberg. Our country and you the citizens deserve better. No longer can we afford to have a radical minority dictate our lives and destroy our freedoms in the name of diversity or whatever the flavor of the month happens to be. Join me each day as we continue to explore solutions to the myriad of problems we face. Until then,

"GOD BLESS AMERICA."

Day 16: Congressional Leadership Meeting with the President

Nine o'clock a.m., the —— room in the White House. Congressional leaders of both houses of Congress are in attendance. Ten members each from the Senate and the House; three from each party leadership; and four members, two from each party, who are junior, first term. The junior representatives were to be chosen at random from among the junior members with the proviso that any junior member chosen could give his or her space to another junior member of his or her party. Twenty congressional representatives were thus selected and are in attendance. Breakfast has just been completed. The various members of Congress are talking among themselves and the vice president. The atmosphere is somewhat light, but the undercurrent bodes a lot of discomfort.

The double doors open. A marine steps in and announces the president. All stand out of respect; President M—— enters the room and greets the assemblage. "Thank you all for coming on such short notice. Please sit down.

"I called this meeting for several reasons. For too long, especially with the last presidency, there has been almost no dialogue between the executive branch and Congress. As I mentioned in my inaugural address to the nation, this administration will have many tasks ahead of it, but the mission will always be the same: return power to the people and away from Washington.

"You all are aware of the low standing all branches of government have with the American public. I want to change that for the better. I want a stronger Constitution and a federal government that supports the Constitution and doesn't find ways to circumvent the Constitution. This will be a huge task, and your responsibility as a representative of the people is to help in that task. The days of crony political deals and incestuous dealings with big business, lobbyists, and the military are coming to an end.

"You have all heard my speeches these past two weeks on proposed amendments to the Constitution, what I call the 'Second Bill of Rights.' Many of you may disagree with many or all of the amendments; some will be violently opposed to the amendments. Unfortunately, this country has been on the 'highway to hell' these past fifty years due to an abundance of progressive legislation and, even more onerous, tens of thousands of pages of federal regulations that supplement the insane laws. For the most part, most of the progressive agenda has been extraconstitutional and, sad to say, our Supreme Court has not acted on the peoples' behalf and reversed many of these so-called 'social laws.'

"I do not expect total adherence to what I have already proposed and will continue to propose. Let's face it, folks, we are not friends—we were elected to do the peoples' will. Our purpose as public officials is not to make friends, not to make scads of money, and not to increase personal power. We are representatives of the people—advisors—and will continue to be. What I do expect is that the fight between Congress and this administration will be civil and respectful. As mentioned in my inauguration address, my two guiding works," he holds up the Bible and the Constitution, "will be the basis of my actions and my proposed legislation.

"Many of you, no doubt, will be appalled at my legislation that will be sent to Congress. If you can prove that any legislation is 'unconstitutional,' then bring those facts to my office and we will go from there. If you 'whine' about your sacred shibboleths that are being destroyed, well, this is only the beginning. I am here to tell you that I will keep the dialogue open at all times between our two branches of government, but as Harry Truman once said, 'The buck stops here!'

"With that in mind, the main purpose of this meeting is to give you all a 'heads-up' on what is coming down the pike. Each of you has a copy of Mark Levin's book, *The Liberty Amendments*, in front of you. That book and those amendments will be the subject of the next several weeks of speeches. Many of those amendments will seem very radical, but I think all are needed if we are to save our country. While each of us in this room are of different backgrounds and party lines, I would hope that we all are patriots in the final analysis and love our country. Many of the ideas behind those amendments will be presented in legislation this office will be sending to Congress. I warn you now, the legislation from this office in the next sixty days will be 'fast and furious.' The legislation will not be huge omnibus bills like Obamacare and TARP. They will be short, concise, and demand action along specific lines.

"Following those amendment speeches will be a month-long series of speeches on paring down the federal government. Topics will include the upcoming federal budget, paring down federal personnel, and a detailed look at most of the cabinet posts and agencies within with specific plans on eliminating or reducing specific agencies. Many of these reductions will take place over the next two years or before. My staff is now working on the next federal budget, which will shock most of you in this room. The people are tired of government-as-usual and are demanding accountability. My first federal budget will be a giant step along those lines.

"Ladies and gentlemen, these reductions will be with the Tenth Amendment in mind. My avowed goal is to return as much power in government back to the states, as defined originally by the Constitution. I know that the states will in many cases themselves rebel, for they too long have been used to feeding at the 'federal trough.' That also will be ending very rapidly.

"Paring down the federal 'leviathan' will be a very detailed and time-consuming job for both our branches. While my speeches will concentrate on the cabinet posts and agencies first, the legislation will continue the pathway and go forward into many of the government's 'entitlement' programs that have grown to enslave our country and destroy the working middle class of Americans who are called on to foot the bill. My speeches will not be limited to Social Security and Medicare but will go into areas such as the

Americans with Disabilities Act and Obamacare. Being a practical man, we will address each of these 'entitlements' and also stress solutions to changing these programs or dismantling them when feasible.

"The next series of speeches will be about the economy and will involve this country's debt issues, now over twenty trillion dollars and counting, not to mention our unfunded liabilities which are over one hundred trillion dollars. Every branch of government has their share of blame for this fiscal irresponsibility. My speeches will be foreshowed by the federal budget speech and legislation and will then go on to examine the Federal Reserve, our fiat currency, taxation, commerce, federal regulations on business, subsidies for agriculture and other business industries, energy usage, exploration, and building a new energy infrastructure for America. All in all, a lot of hot topics.

"My next series of speeches will address another critical aspect of our country: foreign affairs. During this time, I will talk about the 'Masters Doctrine,' which will be defined in detail. Maybe not as famous as the original 'Monroe Doctrine,' the Masters Doctrine will help chart America's relationship with the rest of the world, namely those countries that are our *friends* and those countries that are *not our friends*. In short, ladies and gentlemen, the world will be divided by these categories, and our relationships will be based on these categories. To give you an example, Israel is on our 'friends' list; Iran is not.

"The Masters Doctrine will also include a very changed and enhanced mission statement for our military and will detail the goals for our military. To give you an idea of where I am coming from, 'entitlements' are down in funding terms; military expenditures will be up. The joint chiefs will be expanded to five full branches: army, navy, marines, air force, and coast guard. I will tell you now, there will be no women in the joint chiefs of staff.

"Our State Department will be revamped, and its mission will be changed along the above categories of nations. During the next three years, there will be a number of treaties that will be going to the Senate for approval. These treaties that are enacted will help stabilize the world and will be aggressive for all concerned. The vice president will be meeting with your committees on a regular basis to update Congress on the treaties in progress and our position papers on each of the treaties. Lastly, the number of US embassies around the world will be changing drastically. We will concentrate our efforts and diplomacy in areas of strength, not weakness.

"The last month of speeches will be in the area of American culture. These talks will be totally 'politically incorrect,' as they will examine without partiality how far we as a nation have fallen in the last sixty years, how we have gone from 'one nation under God,' or in other words, *e pluribus unum,*' to a very divided nation falling apart at the seams, all done in the name of the ungodly social dictum 'diversity.' There was a time when we had an American culture; in order to survive we need to find that culture and renew it again. God, patriotism, family, church, work ethic, and of course 'made in America' were once part of our daily lives. This administration is committed to bringing these values and culture back to the mainstream.

"That should cover the main topics that will be discussed over the next two-plus months. I promised the American citizens when I was elected that I would be their advocate in Washington. The first hundred days of this administration will be distinguished along that purpose. Again, I want to stress that it is up to each of us and our colleagues to change the course of our country. We must not be the *Titanic* heading for the iceberg and sinking. History is replete with nations and empires that have come and gone and have fallen on the dust heap of history. America will not be in that category—at least not on my watch.

"I will leave you now to discuss what I have outlined. The folders in front of each of you go into more detail on the various subjects that will be coming up. The vice president will be here to discuss these issues in further detail. I look forward to working with you all to save our country. Until we meet next,

"GOD BLESS AMERICA."

President M—— rises and leaves the room. The room is silent for several minutes, then many conversations start . . .

Day 17: Term Limits

Amendment 11: No person shall serve more than twelve years as a member of Congress either in the House or Senate or a combination thereof. Upon ratification of this amendment, any member of Congress who has been more than twelve years in Congress shall complete the current term and then retire.

My fellow Americans, for too long we have allowed members of Congress to make a career out of being members of Congress. History is replete with instances of congressmen senile beyond their years but still being reelected. Carl Hayden, the congressman from Arizona, was in Congress for over fifty years, from when Arizona became a state until his death. Insane! This has to end. We as a country put limits on how long a president can serve; now it is time to include Congress in those term limits.

Our founding fathers feared many things in formulating our Constitution; one of the major fears was the "professional" politician who by virtue of power, money, position, whatever, becomes a permanent fixture in Washington, working not for the people but for his or her own advantages. As was noted in Mr. Levin's book in 2010, over 85 percent of the members of Congress were reelected.[38] The more these members get reelected, the more powerful they become and the more entrenched they become. Their interests are their continuation of power.

This was not always the case. During the nineteenth century, turnover in Congress averaged over 50 percent.[39] This allowed new members regularly to contribute to the dialogue in Congress. This is no longer the fact. All new members into Congress are now told from the start what they are allowed to do, how to vote, and what committees they can sit on—generally to "sit there and shut up and vote how the powerful leaders tell them to vote." The two-party system is disintegrating into a "republicrat" party consisting of the senior leaders with all the power and the junior members with no power. Any congressman challenging the status quo is quickly vilified and ostracized. Witness the case of Congressman Ted Cruz.

Congressmen, when they finally retire, can keep any unspent election funds that are in their coffers. No wonder there are no poor congressmen! By the way, these are the same congressmen who every few years give themselves generous raises and expense allowances. They have their own retirement fund and, of course, their own health insurance exempt from Obamacare and Medicare and Social Security. A great career path, especially since

---

[38] Mark R. Levin, *The Liberty Amendments: Restoring the American Republic* (New York City, NY: Simon & Schuster, 2013), page 19.
[39] "Reelection Rates Over the Years." OpenSecrets. https://www.opensecrets.org/overview/reelect.php.

they only work part-time—fewer than six months total—when they are in Congress.

The progressives will use the argument that we need seasoned congressmen to better look out for our interests. Sorry, this assumption is not borne out of fact. Look at the growth of the federal government just over the last twenty years under these "seasoned" congressman. The only constant growth "industry" in the US has been government. Over a quarter of this nation's gross domestic product, or GDP, is now with the federal government. Federal deficits have been over $1 trillion each year for the past ten years.[40] Congress is spending not only our money but our children's and even our grandchildren's money. Folks, government does not contribute to the economy, it takes away from the economy. It does not create wealth, it only transfers from one sector to another. It is private enterprise that creates jobs and wealth; government confiscates wealth and moves it to the "entitled" masses, be that who they may. NO MORE!

It is time to rein in our Congress and its members and regain control over the process. Term limits will be a start in the right direction. Until tomorrow,

"GOD BLESS AMERICA."

---

[40] Chantrill, Christopher. "What Is the Total US Government Spending?" US Government Spending.
http://www.usgovernmentspending.com/total_spending_chart.

Day 18: Senate Elections

Amendment 12: The Seventeenth Amendment is repealed. Election of senators shall revert to the state legislatures as prescribed in Article I of the Constitution. Any vacancies in a senator's term more than ninety days, the governor shall appoint an individual for the rest of the term. Any senator can be removed from office by a two-thirds vote of the state legislature.

My fellow Americans, today's topic may appear to be somewhat esoteric, but I assure you it has vast ramifications of controlling our Congress. To start this discussion, it may be beneficial to examine the historical context of the Constitution. Our forefathers feared big government, especially federal government. They saw that unless controlled, big government would lead to totalitarian government and thus to dictatorship. One of the main discussion points in formulating our Constitution was along the lines of controlling "federalism."

The bicameral Congress was the foundation of the states, and thus the peoples, controlling government. Members of the House were to be elected directly by the people of each state. That process has been corrupted over the years by the concept of "gerrymandering," changing congressional districts in states, thus allowing unequal representation in districts galore. This process is usually done by the party in power to further consolidate their positions in the House. The Senate was a different story. Our forefathers wanted another level of control over a federal leviathan. The senators from each state were to be elected by the state legislatures of that state, and thus could also be removed by said legislatures.

To have the states control the election of their respective senators allowed the states direct input into congressional action on a continuing basis, but also served as a check by the states on federal government excess and potential abuse. For 127 years this was the method of electing senators. The Seventeenth Amendment in 1913 changed all that and also removed the states' continued influence and check on the federal government. We all have seen what has happened in the last hundred years. The federal leviathan has grown immensely with almost no countermeasures. The fifty states in our republic have become shells in the federal con game. The feds say "jump," and the states ask "how high?" From immigration, border control, and workplace hiring and firing to education, transportation, welfare, and disability, all states have to bow to the feds. The courts have also contributed to this insanity by continuing to overrule any state initiatives in favor of the federal, even though the Tenth Amendment states otherwise. In all cases, the Supreme Court has ruled that federal law supersedes state law even when not supported by the Constitution. A classic example in the recent past dealt with same-sex marriages; here the federal government via the courts basically nullified the will of the people and allowed same-sex marriage to become law of the land, directly against the will of the people. Another example is the Affordable Care Act, passed by Congress even though the majority of the people in the US—73 percent—did not want it.[41] Senators in many states voted for the act even though the people of that state vehemently opposed it. NO MORE!

We need to go back to what our framers of the Constitution wanted and what worked for over one hundred years. We need to give the states more control over their affairs and increase their

---

[41] "Kaiser Health Tracking Poll: March 2013." Kaiser Family Foundation. March 20, 2013. http://kff.org/health-reform/poll-finding/march-2013-tracking-poll/.

influence on the federal government. The amendment will start the process. No longer will senators be able to snub their noses at their states' wishes in Washington, but they will again be responsible to the states and the people. The other important part of the equation will be the ability of each state legislature to remove a senator for whatever reason by a two-thirds vote of that legislature.

Again, please contact your state representative in the legislature and voice your opinion on this matter. Count on your senators to violently oppose this amendment, but that is nothing new. Thank you for your attention today.

"GOD BLESS AMERICA."

Day 19: Judicial Control

Amendment 13: No person appointed to serve on the Supreme Court shall serve more than twelve years on the court.

Justices on the Supreme Court currently will be divided into three classes by reverse seniority. Each class—first, second, third—shall be retired at the end of their four-year cycle and those justice slots will be appointed and filled by the Senate.

If a vacancy occurs during a justice's term, another will be appointed by the Senate for the remainder of the term.

Federal judges appointed by the Senate will have the same term of office as the Supreme Court. Any current federal judges past the twelfth-year mark will serve out the current year or 180-day mark, whichever is the lesser, and then retire.

My fellow Americans, today's topic will address one of the largest problem areas in our federal government: the "runaway" judiciary. In Mr. Levin's book this was listed as a single amendment, but I have taken the liberty—no pun intended—of making two amendments out of the topic. Tomorrow, I will address the involvement of the states and Congress in judicial oversight.

Our history has been replete with judicial irresponsibility, in many cases not only with not interpreting the Constitution but also in effect rewriting the Constitution and creating new laws, something the Constitution expressly forbids. Article I, section 8 states that Congress and only Congress has the power "to make all laws necessary for carrying into execution the forgoing powers."

The situation has gotten totally out of hand. In the last fifty years, nine individuals—and in many cases, only five individuals— have been deciding the fate of 200 to 300 million Americans, and often badly. I have reviewed already the disaster of *Roe v. Wade*, but the horror continues. States' rights have been totally demolished with court decisions on immigration, voting, border control, and same-sex marriage; our nation has been rent asunder. The list goes on and on. Our website, WH2017.org, will highlight some of the egregious decisions made of the Supreme Court against the will of the people.

These justices have reinterpreted the Constitution and their roles to encompass what they call a "living Constitution." This effectively destroys the Constitution because every law, every part of the Constitution becomes fluid and subject to change on any whim of the Supreme Court. "Women's right to privacy" becomes the rationale for murder. "Discrimination" allows the courts to destroy four thousand years of marriage. "Civil rights" becomes the mantra to destroy states' rights, privacy rights, and free speech. "Diversity" allows the dismantling of laws protecting our borders, language, and culture.[42] (Thank you, Michael Savage, author of *Savage Nation*.)

The insanity goes beyond our borders. Supreme Court justices are even recommending looking into international law and somehow incorporating those laws into their decisions. Even a "conservative" justice, Ms. O'Connor, commented in a speech, "Conclusions reached by other countries and by the international community should at times constitute persuasive authority in American courts."[43] Insane! Thoughts like these lead the way to horrific processes such as Sharia law. In many countries in Europe today where the Muslim population is becoming increasingly visible, residents already adhere not to their country's laws but to Sharia law.[44] The phrase "Euro Arabia" is becoming a reality.

The framers of the Constitution addressed many issues, but the judiciary was an area that, unfortunately, over the years has been become the "elephant in the room." In his book *Men in Black*, Mr. Levin states, "The Court has so fundamentally altered its duties, and so completely rejected the limits placed on it by the Constitution's checks and balances and enumeration of powers, that the justices are in an endless search for extraconstitutional justifications and interventions to explain their activism."[45] NO MORE!

With this amendment, we the people start to rein in our courts. Justices will no longer serve until death but will replaced every

---

[42] Savage, Michael. *The Savage Nation: Saving America from the Liberal Assault on Our Borders, Language, and Culture*. Nashville: Wnd Books, 2002.
[43] Mark R. Levin, *Men in Black: How the Supreme Court Is Destroying America* (Washington, DC: Regnery Pub., 2005), page 21.
[44] "Sharia Law in Europe." BillionBibles.
http://www.billionbibles.org/sharia/sharia-europe.html.
[45] Mark R. Levin, *Men in Black: How the Supreme Court Is Destroying America* (Washington, DC: Regnery Pub., 2005), page 22.

twelve years. The federal justices also appointed will be replaced on a regular basis. Term limits that were recommended for Congress are equally important in this arena.

"GOD BLESS AMERICA."

Day 20: Judicial Decisions

Amendment 14: Upon three-fifths vote of both Houses of Congress, Congress can override a majority opinion of the Supreme Court. Such an override is not subject to presidential veto.

Three-fifths of the state legislatures can also override any Supreme Court decision. This majority of state legislatures cannot be overridden by any act of Congress or the president.

Either the Congress or the state-legislature action must be completed within twenty-four months of the original Supreme Court decision.

All constitutional legal issues regarding any state constitution will be addressed by the USSC alone.

My fellow Americans, today's topic will continue to address judicial activism on the Supreme Court. With this amendment, we the people will continue to rein in the radicalism found in the courts. No longer will Supreme Court decisions be sacrosanct; they will be open to not only congressional review but also the states' review. Decisions can also be reversed on both levels.

The framers of the Constitution defined the role of the judiciary as limited to looking at the constitutionality of a legal question. The role was designed to be limited, definitely not proactive. As Alexander Hamilton said in *Federalist* 78, "The judiciary, on the contrary, has no influence over either the sword or the purse; no direction either of the strength or the wealth of the society; and can take no ACTIVE resolution whatever. It may truly be said to have neither force nor will, but merely judgment."[46]

Sad to say this attitude of the judiciary did not last long. In 1803 Chief Justice Marshall changed the game by stating, "The judicial power of the United States is extended to all cases arising from the Constitution." In effect the judiciary granted itself unlimited power in all realms of constitutional laws.

This, of course, took away any restraints on the judiciary. "Constitutionality" became what the Supreme Court determined it to be, or, in many cases in the past hundred years, what any federal judge determined it to be. Witness the horrific circumstances that happened in the state of California. A state law was passed and endorsed by the people, limiting marriage to a man and a woman. Their state Supreme Court overruled the law, again actively interpreting the state constitution. The people of California then passed an amendment to their state constitution that marriage is only between a man and a woman. Activists appealed to a federal judge, who, by the way, was gay and was involved with a gay activist, overturned the amendment and declared that the amendment was unconstitutional.[47] Immediately after making his ruling, the judge retired from the bench. The Supreme Court did not see fit to throw out the obviously biased ruling and allowed it to stand, thereby opening the state of California to same-sex marriage.

---

[46] Hamilton, Alexander. "The Federalist #78." Constitution Society. http://www.constitution.org/fed/federa78.htm.
[47] Levine, Dan. "Gay Judge Never Thought to Drop Marriage Case." Reuters. April 06, 2011. http://www.reuters.com/article/us-gaymarriage-judge-idUSTRE7356TA20110406.

This activism then led the way for state after state whose constitutions had amendments preventing same-sex marriage to also be overturned. We have seen in the last ten years same-sex marriage become the law of the land, totally bypassing the will of the people in all cases.

The progressives then praise the judiciary for their biased opinions and, of course, their activism in redefining not only the Constitution but the social morals of America. Think of this, folks: as I mentioned before, only a very small minority of any population is homosexual—less than 2 percent. How can a small minority overrule the will of the other 98 percent?

NO MORE! This amendment will address this insanity. It will give you, the people, the tools to take back and control the runaway train called our government. Thank you for your support.

"GOD BLESS AMERICA."

DAY 21: REST

Our Father, Who art in heaven, hallowed be Thy name, Thy kingdom come, Thy will be done on earth as it is in heaven. Give us this day our daily bread and forgive us our trespasses as we forgive those who trespass against us. Lead us not into temptation but deliver us from evil. Amen.

Day 22: Federal Spending

Amendment 15: Congress shall no later than the first Monday in May prepare and present a preliminary budget for the next fiscal year. Said budget is to be finalized by the end of the current fiscal year, October 1st.

The budget shall be balanced each year, total expenses matched by total revenues. Revenues shall not include those received from borrowing, either from the open market or trust funds such as Social Security.

The total federal budget shall not exceed 20 percent of nation's gross domestic product from the previous calendar year.

In case of national emergency, disaster, or war, Congress can suspend the balanced budget for a period of one year.

This amendment shall take effect on the fourth fiscal year after the amendment is passed.

My fellow Americans, the next few days we will address the runaway government both in spending and taxation. As you all are aware, the federal government has had trillion-dollar deficits almost every year for the past ten years. For many of those years Congress ran without a budget in any form, passing continuing resolutions to fund the various aspects of the government. [48] Insanity upon insanity! Instead of addressing the issue with fiscal restraint, the government votes to continually expand its role irrespective to the effects on our nation and the citizens.

We have now an accumulated debt of over $20 trillion and absolutely no means of paring down that debt and making our country fiscally sound. Over the past seventeen years Congress has

---

[48] "History of United States Debt Ceiling." *Wikipedia.*
https://en.wikipedia.org/wiki/History_of_United_States_debt_ceiling.

increased the debt limit fifteen times. The picture is even more horrific. In 2002 our national debt was 58 percent of our nation's GDP. Ten years later in 2012, our debt was 105 percent of GDP. Folks, this debt is now larger than the value of all our nation produces in the private sector.[49]

The Federal Reserve has contributed to this mess by playing a con game over the past ten years—buying up the debt notes, keeping interest rates artificially low, and flooding the markets with dollars. Of course, this cannot be sustained and eventually interest rates will rise and drastically affect the national budget. For each 1 percent that interest rates rise, payments on that interest will increase by $200 billion. Think of this, folks: interest rates fifty years ago were 4 percent; if rates go back to just that level, debt interest payments will be over $1 trillion a year.[50]

All our states are bound by their constitutions to balance their budgets; so should the federal government. It is interesting, however, to note how the disease of fiscal irresponsibility has spread even to the states. Many balance their budgets by including federal grants and transfers as states' revenues. This must stop, and this amendment will hopefully reverse the path we have been on.

With passage of this amendment, Congress has four years to balance the budget. To help matters along, the federal budget will be lowered by 5 percent each year across the board until the budget is balanced. If that is not enough to achieve the balance, in the fourth year the budget outlays will revert to the fiscal year that matches current revenues. For example, the current year's budget

---

[49] "Q&A: Everything You Need to Know About the National Debt." Fix the Debt. http://www.fixthedebt.org/everything-about-the-debt.

[50] "United States Prime Rate History." Fed Prime Rate. http://www.fedprimerate.com/wall_street_journal_prime_rate_history.htm.

is projected at $2.8 trillion.[51] That figure matches with the budget outlays for the year 2007. That year's budget will automatically be the budget for the current fiscal year. Any new departments created since that year will not be funded.

An additional provision in this amendment is the restraint of the federal budget to 20 percent of GDP (here I have modified Mr. Levin's recommendation a few percentage points), a restraint that can only be overridden by both houses of Congress and only in times of dire emergency, such as a world war or national disaster, and then only for a one-year period. As we have stated, the engine for our economy is private enterprise, not government spending. This provision will help that perspective. To rely on government as the answer to all social and economic ills is a fool's game.

Now, of course, the progressives will yell and scream since a vast number of them say the federal budget is sacrosanct, here think entitlements, and limiting those numbers, of course, will limit the powers of the progressives. The federal budget includes vast amounts of entitlement and affects large numbers of our population that are on the government dole; 46 million people on food stamps, 98 million have dropped out of the workforce permanently, and 12 million are on Social Security disability.[52]

The above numbers do not include the millions of Americans on Social Security and Medicare. These mostly retired Americans think that their contributions to the SS and Medicare funds over

---

[51] Chantrill, Christopher. "Federal 2015 Government Revenue." US Government Revenue.
http://www.usgovernmentrevenue.com/fed_revenue_2015US.
[52] "45 Million Americans Rely on Food Stamps, 1 Million about to Lose Them – Report." RT International. February 4, 2016. https://www.rt.com/usa/331216-americans-food-stamps-restrictions/.

their lifetimes have enabled them to some benefits, little knowing that the till is empty and has been for decades. Only IOUs remain.

These numbers are horrific in themselves, but when you add on the illegal immigrants and their families that are in the US to these numbers, the situation becomes unbearable. Many of the above issues will be addressed in the coming weeks. Solutions to these entitlements will be proposed. Many will not be pleasant, but in order to heal this nation from the social diseases we have absorbed, drastic action will need to be taken. NO MORE!

The days of wildly spending our money, our children's money, and our grandchildren's inheritance will be coming to an end. If Congress cannot police itself, we the people will take back control. Have a beautiful week.

"GOD BLESS AMERICA."

Day 23: Taxation

Amendment 16: The Sixteenth Amendment is repealed. Congress shall not tax any individual person more than fifteen (15) percent of that person's annual income from whatever source derived. The only exemption from this tax shall be allowances for charitable donations. Person is defined as a "natural" or "legal" entity.

This deadline for filing annual federal tax returns shall be due on the first Monday before federal elections.

Federal estate taxes are hereby repealed.

No other tax substitutes such as a national sales tax or value-added tax can be instituted.

This amendment will take effect in the fourth fiscal year after the amendment is passed. The IRS will be abolished at that time, to be replaced by a downsized agency by Congress.

Good morning, America. Today we will tackle the immense power of government to tax. Our country has been fighting this monstrosity for over 230 years. In the beginning it was England that unfairly taxed the colonies and eventually led to the Revolutionary War. Our constitution gave Congress the power to tax, but it was a limited power and served to keep the wolves at bay, until 1913 when the progressives won one of their greatest victories and passed the Sixteenth Amendment. Like all progressive legislation, the effect initially was quite small. It is interesting to note that the tax even back then was known as a "progressive tax." The rates started at 1 percent of incomes to $463,283 and went up to 7 percent to incomes over $11 million.[53] As one can see, those income figures in 1913 comprised an ultra-small percentage of the population.

As with all legislation, the amounts and percentages of taxation grew rapidly over the past hundred years. Today the top rate is almost 40 percent, with the tax burden rapidly affecting only the top 50 percent of wage earners. The bottom 50 percent pay no taxes whatsoever. As a matter of fact, the top 5 percent of wage earners in the US pay 59 percent of all federal taxes, and the top 10 percent pay almost 70 percent of the taxes.[54, 55] The picture gets even more dismal when we include state taxes, income, sales, property, and other taxes such as estate, excise, and business. The tax burden is overwhelming.

---

[53] Pomerleau, Kyle. "2016 Tax Brackets." Tax Foundation. October 14, 2015. http://taxfoundation.org/article/2016-tax-brackets.

[54] Saunders, Laura. "Top 20% of Earners Pay 84% of Income Tax." WSJ. April 10, 2015. http://www.wsj.com/articles/top-20-of-earners-pay-84-of-income-tax-1428674384.

[55] "45% of Americans Pay No Federal Income Tax NewsWatch." MarketWatch. February 24, 2016. http://www.marketwatch.com/(S(rnrsydaynixa5x55oiibxm45))/story/45-of-americans-pay-no-federal-income-tax-2016-02-24-17103010?link=MW_story_latest_news.

One hideous aspect of taxation was the implementation of the payroll tax legislation. The government takes its pound of flesh not once a year, but with each paycheck. These monies, your monies, which are withheld and given to the government over the year are, of course, free money to the government. You are not paid any interest for monies collected. If you receive a refund, no interest is paid by the government for your monies they had and used during the year. Insanity!

The tax regulations over the past hundred years have grown to over seventy thousand pages of regulations (over 4 million words) and are growing each year. Over 60 percent of the taxpayers have to hire tax preparers to do their returns due to the complex nature of the laws and returns. Over 6 billion hours per annum are estimated to be needed to complete the required returns.[56] Sheer insanity!

Now, it would be one thing if taxation kept up with our government's insatiable spending, but that has almost never been the case. In recent years our government spending has created annual deficits of over $1 trillion per annum and is still growing.[57] Washington sees no correlation between spending and taxation and, given the choice, will always tax more than less and always spend more. Progressives make light of the late 1990s when the government supposedly had no deficit and surpluses for several years. As usual, when one looks closely, the charade becomes visible. The balancing act was due to the government using monies collected from the SS-trust funds to balance the budget. This

---

[56] Ryan, Tim. "It Takes Americans 6.1 Billion Hours to Prepare Their Taxes, Says Virginia Foxx." Politifact. April 15, 2014. http://www.politifact.com/truth-o-meter/statements/2014/apr/15/virginia-foxx/it-takes-americans-61-billion-hours-prepare-their-/.

[57] Patton, Mike. "The U.S. Debt: Why It Will Continue to Rise." Forbes. September 18, 2014. http://www.forbes.com/sites/mikepatton/2014/09/18/the-u-s-debt-why-it-will-continue-to-rise/#13a9a1134ff1.

subterfuge has been going on since the SS act was created in the 1930s. SS-trust monies were supposed to be segregated and used for SS recipients. The monies have been diverted and have become part of the general-budget balancing act. Those of you who have contributed over the years into SS thinking, as with pension and savings plans, that there are funds available for your use are sadly mistaken. There are not monies, just IOUs, which have about as much value as our national debt. We will discuss SS in the near future and have recommendations on how to heal that particular infection.

When Washington cannot raise taxes without the people revolting, the government resorts to passing legislation with hidden taxes unknown to the people. The Affordable Care Act of 2010, passed overwhelmingly against the will of the people, has fifteen major tax provisions in the act. These provisions have raised Social Security taxes, Medicare-withholding taxes, estate taxes, and dividend taxes. In some cases, the tax rate has been doubled or even tripled. Doubling the tax rate on capital gains, for example, will have disastrous effects on investment capital in the US. Many retirees depend on dividends for supplemental income during their retirement. These rates have almost been tripled, virtually destroying this income source for these retirees. NO MORE!

This amendment will apply a fair rate of taxation on all citizens without exception and will still encourage charitable deductions. I am a firm believer in tithing to the charity of one's choice, and this should always be encouraged. The 15 percent rule will allow all citizens to plan ahead on monies owed for taxes and monies paid to the government during the year. Payroll taxes paid throughout the year shall earn interest at the prevailing rate, either in the form of a tax refund or be used to decrease taxes owed.

This amendment will also stop the insanity of double taxation. Estate taxes are a prime example: individuals pay taxes on their income and business throughout their lives; to tax the estate thereafter is wrong. We pay SS taxes on "after-tax" income and then are taxed when we get the income. NO MORE! Dividend tax is another example of double taxation that will be stopped.

The filing of tax returns will move from April fifteenth to the first Monday in November before federal elections. We the people should have the opportunity of relating our tax burden with our elected officials.

Lately, many other forms of taxations have been proposed to replace our current system. However, with each proposed new method, there is no guarantee that the current system will be replaced or that the new taxation method will just be added on to the overall tax burden. The states are infamous for this. State income tax deficits lead to state sales tax, which is added on to state property taxes; nothing ever gets repealed or replaced, only increased. Of course, with the states, these new or additional methods of taxations only increase the opportunity to spend more.

Lastly, with the full implementation of this amendment, the IRS will be formally dissolved. What started out as a necessary agency has grown into an incredible government leviathan, a horrible monster that serves to wreck numbers of people's lives and is now even into spying on our citizens. Its regulations almost totally circumvent the Constitution and the Bill of Rights. Citizens are guilty unless they prove they are innocent; property is seized without due process. Congress, the branch that is supposed to legislate taxation, has lost all control over the IRS and has proven reluctant to even supervise its actions. This must stop! Congress will have four years to replace the IRS with a controllable agency, downsized and limited in power and scope.

Thank you for your attention.

"GOD BLESS AMERICA."

DAY 24: DOWNSIZING THE FEDERAL LEVIATHAN

Amendment 17: All federal departments and agencies must be reauthorized by Congress every three years by a majority vote of both houses of Congress. This authorization is not subject to presidential veto.

All executive-branch regulatory agencies and their regulations that have an economic burden of over $100 million as determined by the Government Accountability Office (GAO) shall be reviewed by a joint committee appointed by both houses of Congress. Any regulation over that above amount shall be approved or disapproved by the committee. The committee's actions are not subject to presidential override.

If the committee does not act within six months of said regulation submission, the regulation is considered disapproved and will not be implemented.

Good day, my fellow Americans. Today we will continue to address the leviathan called the federal government. Our government has grown and continues to grow due to the vast bureaucracy that has been created and is not subject to any congressional or electoral process. The federal government now employees over 2.7 million people, not including the military.[58]

These bureaucrats continue to make a career out of government. And why not? The average pay of a federal employee is twice what his or her counterpart in the private sector makes.[59] The retirement

---

[58] "Historical Federal Workforce Tables: Total Government Employment Since 1962." US Office of Personnel Management. Accessed June 22, 2016. https://www.opm.gov/policy-data-oversight/data-analysis-documentation/federal-employment-reports/historical-tables/total-government-employment-since-1962/.

[59] Harrington, Elizabeth. "Study: Government Workers Make 78 Percent More Than Private Sector." *Washington Free Beacon.* October 8, 2015.

is more than ample, and the health benefits are amazing because they have their own health insurance. Plus, the final kicker, if we actually need one, is that many government employees double dip; that is, they "retire" from one federal job and start at another comparable government job immediately—while still earning retirement from one job and salary from the current job. Government employees can make up to $500,000 a year in this scenario. Life is good for them, to be sure! The other side of this coin for higher-up federal employees is that they retire and immediately start a lobbying job to continue influencing the department in which they had a career. Government employment is no longer a service to the people, but a career path vastly better than the private sector.

Another problem, of course, is the fact that once a government employee passes a certain amount of time in their job, with civil rights legislation and union involvement, they virtually can never be fired unless it is for some egregious offense like murder, espionage, or mass embezzlement.

This amendment will allow, for the first time, congressional supervision of the regulatory process and regulatory agencies in the government, especially the executive branch. As I mentioned in my inaugural address a while back, there are now fifteen major agencies reporting to the executive branch. Over 630,000 people are employed by these agencies.[60] Most have been operating autonomously with almost no supervision either by the Oval Office or congressional oversight.

---

http://freebeacon.com/issues/study-government-workers-make-78-percent-more-than-private-sector/.

[60] "Historical Federal Workforce Tables: Executive Branch Civilian Employment Since 1940." US Office of Personnel Management. Accessed June 22, 2016. https://www.opm.gov/policy-data-oversight/data-analysis-

While the aforementioned are significant problems, the elephant in the room is the situation where these agencies promulgate regulations on their own with almost no congressional oversight. A single law passed by Congress can virtually grow into thousands and thousands of regulations overnight. These regulations are often draconian and allow federal agencies almost absolute power over the people. The judiciary has not helped matters at all, most often siding with the agencies in cases of oppressive regulations. A classic case is the Environmental Protection Agency, or EPA, originally empowered by Congress in the 1970s. This agency has grown tremendously in power and scope. Originally designed to control water pollution, it now controls vast areas in almost all industries in the US. The biggest grab, of course, is now to control carbon emissions. Think of this, folks: carbon dioxide is a normal and essential part of life on earth. Plants require it to grow and humans exhale it in every breath. It is a minute part of the atmosphere—less than 0.04 percent[61]—but a very necessary part. It meets no definition of pollution, but through propaganda and falsified data, CO_2 has become a villain on earth. A former vice president has made hundreds of millions of dollars propagating this myth as truth. Now, I do not fault anyone making money legally in the US, but fiction is fiction. The CO_2 pollution myth is just that, a myth. This has not stopped the EPA from getting involved and promulgating its enhanced regulations to cover this new source of "pollution."[62] I wonder if they want to regulate how

---

documentation/federal-employment-reports/historical-tables/executive-branch-civilian-employment-since-1940/.

[61] "Atmosphere of Earth." *Wikipedia*. Accessed June 22, 2016. https://en.wikipedia.org/wiki/Atmosphere_of_Earth.

[62] "Carbon dioxide in Earth's atmosphere." *Wikipedia*. Accessed June 22, 2016. https://en.wikipedia.org/wiki/Carbon_dioxide_in_Earth%27s_atmosphere.

many breaths each human can take, thus controlling the CO_2 emissions more effectively.

Another "Obamanation" is, of course, the Affordable Care Act, which is neither affordable nor healthcare. The act itself empowered over 150 new agencies and enhanced bureaucracies. Currently, over 20,000 pages of new regulations have come about through the law, not to mention additional tax burdens on the American public. Did you realize that the act provides for a 3 percent federal tax on every building sold in the US after 2014?[63]

NO MORE!

This amendment will start the process of reinstalling congressional control over the various federal agencies. Congress has, quite frankly, largely abdicated its role and needs to redirect its energies according to the Constitution, which states, "Legislative powers rest solely with the Congress." God bless you all, and

"GOD BLESS AMERICA."

DAY 25: COMMERCE

Amendment 18: Congressional power to regulate commerce is not absolute and is a specific grant limited to interstate commerce and trade between states.

Congressional powers to regulate commerce do not apply to any commerce within a state, whether or not said commerce can have effects beyond the state's borders.

No entity can be compelled to engage in any commerce or trade.

---

[63] "ObamaCare Tax: Full List of ObamaCare Taxes." ObamaCare Facts. Accessed June 22, 2016. http://obamacarefacts.com/obamacare-taxes/.

Good morning, my fellow Americans. Today's topics continue our examination into the federal government's encroachment into our daily lives. This particular topic, which may sound innocuous, is actually almost all pervasive in our economic environment today. The phrase in the Constitution simply states that "Congress shall have the power to regulate interstate commerce."

While seemingly a very nonthreatening phrase, it had grave implications for the young US at the writing of the Constitution. Many states had become like little countries on their own, some printing their own currency and others making treaties with foreign powers, not all of which were very friendly with their neighboring states. These states enacted numerous taxes and tariffs on goods coming to their state from other states, thereby greatly restricting free trade among the states.

The Constitution was formulated to promote states' rights versus federal rights. This clause was never designed as an all-powerful tool of the federal government as it is today, but to be very restrictive. Thomas Jefferson said in 1791, "The power given to Congress by the Constitution does not extend to the internal regulation of the commerce of a state . . . which remains exclusively with its own legislature, but to external commerce only."[64]

In fact, commerce excluded such activities as agriculture, manufacturing, and labor and dealt specifically with movement of commodities throughout the states. However, as we shall see, these restrictive definitions have been totally cast aside, like much of the Constitution, by our progressive government and the Supreme Court. Indeed, the clause was to promote commerce, not restrict it.

This narrow legal viewpoint of interstate commerce held sway until the 1930s. The Supreme Court ruled in 1933, overturning a

---

[64] Mark R. Levin, *The Liberty Amendments: Restoring the American Public* (New York: Simon & Schuster, 2013), page 119.

federal law setting wage and price controls on poultry, even when the activity was intrastate. The court declared that "If the commerce clause were construed to reach all enterprises and transactions which could be said to have an indirect effect upon interstate commerce, the federal authority would embrace practically all the activities of the people."

Unfortunately, this narrow ruling of the Supreme Court did not last long. The progressives under FDR struck back, and a few years later the Supreme Court reversed its legal thinking with the *Wickard* case. This case involved a quota placed on a farmer whose product never went out of state. The Supreme Court ruled in favor of federal control. The court stated, "Even if appellee's activity be local and though it may not be regarded as commerce, it may still, whatever its nature, be reached by Congress if it exerts a substantial economic effect on interstate commerce . . ."[65] As a result, virtually any economic activity over the last eighty years can be said to affect interstate commerce.

The Supreme Court continued in this vein when in 1968 it ruled that labor conditions in state-run hospitals, schools, and care facilities can effect commerce and are thus under federal control. Today, virtually every activity in the US has federal control to some degree. Every business is controlled in some way: wages, hiring, firing, zoning, EPA controls, building standards, emission controls. The list is endless. All the above is promulgated by Congress and the interstate commerce clause of the Constitution. Recently the Affordable Care Act was considered under the realm of the interstate commerce clause with respect to the individual mandate for health insurance in the act, which, as stated, mandates insurance of all citizens. This type of mandate is of course nothing

---

[65] Mark R. Levin, *The Liberty Amendments: Restoring the American Public* (New York: Simon & Schuster, 2013), page 130.

new; witness the Social Security mandate and the Medicare mandates on all citizens. NO MORE!

This amendment will help put an end to this federal insanity and hopefully return to the states their authority to regulate the affairs of their citizens and not the federal government.

"GOD BLESS AMERICA."

DAY 26: PRIVATE PROPERTY RIGHTS

Amendment 19: The Fifth Amendment is changed to add the flowing phrase: "Private-property rights are predominant and will prevail whenever possible over the right of eminent domain (ED). All properties taken by government shall be compensated under the open-market system."

Eminent domain shall only be instituted in the case of war or national emergency. ED must be ratified by two-thirds of the state legislatures or, in the federal realm, a majority of both houses of congress.

Just compensation of taken land shall be on fair market value at the time of ED.

Good morning, America. Today we will undertake another sensitive topic: private property rights. These rights form the basis of our Constitution and hence our freedoms as a people. John Adams said it well: "The moment that the idea is admitted into society, that property is not as sacred as the laws of God, and that there is not a code of law and public justice to protect it, anarchy and tyranny commence."[66]

---

[66] Mark R. Levin, *The Liberty Amendments: Restoring the American Public* (New York: Simon & Schuster, 2013), page 140.

Sadly, today the federal government has severely encroached upon all aspects of private property rights. Numerous civil rights laws have been enacted to suppress private property rights. The laws now protect all sorts of animal, plant, and other lifeforms and take precedence over our private property rights. As with interstate commerce, federal control of your property is becoming paramount, whether it be a business, a farm, your home, or a commercial building. For example, under the Americans with Disabilities Act, a private property owner must modify his property to accommodate people with disabilities. His home and business must accommodate the disability, and now must accommodate "service animals" who accompany a "disabled" person. Of course, the definition of "disabled" is whatever a person wants it to be, as well as the definition of a "service animal." Their rights supersede your rights. In California, landowners must set aside property for so-called endangered species, even if it's productive farming land.

NO MORE! This amendment will bring back into focus our private property rights, which shall be sacrosanct again. Have a good day, and

"GOD BLESS AMERICA."

DAY 27: STATES' RIGHTS (PART 2)

Amendment 20: State legislatures may adopt amendment(s) to the Constitution upon approval of two-thirds of said state legislatures.

Each state legislature adopting an amendment must use the exact wording as any prior state legislation.

The states have a six-year limit to gain the necessary number of states (thirty-four) to ratify the amendment.

Any amendment adopted thusly cannot be overridden by Congress, the president, or the Supreme Court.

My fellow Americans, today we will reaffirm Article V of the Constitution, which allows the states directly to propose amendments to the Constitution, bypassing Congress altogether. While Article V accomplishes much, it will only be used in extraordinary times such as these since it takes two-thirds of the states to call a convention and three-quarters of the states to ratify amendments proposed by said convention. This, as I have repeatedly said, is the necessary first step to stopping the insanity of government.

However, on a continuing basis and given the broad abuses of Congress, the president, his executive orders, and the radical and runaway judiciary, it will be necessary on an irregular and hopefully infrequent basis for the states to continually step up to the plate and propose new and ongoing amendments to stop radical abuses as they crop up, and, believe me, they will continually crop up. The changes I am proposing and will continue to propose during the next two months will help stop a lot of the abuse, but like an infection in the body, unless we are diligent, the infectious agents will arise again to try and destroy the host. Make no doubt about the enemies we are facing, folks. They are not our friends; they are out to destroy this great nation of ours and we must continually be on our guard. They are in our country; many call themselves citizens, but their hatred for who and what we are as a nation knows no bounds. Like vicious weeds in the garden, they will never go away; they may lie dormant as in winter, but come spring . . .

With this amendment, any state legislature can propose a possible amendment to the Constitution. Each state thereafter when considering the amendment can also pass the said amendment. During the process, the wording of the amendment cannot be changed; if it is changed in any way, the process starts all over again. Several states can meet and decide on common wording; however, there is a six-year time limit in getting the required states to adopt the amendment or not. If two-thirds of the states approve within the time frame, the amendment is certified and becomes part of the Constitution.

The necessity of this amendment is apparent. It reinforces the Tenth Amendment to a large degree and gives back to the states (and thus the people) the power to override legislation arising out of Washington from either of the three branches and stop insanity as it arises. Take again the infamous illustration, the total overruling of the people in the arena of same-sex marriage. Thirty-seven states had amendments to their state constitutions stating simply that marriage is between a man and a woman. In each case, one person in the federal judiciary decided against the people and ruled that same-sex marriage must be allowed, based solely on his or her "activist interpretation" of the Constitution. NO MORE! The states will now be able to fight back against this radicalism and directly affect the Constitution.

The progressives will, of course, cry wolf and proclaim dire consequences if the states are allowed such power. The reason behind their cries is not concern for our nation, but a situation where their power diminishes while the people's power increases. Here it is useful to go back historically to the enactment of the Constitution. Our forefathers feared a large federal government before all else. The Constitution was written expressly to limit the federal leviathan but at the same time preserve the power of the states. As Mr. Levin stated in his book, *The Liberty Amendments*, "In *Federalist* 39, James Madison argues that the federal government has only 'certain enumerated' powers and the states retained 'residuary and inviolable sovereignty' over all else."[67] The framers

---

[67] Mark R. Levin, *The Liberty Amendments: Restoring the American Public* (New York: Simon & Schuster, 2013), page 140.

knew that each of the states would have their own character, their own population, their own economies, and their own thoughts. The proliferation of many states continually serves to constrain the states in actions that would become interstate or national. Even with this amendment, two-thirds of the states would have to agree on the amendment—a formidable task at best.

Again, I would remind you all, as we go through these rough-and-tumble days together, to contact your state and federal representatives and pronounce your thoughts to them. The more of you who sound the alarm, the more they will be forced to listen. Have a beautiful day and remember,

"GOD BLESS AMERICA."

Day 28: Rest

Our Father, Who art in heaven, hallowed be Thy name, Thy kingdom come, Thy will be done on earth as it is in heaven. Give us this day our daily bread and forgive us our trespasses as we forgive those who trespass against us. Lead us not into temptation but deliver us from evil. Amen.

Day 29: States' Rights versus Congress

Amendment 21: All legislation passed by Congress will have a minimum of thirty days before being signed into law by the president. This minimum can only be overridden by a two-thirds majority of both houses.

Upon three-fifths vote of the state legislatures, the states can override any federal statute.

Upon three-fifths vote of the state legislatures, the states can override any executive order or regulations that have a cost burden over $100 million.

This override cannot be overturned by the president, Congress, or the Supreme Court.

The states' override authority is valid for twenty-four months from the day the legislation is enacted into law.

Good morning, my fellow Americans. Last week we proposed an amendment to allow states direct authority to change the Constitution. Today we will go further and propose another amendment which will give the states control over federal legislation. Again, as before, we need to look back at history and what our forefathers intended when they were formulating the Constitution. They feared a large federal government, and what they feared is what our government has become. Bills passed by Congress and passed into law now can number one thousand, two thousand, up to three thousand pages, and no one in Congress even bothers to read the law. They, at the most, are given bullet points from the legislation by their staff, and few even bother to read the bullet points. The situation goes ballistic when the law is passed. Here the federal bureaucracy takes over, and two thousand pages of law become twenty, thirty, forty thousand pages of regulations controlled by the administrative arm of the federal government. That is not the end; as each year passes, thousands of pages of new regulations are promulgated with this act. These regulations have the effect of law but totally bypass Congress, the only branch that is empowered by the Constitution to make law. Here again we have another fine example of this insanity, the Affordable Care Act, which is neither affordable nor healthcare. It is instead a giant step toward socialism and, in this case, socialized medicine. To make matters even worse, who is in charge of enforcement? The IRS. The IRS has had to hire thousands of new agents just to enforce the policies of this act. The act includes at least fifteen hidden new taxes on the American public to pay for aspects of this bill. This act is destined to merge into a national healthcare plan, and it is mandatory for all peoples in the US. The progressives say nothing about the fines on those who ignore the law and the increasing fines every year. The progressives tout the millions who have joined but do not say that the vast majority are at the low end of the economic ladder and are subsidized by the government. The middle class is forced to pay outrageous monthly payments and now have huge deductibles, some up to $10,000 per annum. Remember, folks, that deductibles must be met before any insurance kicks in. In the interim, it is cash for each medical visit or emergency.

Other aspects of this act are equally as horrible. We built our healthcare system on the free enterprise system — that is, the profit motive. It may sound trite, but the capitalist society directly contributes to the quality of our healthcare. Take that away and very quickly supplies become limited, medicine becomes limited, medical care becomes limited, and hospital care becomes limited. We are seeing this in the Medicare field. Thousands of doctors are no longer taking Medicare insurance. If patients want a doctor, they have to pay cash. Canada, our neighbor to the north, has this type of insurance; two years for elective surgery, and an MRI can take up to a year. Why, you ask? Simply because the reimbursements decrease each year while the patient's increase. What has happened with Canadian patients is that they come to the US for healthcare. That will, of course, end soon with the ACA.

To further illustrate this insanity, again let us look at the new "insured." Most of these millions are subsidized and will always be subsidized. Not mentioned also are the millions of illegals who are covered under the act and of course pay nothing for their care. The millions of people in the middle class whose premiums have skyrocketed are also not mentioned. The millions of middle-class people who have lost their insurance and have been forced into the government programs are also not mentioned. The cost for the

ACA explodes each year, now over a $1 trillion over ten years and soaring.[68] Insanity upon insanity. Former President Bill Clinton illustrates the progressive thoughts when he said, "It's not important to be perfect here. It's important to act, to move, and to start the ball rolling. There will be amendments to this effort, whatever they pass, next year, and the next year, and the year after . . ."[69]

All the above will, of course, be mainly supplied by the huge government bureaucracy, who will be writing more and more regulations—new regulations to supplant the old regulations and more regulations to supplant the previous; all totally unsupervised by Congress, the president, or the Supreme Court.

Currently there are about 550 members of Congress in both houses. Their "staff" now numbers over thirty thousand and grows daily. Heck, most congressmen do not even know how large their staff is or who is on their staff. The point here is, as Mr. Levin stated in his book, "Although citizens vote for their members of Congress, these members legislate in a manner that denies the people to a transparent, orderly, and predictable lawmaking system, thereby avoiding true public scrutiny and input. Therefore, government decision-making becomes more centralized and power more concentrated."[70] NO MORE!

This amendment will address some of this abuse of power and start allowing the states and the people more access and more control over the federal leviathan. No longer will two-thousand-page bills be

---

[68] "Conflating Costs of the ACA." FactCheck.org. February 6, 2015. http://www.factcheck.org/2015/02/conflating-costs-of-the-aca.

[69] Slack, Megan. "Former President Bill Clinton Explains the Affordable Care Act." *The White House*. September 3, 2013. https://www.whitehouse.gov/blog/2013/09/03/former-president-bill-clinton-explains-affordable-care-act.

[70] Mark R. Levin, *The Liberty Amendments: Restoring the American Public* (New York: Simon & Schuster, 2013), page 3.

passed into law that no legislator even bothers to read. No longer will the executive branch be able to issue executive orders without any oversight and control. As Thomas Jefferson said long ago, "It was by the *sober sense* [italics mine] of our citizens that we were safely and steadily conducted from monarchy to republicanism, and it is by the same agency alone we can be kept from falling back."[71] Good day!

"GOD BLESS AMERICA."

Day 30: The Right to Vote

Amendment 22: In order to vote, citizens in every state, territory, and DC shall produce valid photographic identification documenting evidence of their citizenship.

Such evidence shall be issued by the state of their residence at no cost to the citizen.

Early voting is restricted to thirty days prior to the elections. Mail-in ballots shall be accompanied by a valid registration to vote in order to be eligible.

All ballots shall be in English only.

Any person attempting to vote who is not a citizen or has falsified documentation will be guilty of a felony and shall be deported immediately. Citizens with false documentation will lose voting privileges for a period of not less than five years.

Good morning, my fellow Americans. Today we examine further our responsibilities as citizens of the US, this one being the right to vote. Voter fraud has been increasing dramatically over the

---

[71] "Thomas Jefferson Quotes About Monarchy." AZ Quotes. Accessed June 22, 2016. http://www.azquotes.com/author/7392-Thomas_Jefferson/tag/monarchy.

past fifty years and has been aided by progressives in Congress and a radical Supreme Court. Much of this voter fraud stems from those who are not citizens or are not allowed to vote due to criminal acts. In state after state, close elections take drastic changes in the last second due to "missing votes" that have appeared out of nowhere. The progressives are famous for this. Remember the case of Senator Franken in Minnesota? He lost the election by under a thousand votes, but after *three* recounts, somehow enough votes surfaced and he won by less than three hundred votes. Strange how quickly that last recount was certified. Insanity!

Again, the progressives will lament that having to produce valid ID will discriminate against the poor and the minorities. Nothing could be further from the truth. Try buying liquor anywhere in the US and not having to produce a photo ID. All driver's licenses are photographic and must be produced when stopped by the police. No one says anything about those instances, but voting seems to be different. Voting is one of the most important duties of any adult citizen, and the progressives want anyone to be able to vote without adequate documentation. Driver's licenses used to be a valid ID, but now with Supreme Court rulings, illegals can obtain a driver's license. My solution there is that every state, when issuing DL to illegals, have in bold, red letters on the licenses NC—noncitizen—on the front and back of the license.

The situation has gotten even worse everywhere with early voting, same-day registration, online registration, ballots published in non-English languages, and the use of provisional ballots. The new talk is to increase online voting using smartphones, the internet, and desktop PCs. Total insanity, since with each new voting method, control becomes less and less. The internet is totally open to the hackers, both government and independent, and, yes, even foreign interests, government and otherwise.

The right to vote has to be protected at all costs. Obtaining valid photo ID is not discriminatory and will help insure that voter fraud is minimized. A 2012 Rasmussen poll showed over 82 percent of those polled believed that a photo ID should be mandatory in order to vote.[72]

Unfortunately, as with many areas of our lives, the right to vote has suddenly become a civil rights issue when it's not. The amendments to the Constitution (XV, XIX, and XXIV) already addressed the valid issues to voting. Establishing a valid ID to vote is not a civil rights issue. No citizen is forced to vote as in other countries, but if one does elect to vote, one must be eligible and prove that eligibility. States that have passed voter-ID indicatives (Pennsylvania and Arizona are two examples) have run into the gamut of federal interference in initiating the laws. It is interesting to note here that in 2005 the GAO found that in just one federal district, over thirty thousand people called for jury duty from voter registration records, 3 percent of whom were not citizens.[73] The number may not seem high, but multiply that by all the federal districts, and the numbers mount. In Colorado, after cross-checking voter registration records against DL records, over eleven thousand were not citizens, and over half of them had voted. NO MORE!

This amendment will restore balance to the voting process and put control over the voting process again. It will not solve all the problems, for there is much work still to be done. A 2012 analysis by the Pew Center showed that nationwide over 2 million deceased individuals still remain on the voter-registration lists. Almost 3

---

[72] "Support Remains Strong for Showing Photo ID Before Voting." *Rasmussen Reports*. June 3, 2015.
http://www.rasmussenreports.com/public_content/politics/general_politics/may_2015/support_remains_strong_for_showing_photo_id_before_voting.
[73] Mark R. Levin, *The Liberty Amendments: Restoring the American Public* (New York: Simon & Schuster, 2013), pages 197–98.

million people have registration in more than one state. To make matters worse, it is estimated that almost 25 million voter registrations are no longer valid or inaccurate.[74] I urge each state to review their registration methods to correct these sources of potential voter abuse and fraud. Thank you all for listening today.

"GOD BLESS AMERICA."

DAY 31: THE CONSTITUTIONAL CONVENTION

Good morning, my fellow Americans. Today marks the end of the first phase of my one-hundred-day mission to address the significant issues of our times and propose solutions to those issues. During the past thirty days we have examined Article V of the Constitution, which allows the states to bypass Washington and vote to convene a constitutional convention for the sole purpose of proposing and passing amendments to the Constitution to address many of the issues that we have been talking about these last thirty days. The process is cumbersome, because a total of thirty-four states have to propose the convention and have their state legislatures pass the resolutions. A convention site must then be chosen, as well as a time for the convention, and the convention itself, I can assure you, will be convoluted at best. The amendments that this office has suggested since my inauguration and others, I am sure, will be hashed and rehashed until resolution. Whether one amendment or a multitude of amendments are passed by the convention, they will still need to be ratified by at least thirty-seven states in order to become law.

---

[74] Liptak, Adam. "Voter Rolls Are Rife With Inaccuracies, Report Finds." *New York Times*. February 14, 2012.
http://www.nytimes.com/2012/02/14/us/politics/us-voter-registration-rolls-are-in-disarray-pew-report-finds.html?_r=0.

But think of this, folks: the beauty of the convention and the amendments is that Washington has no control over the process. No executive order can be made by the executive branch stopping the convention, no state or federal judge can issue an injunction forbidding the convention, no Supreme Court can decide to overrule the convention or the amendments that are finally ratified. We the people will have the opportunity, as we did in 1776, to say "NO MORE" to tyranny and oppression, "NO MORE" to taxation without representation, "NO MORE" to the federal leviathan ruling every aspect of our lives, "NO MORE" to radical judges overruling the will of the people in the name of who-knows-what, "NO MORE" to losing our freedoms as citizens in the name of "diversity." The discourse will be fast and furious, as the progressives have had control over many of our institutions, education, the media, and government for the past fifty years and are not going to relinquish control easily, but they will relinquish control eventually.

This process to freedom will take some time, but given the will of the people, it is possible within the next twenty-four months that all these changes can become part of the America I know and love. Here again, I *urge* you all strongly to contact your state and federal representatives and voice your opinions on these issues. Whatever your opinions are, they need to know very solidly what those opinions are. Get involved, folks, sign petitions, call your friends, have chats after church, at home, wherever. The more that you, the people, arise, so too will our country start to rise again, like the phoenix bird of legend arising out of the ashes to reclaim our land and nation.

As I sign off for the day, it will be just for the day. We have two more months of dialogue to reach the one-hundred mark. Starting tomorrow we will be addressing more problems and solutions to those problems. Unfortunately, with the convention and the amendment process, there will be a time lag to implementation. Sad to say, some solutions will not wait the process. Therefore, starting tomorrow I will address specific actions that I, as president, am prepared to take and some actions I am hoping that Congress will take and I can sign into law. While I am prepared to work with the houses of Congress, unless action is forthcoming, other actions will need to be implemented. Sorry, folks, about that last sentence; I am sounding like my predecessor. The inertia in Washington is immense and has been ongoing for over fifty years, maybe more. As I started this journey, I have always prayed for guidance from our Lord, God, and will continue to do so. I also urge each of you to pray as often as possible for God's guidance in our lives and for our leaders that they may come to their senses and do the right thing. Until tomorrow . . .

"GOD BLESS AMERICA."

SECTION 4

DOWNSIZING THE GOVERNMENT

(PART 1)

Day 32: Meeting with the Fifty State Governors

Location: The rotunda in the White House, used for large events. The room is overflowing with the representatives of all fifty states for a two-day conference on the State of the Union and the examination of possible solutions to the morass and lethargy that is infecting the USA. Most of the states' governors are in attendance, with a few lieutenant governors representing primarily "blue" states. Everyone is gathered around their tables, chatting with other governors and government officials. The main door opens and a marine guard enters and announces the president. President M—— enters the room, which has become quite silent.

"Good morning, ladies and gentlemen. I am so glad you all could attend this important conference on such short notice. Please be seated.

"You all, I assume, have been listening to my daily speeches to the American public these past thirty days, and I am sure you have many views on the topics that have been discussed. Many amendments have been outlined and remain to be debated. More importantly, though, is the constitutional convention that will decide those amendments or others. This convention will be the major topic of this conference.

"Of equal importance will be the hot-and-cold relationship between the federal government and the fifty states. Hot in the sense of federal encroachment on states' rights circumventing the Constitution, and cold with respect to the states' acquiescence to much of this infringement. I am not here to castigate anyone; I am here to open a dialogue again with the states and you as representatives of your states to endeavor to move back to the original intent of the Constitution, which was a limited federal government and a vibrant Tenth Amendment to protect states' rights.

"The third topic will be our moribund economy and how we as a nation can restore vim and vigor to our nation's vast enterprises, which are private, not public. We all share some of the blame over the past fifty to seventy years of moving away from a free-market nation to an 'entitlement' nation. This must stop on both ends. Some of the states are well ahead of the others and exhibit vibrant economies: Alaska, North Dakota, Texas, and Wisconsin come to mind. However, too many states, like Michigan, Ohio, California, and New York, have been on the dole for so long that their independence is gone. Even worse, a vast number of our cities around the nation are cesspools of 'entitlement' mentalities—or worse, 'sanctuary' cities—ignoring the laws of our nation, not the least of which is the city you are in now, Washington, DC.

"As you all can see, we have a lot to discuss. Before we begin, I have asked the reverend to lead us in a short prayer, asking for God's blessing on this meeting."

The reverend stands and says, "Dear Lord, bless this momentous endeavor and these statesmen in their efforts to stabilize our nation and move to the correct pathway, back to a sense of purpose and resolve in following Christian values and the Ten Commandments. Amen!"

"Thank you, Reverend. Now let us begin on the important issues that brought us here today. In front of you all are folders highlighting the convention process and what is needed to convene this convention and how quickly we need to move onto this task. At this juncture, let me introduce a very learned scholar in this regard, Mark Levin, also the author of the book *The Liberty Amendments*, a copy of which is before each of you. Feel free to take the copy with you and study it at your leisure. I would suggest again that the debate on possible amendments is not the purpose of this conference; those amendments will be debated at the actual convention. Our purpose here is to gain your support for this constitutional convention and develop a strategy for getting the states' approvals for the convention. Gentlemen and ladies, we need to start the pathway back to the Constitution and back to sanity. Our nation has strayed greatly from what our forefathers envisioned and what has guided us for almost two hundred years. The past fifty years have been a horror of progressive legislation getting into every aspect of our lives. Extraconstitutional legislation has become the norm of Washington, much to the detriment of the American people.

"I will leave you now in Mr. Levin's capable hands as well as those of my vice president, who will monitor and moderate the discussions. I will return this p.m. to start the discussion of our other topics. Again, thank you all for being here. Together we will save our nation."

After lunch, President M—— returns to a very vocal crowd. Groups here and there are arguing visibly on the convention process. The vice president enthusiastically says that the discussions have been hot and heavy, but the consensus has been to support the convention by the majority of those present. Mr. Levin also is quite impressed at the response. He states that more has been accomplished in the last four hours than in the last two years that the convention idea has been debated.

President M—— assumes the floor and says, "Thank you all for your thoughts, as we all know journeys of significance often start with small steps.

"I would like to discuss now the second major topic for this conference: the relationship between the federal government and the states. As you all know, this Constitution," President M—— holds up a copy, "is my guiding light. As the weeks evolve you will see much in the federal realm either decreased, changed, or eliminated. Much of what will happen then will revert to the states' responsibilities. For example, one such issue at random is the insanity of same-sex marriage. This is an issue of states' rights and not a dictum of the Supreme Court. This administration will address many aspects of our governance and how to revert those issues to the states. But with such a return will also come responsibility and action. The federal government will step aside on many issues, but you all will need to pick up the banner and proceed. The journey will be hard, arduous, and, in many times, expensive. This is our nation that we are trying to repair; the tasks are great, but the reward will be a strong, vibrant nation again. Those of you who are on the healthy pathway already will continue; those of you that look to the federal government for all the answers will not find any help in this direction. Smaller government means just that—smaller government.

"One of this administration's greatest tasks will be to balance the federal budget as soon as possible. The states already have laws on the books regulating that their budgets are balanced each year. However, many states have been playing a con game, balancing their budgets by using federal monies in various aspects of their state budget: transportation, healthcare, welfare, the list goes on and on. You are all on notice that as the federal government budget is pared down, the monies will need to be generated through the states, not the federal government. In many cases, the states involved will need to take a hard look at their various programs and make adjustments as necessary. Arizona, for example, receives a huge amount of their indigent healthcare monies from the federal government. That will cease rapidly. We must learn to live within our means; the sooner the better.

"There is a red folder on your tables that highlights some of the federal and state interdependence that has evolved over the past sixty years. The vice president will moderate the discussions on these topics for now. As I mentioned, the changes are coming; one of the vital purposes of this meeting is to not only inform you all on these changes, but to prepare you and your states for the future. I will return in a short while since affairs of the nation still must be addressed and demand my attention. One thought before I leave— feel free to form individual groups for specific discussions on aspects of what is being presented here. I would encourage all of you as heads of your states to establish lines of communication between you and other governors to help resolve many issues that will evolve over the next four years and beyond."

Later on, the president returns to another very vocal setting. Surprisingly, the room and the people involved in the conference seem calmer than before. Many governors have split off into separate groups discussing various aspects of the changes that have been presented. While the discussions are very energetic, the mood is strangely upbeat. The vice president comes over and mentions to the president that the conference continues to be extraordinary in that so many of the governors, even those who are hardcore progressives, are enthusiastic about bringing positive changes to their states and reviving their economies.

The president smiles and calls the meeting to order again. "Thank you all for your cooperation. I sense that we are making progress and that our nation will benefit greatly from this meeting. Now to the last major topic, namely how to revive our economy. My administration is committed to helping you all as much as possible. We will be addressing a more positive and smaller taxation and a much smaller regulatory federal government. Many agencies that have been a total bear for the economy will very rapidly be terminated. The next thirty days will highlight some of the major regulatory changes that are coming down the pike.

"The vice president will handle the discussion on improving the economic status of the states. As we mentioned already, some states have progressed on their own to achieve a better standard of living for all concerned. The VP will fill you in on specific actions we will be pursuing to enhance our economy and strengthen our republic. The blue folder in front of you details some of the 'hot' topics that will be emerging over the next few weeks. The list is not all-inclusive; I have to leave a few surprises for everyone. I promise you all that each governor will receive advance copies on upcoming speeches and their significance to their state.

"I will return in a little while and we can sum up the major aspects of this conference. Before I leave, I would like to mention a major influence for our world and why we need to address this issue. I would refer you to the other book on your table, by Harry Dent, *The Demographic Cliff.* Folks, to have a vibrant economy, to have a vibrant nation, to have a vibrant world, we need to have the next generation to carry on the banner of our society. The insanity of limiting our families, limiting children, as well as the abortion issue of killing our babies must end. Each state must foster the family; having children should be viewed with joy and not shame and derision. Men and women should be encouraged to start families and have children. In a nation where there are four times as many pets as children,[75] insanity reins. Pets are not the future, our children are. The importation of migrants will also never be the answer, as you all well know. I urge all of you to meet with the legislature, the churches, the family organizations, and our businesses to promote our families, our children, and therefore our society."

President M—— stands and leaves the room. As he leaves, he looks at the governors and states simply,

"GOD BLESS AMERICA."

---

[75] "Pet." *Wikipedia.* Accessed June 22, 2016. https://en.wikipedia.org/wiki/Pet.

DAY 33: PARING DOWN THE FEDERAL LEVIATHAN (PART 1)

Good morning, my fellow Americans. Today we will start on the next chapter in regaining our country, that is, paring down the government. Over the next thirty days we will look at specific areas of government that will not only be pared down but also, in many cases, eliminated totally. Some of these areas are dictated by law, and I will be urging Congress to act and either abolish the law or simply defund the agencies involved in the law. Any such acts by Congress will be signed by me as soon as possible.

We have discussed over the last month how the government intervenes into virtually every aspect of our lives. Two famous books written seventy years ago, *Brave New World* and *1984*, predicted very accurately the how and the means government—called "Big Brother"—would gain control and thereby dictate our lives. I remember reading the books while in school; they were then regarded as pure fantasy. My attitude then was, "Nice fiction, but it will never happen here." Boy, was I wrong. I also remember visiting Russia when I was in college: reading the propaganda in the newspapers, listening to the propaganda on the radio, the TV, and in the movies, and laughing at the gullibility of the Russian people under communist control. What I also noticed was the palpable fear the people had not only of the government, but also of their friends, their family, and their neighbors. If you wanted to discuss anything controversial, a Russian would meet you outdoors where "they could not hear you." When I asked who "they" were, the Russian would just roll his eyes.

Returning back to the States, I remember thanking God that I lived here in the US and not there. Their society was very stratified. If you toed the line or were a member of the party, the ruling class, the goodies came your way. Otherwise, if you did not toe the line, people just disappeared. I also very naively thought that what I witnessed could never happen here in the US. Fast-forward fifty years, and the US is rapidly becoming the USSA, the United Socialist States of America. "Big Brother" is here and we are living in the "brave new world." Think of all the government agencies that have a say in your life: the EPA, the IRS, FCC, Federal Aviation Administration (FAA), Homeland Security, Federal Drug Administration (FDA), NSA, Immigration and Naturalization Service (INS), Federal Reserve, and the Bureau of Alcohol, Tobacco, Firearms, and Explosives (ATF). The list goes on and on. Many of the above acronyms may seem foreign to you. Just plug them into Google on the computer, and you will find out what they mean and how these agencies influence your life.

The scandals of the prior administration involving the IRS, NSA spying, and Homeland Security have been largely hushed up and are still being hushed up. Hopefully in my administration, light will finally shine on these actions against the American people and more importantly have these agencies eliminated from the scene. Their purpose is not national security, not the welfare of America or the people, but control over all of us. This will stop, I assure you.

Now, a brief outline on the coming days' problem solving. The next week I will be addressing the government leviathan at large, looking at major changes in the budget, the cabinet, the federal bureaucracy, taxation, and the executive branch. The following week will involve specific cabinet agencies detailing my solutions to each agency. The list is long and will involve a lot of hollering by the progressives as I eliminate, change, and pare down dozens of agencies and institutions that have cropped up like weeds in your garden and have to be pulled up by the roots and cast aside. This will be painful to many whose careers have been made by continuing the bureaucracy to which they are aligned and following these pathways to the detriment of the citizens of this country. This was not the role of the federal government that our forefathers desired when formulating the Constitution, but it is what has evolved. In retrospect I am amazed how the foundation of our country, the Constitution, has even survived these past two-hundred-plus years. But have no fear, my fellow Americans, the Constitution will be protected, and with the amendments that I have already outlined the Constitution will be strengthened to get us another two hundred years, God willing. These changes I will be proposing over the coming days will be fast and furious: fast in the sense that eliminations will start within the next ninety days, and furious in the sense of the rage that the progressives will shout as one after another of their "holy" programs will bite the dust. "Dire straits" will be shouted from the ramparts, that America is being destroyed. The truth be known, folks, America has been succumbing to these infections for over fifty years. It is only because America was so healthy that we have resisted so far. But like all infections, the host, unless helped by antibiotics, diet, and exercise, will eventually be destroyed. We will not let that happen. Already my mailbags are full of your responses to the amendments that have been proposed. The response has been overwhelmingly favorable. I will share with you over the next thirty days some of the response categories—good, bad, and otherwise—as well as excerpts from various people that have put in their comments. Have no fear, I will include the good, the bad, and, yes, even the ugly. I have already been accused of many things; Congress is in an uproar about possible impeachment. As I stated in the beginning, folks, my two advisors are the Bible—God's word—and the Constitution. So the devil can have his best shot; in all, God's will shall prevail. Take care, folks, the roller-coaster ride will start again tomorrow. Until then,

"GOD BLESS AMERICA."

DAY 33: PARING DOWN THE FEDERAL LEVIATHAN (PART 2)

Continuing our discussion, now we will begin to tackle the task of decreasing the federal government and, in many ways, dismantling many of the egregious aspects of the government that have grown unabated over the last eighty years. The federal leviathan, as I have already illustrated in prior talks on the amendments, is voracious. The economy may have its ups and downs, but the federal monster grows each and every year, unfettered by the normal constraints of society and owing no allegiance to any particular group, save, of course, the professional politicians who continually feed the monster year after year after year. The once ferociously proud America that I grew up in has been replaced by an "entitlement" society, feeding on the ever-dwindling middle class who still believe in the American dream of working and making a life for oneself and family. This is a class of Americans who still believe in God, traditional marriage, and work ethic.

To recap what we have said before, the amendments, if instituted, will serve to finally bring the beast to leash. However, that process will take some time. In the interim, I, as your president, will start the process to corral the beast. I will be presenting legislation for Congress to enact to further stop the insane growth of the federal government. I will be meeting with Congress to get some of these critical items passed. Given, however, the history over the last fifty years and especially the last seventeen years, success is in question. Again I urge all of you, the citizens of this great nation, to get in contact with your legislators and voice your opinions on these changes and your fears for the future of our country. Your voices need to be heard.

As for me, the first step will be my budget for the upcoming fiscal year. As I mentioned in day twenty-two, Amendment 15, my budget will first look at this year's revenues, with the exception of extra budgetary items such as Social Security payments and Medicare payments. Those revenues will be matched for the budget year in with the expenses equaled this last year's revenue. That by my calculations comes out to 2007. That year's budget is what I will present to Congress. Whatever agencies were in place and what their budget constraints were will now be again. If personnel have to be cut, so be it. If new agencies have sprung up in the interim, they will be eliminated. The only exception in this last regard is if the agency can be shown to be critical for our nation. In that case the agency will stand, however, cuts equal to the agency's budget will need to be made elsewhere. There will be no exceptions in this regard. If Congress can act within the budget, I will sign it into law. If they try to override the budget, I will veto it. We will start living within our means. Every family in the US has to live within its budget, so should your government. The budget will have ongoing transfers to the states for roads, education, Medicare, Medicaid, and the like. Those already in the budget will stay. However, the states are put on notice that such grants, transfers, and the like will be on the chopping block within the next two years. As we get the federal governmental house in order, so should the states. The continued feeding frenzy at the federal trough will be coming to an end.

Part of the federal leviathan is, of course, the federal bureaucracy. I am announcing a freeze on federal wages except those paid to the military. I am also announcing a freeze on all federal hiring for at least two years. The government is overpaid and overstaffed and that shall be coming to an end. The latest estimate from the Congressional Budget Office, year 2012, shows a 46 percent increase in federal pay over comparable private pay. Federal wages, again except for the military, will be reduced by 5 percent each year for the rest of my term. A committee will be formed to look at the federal retirement plans in effect and incorporate them into the Social Security Network. Alternative pension plans which employees can contribute to will not be affected. Federal employees over the age of 65 will be incorporated into the Medicare program. Private health plans will no longer be allowed unless paid for by the federal workers.

Folks, working for the government was never meant to be a career path. The cushions that have arisen in this regard will be dismantled. Thank you for your attention.

"GOD BLESS AMERICA."

DAY 34: JUSTICE DEPARTMENT (JD)

Good morning, America. Today we continue our journey into the federal leviathan. I will beg your pardon and start with a cabinet position that will not decrease in size, but will have its mission changed and reverted to its traditional approach—that of upholding the laws of the Constitution. This department, the Justice Department, has become like so many other cabinet posts—highly politicized and partisan. It has lost all aspects of its purpose in order to uphold, or in many cases not uphold, the laws of our nation and Constitution. This will change drastically during my tenure in office. The last two attorney generals, or AGs, appointed by my predecessor have done little to uphold our Constitution and have avowed to not only not uphold the laws, but to ignore any laws that did not meet the progressive agenda. NO MORE!

The new AG has already been appointed and will steer the course that we have set for the agency. As of today the Justice Department is out of the civil rights litigation business and will be focusing on the real legal issues of the day. All civil rights legal issues will automatically revert to the states' judicial systems until such time that legislation or amendments to abolish the civil rights quagmires can be accomplished. All ongoing CR legal issues will immediately be terminated and, where applicable, remanded to the state in which the suit is being tried.

The mission of the JD will focus on four main areas of constitutional law. The first area will be the review of all federal cases and military cases over the past ten years in which innocent people ran afoul of the federal leviathan and have been incarcerated because of said infractions. For example, there are a number of military personnel incarcerated because their actions were not politically correct. There are border agents incarcerated because of the same. As those cases are investigated, these personnel will have a presidential pardon immediately where applicable. I have already reviewed the new rules of engagement for the military and those shall nullify any PC rulings made prior. There are many on the state, local, and federal level who have been harassed by federal and state authorities because of their beliefs. Those cases will be reviewed and judgments changed where necessary. To me, criminal action such as the Waco massacre in Texas and the Ruby Ridge siege in Idaho clearly show federal illegality and malfeasance. Such cases, if within the statute of limitations, will be investigated, and the involved federal authorities will be prosecuted.

There has been a tradition that the president, before leaving office, posts a number of presidential pardons. Again, this practice had some good intentions but over the years has only served to release clear felons who were friends of the president or party contributors. NO MORE! That practice is hereby abolished. There will be pardons throughout my presidency, but they will be on a case-by-case basis and will be done to stop injustice whenever possible. Lastly, in cases of "civil" issues where innocent businesses and personnel were harassed by "agenda" groups (such as the gays, the pro-abortionists, the blacks, the media, and the women's liberation groups), the JD will be instructed to bring suit against those special-interest groups in violation of constitutional law.

The second area of focus will be the broad spectrum of the illegal-immigration issue. This is a multifaceted legal issue. The first emphasis will be the "sanctuary" cities and states throughout the USA. There are currently over three hundred such sites nationwide. As I have already mentioned, these "sanctuary" sites will have all federal monies immediately suspended for a period of five years. These monies include all grants, transfers, block aids, and emergency funds covering all medical, transportation, police, housing, welfare, and the like. Private institutions, such as churches and nonprofit industries, will immediately cease these illegal activities or be prosecuted to the full extent of the law. In addition, any tax exemptions will be immediately nullified. There will be no appeal to this suspension. If these sites, institutions, and the like still do not comply with federal and constitutional laws, federal marshals shall be dispensed to these sites and will be responsible for the apprehension of all illegals and those US citizens involved in their "sanctuary." Illegals will be deported forthwith; all families associated with the illegals will lose any visas to stay in the USA and will also be deported. Folks, we are a nation of laws, and "sanctuary" sites will be abolished. This is the USA, not Mexico, not China, not South America. If the federal marshals cannot handle the situation, the military will be made available.

The "sanctuary" sites are just one part of the problem. As I mentioned on day nine, the border patrol will be issuing fines for those industries who knowingly hire illegals. If these fines do not work to curb the activity, these industries will be prosecuted in federal court for those offenses.

Lastly, the JD will be working with financial institutions in the matter of illegals transferring funds outside the USA. Any funds transferred by illegals to other nations will be subject to confiscation. Institutions that facilitate such transfers will also be subject to fines and prosecution.

The third area of focus, my fellow Americans—and this is a biggie—is the area of public malfeasance. Every poll taken over the past twenty to thirty years has shown a downward spiral in the public's confidence and trust in our government. It does not matter what branch; all trust is abysmal. Every politician is seen feathering his or her cap and becoming rich in their line of work. Graft is rampant and often hidden by the powers that be. The joke used to be, "How do you know when a lawyer is lying?" Answer: "His lips are moving." For lawyer, now substitute politician. The game has continued unabated; politicians, many of whom are clearly felons in office, skate by and obtain a "get-out-of-jail" card by retiring from their office. Once in a blue moon, an elected official does something egregious enough to be prosecuted in office. That is a rarity.

Therefore, I am instructing the Justice Department to start investigating those public officials, those still in office or those who have left office, who have repeatedly and with malice distorted and not upheld their oath of office. People like a former House representative, who for many years used taxpayer monies in the millions to jet back and forth on Air Force planes to her home state on a weekly basis. The senator whose husband made millions from contracts shuttled to his company though the senator's connections. The senator in the western United States whose son profited in the millions by the senator's maneuvering of land grants. The attorney general who explicitly stated that he would not uphold constitutional laws with regards to gays, illegals, and the like. The Supreme Court justice who biased her position on Supreme Court cases before even hearing these cases, clearly ignoring her oath of office. The gay federal judge who overruled the California amendment to gay marriage, again clearly a conflict of interest, but who did not recuse himself from the case. The number of other federal judges who have abused their power by deliberate misinterpretations of the Constitution. The cases abound. Some will be reprimanded by Congress for impeachment proceedings if they are still in office. Others will be tried in federal court for dereliction of office and malfeasance where applicable. Restitution will be demanded for those who profited monetarily by their office. Folks, these officials need to be prosecuted, their crimes brought to light, and restitution made to the American taxpayer. The infractions go up to the highest office. Presidents have spent far in excess of what they were allowed, and no restitution has ever been made. This shall stop here.

The last area of focus for the JD over the next four years is not well known to the American public but has had dramatic repercussions on our society. This area deals with enormous "nonprofit" foundations existing in the US today. A historical look at this phenomenon would probably be in order. After the US passed its "income tax" amendment in 1916, many wealthy families then and now face the problem of how to leave their wealth to succeeding generations and not have it taxed away by the government. Many wealthy individuals—Rockefeller, Mellon, Ford, and Carnegie, to name a few—also wanted to give back to society in the form of philanthropic charities to help the unfortunate in life accumulate and save some of the fruits of their labors. Thus, foundations were formed. As mentioned, most were philanthropic in nature, and as taxes became an issue, these foundations, in order to continue their tax-exempt status, had to maintain a percentage of charity done each year. The problem was with succeeding generations. The foundations stayed and grew, but the original intent was subsumed by later trustees who moved the purpose and intent of the foundations to other realms.

There were few rules from the government pertaining to foundations, and none looked at the spending of their inheritance, just the amounts. What has happened in the last fifty to seventy-five years is that these foundations (and there are dozens, each with billions and billions of dollars) have become extremely radicalized and progressive in their operations. Take, for instance, the Gates Foundation, worth over $50 billion in investment power, with almost no oversight as to where the money goes and for what use.[76] The ongoing scandal with the Clinton Foundation and its unbridled use and misuse of donated monies is a prime example of how little is known about these foundations.[77] Their power is enormous and all under the radar. They now influence the most progressive agendas, such as gay rights, abortion issues, immigration issues, civil rights, and the like. They also fund and thereby influence political elections through the use of sham organizations, which in most cases are very progressive.

I would recommend an excellent book, *The Federal Leviathan* by David Horowitz, which exposes these foundations and their massive influence on public opinion and on our society in general. With the above in mind, I will be directing the JD to be active in the research into these various foundations and prosecute accordingly if federal laws have been broken. Based on their findings, I will be proposing legislation to Congress to limit these foundations to philanthropic endeavors.

I am sorry I have been long-winded, America; I will try and be more succinct in the future. Until tomorrow,

"GOD BLESS AMERICA."

---

[76] Belluz, Julia. "The media loves the Gates Foundation. These experts are more skeptical." *Vox.* June 10, 2015. http://www.vox.com/2015/6/10/8760199/gates-foundation-criticism.

[77] Farley, Robert. "Where Does Clinton Foundation Money Go?" FactCheck.org. June 19, 2015. http://www.factcheck.org/2015/06/where-does-clinton-foundation-money-go.

Day 35: Rest

Our Father, Who art in heaven, hallowed be Thy name, Thy kingdom come, Thy will be done on earth as it is in heaven. Give us this day our daily bread and forgive us our trespasses as we forgive those who trespass against us. Lead us not into temptation but deliver us from evil. Amen.

Day 36: Unions

Good morning, my fellow Americans. Today's topic will look at another aspect of the federal bureaucracy and its infiltration by another destructive force, the unions. In 1962 President Kennedy signed an executive order allowing government employees to unionize. This has led to an intolerable situation where in all levels of government—federal, state, and local—wages increase every year, the unions get more and more powerful, and, of course, the bureaucracy increases geometrically. This is insane. The conditions that led to the private sector being represented by unions do not exist in the government. To allow the unions to virtually dictate their terms each and every year is intolerable. NO MORE!

I am, effective immediately, repealing the abovementioned Executive Order 10988. Unions will no longer be allowed to represent any governmental workers. Hiring, firing, and wages will be determined on the merit system. Unions will have thirty days to finalize their involvement with government employees. No longer will the system allow incompetent workers, overstaffed workers, and the patronage benefactors to be continually employed because the unions control the workplace. FDR, a vociferous progressive, had his qualms about the unions being allowed to get into the government sector. He said in 1937 that collective bargaining in government is "unthinkable and intolerable." It is interesting to note that in all private industries, union representation has been decreasing for the last fifty years. Currently only 10 percent of the workforce in the US is unionized.[78] However, the major growth in union participation has been in the government sector over the last fifty years. We the taxpayers are paying the price. Look, for example, at the Postal Service. Do you realize that 75 percent of the US Postal Service, or PO, budget is wages?[79] FedEx and UPS, both private enterprises, have wages at only 40 percent of expenses.[80] These companies are not unionized. The USPS has been unionized since the 1960s, and, of course, has never run a profit.[81] Every few years like clockwork the USPS goes back to the federal trough to raise their rates. The unions totally dictate the wage scene, and the benefits, of course, are superb. I will be addressing the situation with the USPS in greater detail in a further talk.

Look, folks, at what broke General Motors: wages, specifically unionized wages. The benefits and wages to the union worker average over seventy-five dollars an hour, not counting overtime.[82]

---

[78] "Union Members—2015." Bureau of Labor Statistics, US Department of Labor. January 28, 2016. http://www.bls.gov/news.release/pdf/union2.pdf.

[79] "Locality Pay." US Postal Service Office of Inspector General. February 7, 2014. https://www.uspsoig.gov/sites/default/files/document-library-files/2015/rarc-wp-14-008_0.pdf.

[80] "Pay Tables – Postal Positions in General." Postal Jobs Authority. Accessed June 22, 2016. http://www.postaljobsauthority.com/pay. Also see "Average Salary for Federal Express Corporation (FedEx) Employees." PayScale. Accessed June 22, 2016. http://www.payscale.com/research/US/Employer=Federal_Express_Corporation_(FedEx)/Salary.

[81] Minaya, Ezequiel. "USPS Posts Annual Loss, Though Revenue Rises." *Wall Street Journal*. November 13, 2015. http://www.wsj.com/articles/usps-posts-annual-loss-though-revenue-rises-1447433323.

[82] Farley, Robert. "Big Three hourly wages inflated." *Politifact*. January 13, 2009. http://www.politifact.com/truth-o-meter/statements/2009/jan/13/spencer-bachus/big-three-wages-inflated/

The pension plan liabilities just for GM are over $80 billion. [83] Comparable wages for Toyota and other foreign manufactures are half of the wages GM has to pay. Of course, in the last bailout, the government gave even more control to the unions courtesy of my predecessor and Congress, all influenced of course by union contributions to Democratic Socialist Party, or DSP, campaigns. NO MORE!

The union days are past; they served a purpose long ago, but now they exist just to enrich their own coffers, at the expense of the taxpayers. We shall move ahead.

"GOD BLESS AMERICA."

Day 37: Taxation

Hello, all of you listening to my broadcasts. There are many of you, because as you can see in the corner of my office, there are a multitude of mailbags full of your letters and comments since I have begun my presidency. It is encouraging to this office that you, the American citizenry, are becoming more and more vocal. It is only through your participation that we can correct the disastrous path this country has been on and bring some normalcy and tradition back into our nation.

Today's topic will be near and dear to your hearts—namely, taxation. I had mentioned this on day twenty-three with the proposal for an amendment eliminating the Sixteenth Amendment and replacing it with a flat tax. I will be proposing this to Congress, but as I have stated many times before, the progressives have

---

[83] Geisel, Jerry. "General Motors pension plan funding improves in 2015." *Business Insurance.* February 4, 2016. http://www.businessinsurance.com/article/20160204/NEWS03/160209897/gener al-motors-pension-plan-funding-improves-in-2015.

grown rich on taxation. Any movement other than by amendment will probably be defeated either in Congress or by a Supreme Court dictum. In the interim, there are changes to the tax system that ease some of the burden that is now placed on the American public. Today we will address the major changes that I will propose to the Congress.

First, I will address the capital gains tax. At 20 percent, it is burdensome and directly decreases investment in the economic machine of our country, capitalism. Studies have shown consistently that for every 1 percent rise in the capital gains tax, there is a 4 percent decrease in GDP. On the flip side, for every dollar decrease in capital gains taxation, there is a $1.30 increase in GDP. [84] Folks, investment and capitalism are what grow our economy and most importantly grow jobs that continue to stimulate the economy. Government intervention contributes nothing to the growth of our economy; it instead serves to decrease the economy. Our latest "recession" has lasted over eight years, the longest save for the horror of the 1930s. Sad to say, the scenarios are essentially the same; FDR then tried a multitude of governmental programs over eight years, spending what then amounted to billions of dollars, to stimulate the economy. Nothing worked. What worked finally was a war, which created millions of jobs and ended the Depression.

Our nation has been trying the same tactics since 2008. The government has thrown $10 trillion these past eight years at the problem, and we still have anemic growth. The unemployment has not gone down, even though the numbers look positive thanks to

---

[84] Beach, William W., Rea S. Hederman Jr., and Guinevere Nell. "Economic Effects of Increasing the Tax Rates on Capital Gains and Dividends." The Heritage Foundation. April 15, 2008. http://www.heritage.org/research/reports/2008/04/economic-effects-of-increasing-the-tax-rates-on-capital-gains-and-dividends.

government tinkering with the unemployment index. When you look closely, the numbers are horrible. Ten million jobs have been created in the US since the year 2000, the smallest number for any generation since our founding.[85] What is even more horrible is that we have allowed into our country since 2000 over 20 million legal and illegal aliens.[86] These numbers are lousy, folks; we do not have enough jobs created for our own population, and yet we have the insane idea that importing immigrants will solve the problem. The progressives claim that the immigrants take the jobs no American wants. That is also a canard. The immigrants do not go into the fields, folks, they go into the trades of construction, manufacturing, retail, service industries, resorts, restaurants. Go to any hotel, upscale or not, and look at the service people. English is not their spoken language. The immigrant issue was partially addressed on day six with the citizenship changes. I will address more in the coming weeks.

Back to the capital gains tax. Private enterprise needs investment capital not only to sustain growth, but also to provide continued funds to start new enterprises. These new companies provide new and expanded goods and services for our economy. In providing these services, they create jobs, jobs, jobs. These jobs provide not only for additional workers, but directly provide additional taxes to run the various federal, state, and local governments. Our government cannot create jobs; our government can only transfer wealth from one sector, the private sector, and

---

[85] Irwin, Neil. "Aughts were a lost decade for the U.S. economy, workers." *Washington Post.* January 2, 2019. http://www.washingtonpost.com/wp-dyn/content/article/2010/01/01/AR2010010101196.html.

[86] Greenberg, Jon. "Economist: Immigrants have taken all new jobs created since 2000." *Politifact.* December 2, 2014. http://www.politifact.com/punditfact/statements/2014/dec/02/peter-morici/economist-immigrants-have-taken-all-new-jobs-creat/.

spread it around to the entitlement sector. Remember, folks, the name of the game is simply "jobs."

What entices individuals and companies to invest in established and new companies on a continuing basis is simply the profit motive. Investing in a new company with a new idea is extremely risky. Only five out of a hundred companies actually survive.[87] So in order to have the investment, the rewards must be substantial. Microsoft was created out of a garage—a whole new idea in computer software. Their future is looking bright, but the risks were very substantial. The early investors in Microsoft risked their funds (investments) for the potential rewards that they imagined. The investments paid off; to date, Microsoft has created a number of billionaires, but what is not commonly known is that over twenty thousand Microsoft employees have become millionaires over the years.[88] One man with a vision has created more wealth than our government in over two hundred years. This wealth, along with the wealth of people who have and are working for Microsoft, continues to stimulate the economy not only of our nation, but of the world. The government cannot do anything like this; most often our government only serves to hinder the progress.

Now going back to investors: they risk their monies in order for a hoped-for reward that exceeds their risk capital. Many investors relate that out of maybe ten investments, if only one or two pan out, they are ahead of the game. However, given the risks of the investment game, if one adds on an onerous tax rate on the one or

---

[87] Wagner, Eric T. "Five Reasons 8 Out Of 10 Businesses Fail." *Forbes.* September 12, 2013. http://www.forbes.com/sites/ericwagner/2013/09/12/five-reasons-8-out-of-10-businesses-fail/#2e41a7495e3c.

[88] Weinberger, Matt. "Microsoft millionaires unleashed: 12 Microsoft alums who spent their money in the most magnificent ways." *Business Insider.* August 8, 2015. http://www.businessinsider.com/microsoft-millionaires-who-spent-their-money-magnificently-2015-8.

two investments that do pay off, investment capital is decreased dramatically and new funds dry up quickly.

Our current tax rate of 20 percent is, of course, way too high. It was raised in 2010 as a new revenue source.[89] However, as with all misplaced actions, the tax revenues have not even come close to projections. The effect on the private sector is even more alarming. For the first time, in 2014, more private companies failed than were started nationwide.[90] A horrible statistic, but telling in the insanity of government intervention.

To help correct this insanity, I will propose legislation to decrease the capital gains tax to 12 percent for short-term investments (under one year) and 10 percent for investments on a long-term basis (over one year). As before, capital losses can be used to offset capital gains.

Next, let us look at the other egregious tax, the estate tax, currently at 40 percent for estates over $5 million.[91] Talk about insanity. Much of the wealth in the US is in the hands of owners of private businesses, farms, stores, restaurants, and manufacturing plants. The valuation of these businesses may be in the millions due to land, equipment, and inventory. However, that wealth is not liquid and serves to continue the business. Taxation on such assets can often be paid only by liquidation of the business. Insanity! This horror, coupled with the fact that the business paid taxes throughout its existence and the owners also pay taxes on their profits throughout the years, adds to the insanity. In many cases, the businesses are handed down to the next generation, hoping to

---

[89] Bell, Kay. "A look at long-term capital gains tax rates." Bankrate. April 5, 2016. http://www.bankrate.com/finance/taxes/capital-gains-tax-rates-1.aspx

[90] Clifton, Jim. "American Entrepreneurship: Dead or Alive?" Gallup. January 13, 2015. http://www.gallup.com/businessjournal/180431/american-entrepreneurship-dead-alive.aspx.

[91] "Estate tax in the United States." *Wikipedia*. Accessed June 22, 2016. https://en.wikipedia.org/wiki/Estate_tax_in_the_United_States.

continue the enterprise. This unfortunately goes by the wayside because of the onerous taxes demanded by the government.

Of course, what happens in reality is that the very wealthy find the means to move wealth away from our nation and thus avoid taxation. The middle-class businessperson, however, will end up paying and paying.

To correct this insanity, I will propose to Congress to eliminate the estate tax on all people whose estates are comprised of ownership in businesses, real estate, and any other private property. Estate taxes for inherited wealth will only be taxed for the first generation. The tax rate shall equal the capital gains tax rate.

Next, I will address the dividend tax rate, another double-taxation ruse that serves to decrease investments and also directly affects millions of retired people who rely on dividends for income during their later years. This also is intolerable and serves no purpose except to hinder our economy and hurt many of the American public who rely on that income for existence.

I will propose that the dividend tax be eliminated for individuals. Dividends of other entities, corporations, and pension plans will be taxed at the capital gains rate.

Now, let us look at the income tax rates across the board. It is well-known that increasing the tax burden not only hinders the economy, but decreases the investment pool and really does not increase taxable revenues since many will simply hide their income in whatever they see fit. The current top income rate is 39 percent for top-end income earners.[92] I propose to Congress to lower this top-income rate to 25 percent and adjust the other income rates downward.

---

[92] Pomerleau, Kyle. "2016 Tax Brackets." Tax Foundation. October 14, 2015. http://taxfoundation.org/article/2016-tax-brackets.

Lest I forget, a major component to the economic engine in the USA is, of course, our corporations, large and small. The top corporate tax rate is currently at 38 percent. This is a major reason why so many corporations have relocated much of their operations overseas.[93] This office will propose lowering the corporate tax rate to 20 percent maximum with the long-term goal of further reducing the corporate tax rate to 10 percent within five years. We need to get the manufacturing engine restarted in the USA, not overseas.

I will also propose that earned income tax credit be eliminated entirely. It also serves no purpose but to increase the burden on those who are already paying most of the taxes. Folks, the top 1 percent of earners pay 24 percent of total income taxes. The top 20 percent of wage earners pay 84 percent of all income taxes.[94] That is insane!

As I stated earlier in my talks, it is grossly unfair where almost half of the wage earners in the US not only do not pay taxes, but get income credits to boot. That shall end. I will propose to Congress a minimum tax of 2 percent on gross income under $50,000 and 5 percent of all gross income over $50,000. The alternative tax method currently in use shall be abolished.

As you all can see, my proposed tax legislation will be comprehensive and hopefully will stimulate the economy and thus increase what we all desire—more jobs. Decent jobs, not part time, not government jobs, not dead-end jobs. Jobs are the mark of a vibrant, growing economy, not more people on the dole, not more permanently unemployed people, not more on welfare, not more

---

[93] Pomerleau, Kyle. "Corporate Income Tax Rates around the World, 2015." Tax Foundation. October 1, 2015. http://taxfoundation.org/article/corporate-income-tax-rates-around-world-2015.

[94] Saunders, Laura. "Top 20% of Earners Pay 84% of Income Tax." *Wall Street Journal*. April 10, 2015. http://www.wsj.com/articles/top-20-of-earners-pay-84-of-income-tax-1428674384.

on disability, not more on Women, Infants, and Children (WIC), and not more standing on the street corners begging for handouts. What we all in this country want is to be able to work productively, provide for our families, and be a part of an energized economy so that we can plan for the future and have the jobs that will sustain the future. Thank you for listening today.

"GOD BLESS AMERICA."

DAY 38: CABINET ROLLBACKS

Good morning, my fellow Americans! As the week progresses, so shall we. To this point, I have addressed the government in general terms. In the next two weeks I will address specific agencies that will either be reduced or eliminated. Many of these agencies are part of my cabinet, so it is fitting that cuts to the federal leviathan should start with the executive branch.

During the Civil War and afterward, Lincoln's cabinet numbered seven. Imagine, one of the most horrendous wars we as a nation have ever engaged, and there were only seven cabinet members. Today, of course, the cabinet positions have grown geometrically as the encroachment of government grows into every aspect of our lives. Fifteen major cabinet positions, employing over seven hundred thousand people, not to mention any number of pseudo-cabinet agencies that have arisen. Each day for the next few weeks we will examine every cabinet position in turn and propose solutions on how to either eliminate the cabinet post and the agencies involved or severely reduce its scope of operations. There will be "weeping and gnashing of teeth" as changes will be made in these agencies. The status quo for so many years will no longer be valid. I might reiterate here that my main purpose in these changes is not only to reduce the federal leviathan, but mainly to transfer back to the states and you, the people, control over many aspects of your lives that are now being controlled by "Big Brother" in Washington. This will require that the states step up to the plate and take over the tasks that will revert to them. This will not be easy or simple. Many states have been at the federal trough for so long that the thought of managing their own affairs is foreign to them. Witness the State of California. You, the people, need to harass your representatives, if necessary, to do the jobs you elected them to do.

Most of the changes to eliminate a particular cabinet will require congressional approval since the cabinet post was originally created by congressional legislation, and I will be working with the leadership of both houses to rescind the original legislation. This can be a lengthy process. In the interim, I will be reducing the agencies in both their mission and involvement with the American public. This will include personnel reductions. It is time for many in the government bureaucracy to return to the private sector and get a real job. In many cases, monies that were allocated on the federal level will revert to the state level; how well the states respond will be their responsibility.

Cabinet posts illustrate the horrific concept of "incrementalism." As with many laws passed in the last 150 years, the original intent of creating cabinet posts may have had some validity, but over the years, that validity has passed. However, the cardinal rule of government is that once a government post is created, it stands in perpetuity; the government will just change the mandate or, in many cases, add new mandates to the post. So instead of vanishing, the government posts grow into behemoths. NO MORE! If Congress refuses to work to trim these cabinet posts and agendas, this office will simply decrease each cabinet post until it becomes inconsequential.

The Supreme Court will also of course be involved since there will be legal actions on many of the changes I will be instituting. The changes for myself will actually be somewhat easy since these cabinet posts and agencies are under my authority in the executive branch, and this gives me the control over not only their budget, but also their responsibilities and their ultimate functions on behalf of the American people. The last part of that sentence is quite tongue-in-cheek since many of these agencies have long lost having a purpose to serve the American public and now only serve their own interests.

The order in which I will address each of these agencies and cabinet posts will be of my own choosing. I will endeavor to start with the most egregious and work my way through the maze. The people I have appointed to the cabinet posts have already been informed of what is coming down the pike. They are all on board with the changes that will come and also desire less, not more, government. None are career-government types; they come from private and public sectors and are diverse in their abilities and knowledge. After their term in office is complete, they will return to the private sector. They have been chosen as the apostles were chosen, if I may use the Bible as a source of inspiration, to proclaim the "good news" and to work to revive our Constitution.

Lastly, I would like to say that we have an outstanding tool available to each of us: the internet. I urge you, the people, to access the internet to examine each of these cabinet posts in detail, their purposes, the multitude of agencies under each cabinet, the personnel working in the agencies, and especially the millions and billions of your tax dollars involved with these agencies. Have a great day, and

"GOD BLESS AMERICA."

Day 39: Department of Education (Part 1)

Good morning, my fellow Americans. Today I will address an aspect of government that is near and dear to my heart: education. When I was growing up, I was fortunate for many years in elementary and high school to attend a Catholic school. I remember to this day the discipline invoked by the nuns and priests who taught us. It was not unusual to have two to four hours of homework each night. Memorization was an integral part of our education. In English, I memorized much of Poe's famous poem "The Raven," as well as many passages from Shakespeare. In Latin, I memorized many of Caesar's speeches. The classics were taught in English literature. Two years of American history were taught. Penmanship was taught in elementary school. Physical sciences were stressed. Grades were important, and all were measured by the grades received. There were no points for effort. Math was "one plus one equals two," not what one thought it should be. If one did not pass a grade, one repeated that grade until one could pass. There were no "English as a second language" classes. There were no bilingual classes, except for the foreign-language classes one was required to take in order to graduate. The dress code was strict. There were no jeans, T-shirts, and no shorts for either boys or girls. A student had no access to phones during school. Meals were either what was brought to school or bought at school. There were no vending machines at school. All this was, of course, at the Catholic school. Religion was a part of the education. The Baltimore Catechism was studied regularly, as well as attendance at Mass. The boys and girls were taught courtesy; the girls all wore shirts and the boys all wore sport coats. Foul language would get one expelled. If one was expelled, that was the end of one's Catholic schooling. This was especially important since the parents were paying for the schooling. The penalties were harsh, but the students graduating were top notch. Many went on to the top colleges in the US. It was the best of times!

My last year in high school, I, unfortunately, due to financial circumstances with my family, had to transfer to a public high school. Even back in those days the differences were immense. From two hours of homework a night, I did what little was assigned while waiting for the bus. I remember my father asking about my homework, and when I told him, he just shook his head. He then improvised additional homework assignments in several subjects. The sum total was that with little effort, I graduated near the top of my class.

I tell you all this because in the intervening forty to fifty years the situation has just gotten worse in our schools. At least back then, control in the schools was on the local and state levels and parents had some say in the education of their children. However, all that changed in 1977 when, under a progressive president and a very progressive Congress, the government "federalized" education and created the Department of Education. All has gone to hell, pardon my language, and is still on the "highway to hell."

Curricula are now chosen in Washington, and every facet of education is controlled by the federal leviathan. Let us look at a typical school in America today. First, the structure is no longer simple. The new school complexes cost hundreds of millions of taxpayer dollars to erect and contain indoor pools, tennis courts, gymnasiums, computer facilities, online-course computers for the students, and acres of student parking. Amazing! Let us look inside these schools and what is being taught. English literature is no longer devoted to the classics.[95] Now it is black literature, gay

---

[95] Godsey, Michael. "The Wisdom Deficit in Schools." *The Atlantic*. January 22, 2015. http://www.theatlantic.com/education/archive/2015/01/the-wisdom-deficit-in-schools/384713/.

literature, Hispanic literature; the classics are almost gone.[96] Political correctness rules the schools. Sex education goes way beyond the birds and the bees; now the agenda includes all from straight sex to gay sex to all forms of sexual persuasion. Gay and lesbian clubs are in many schools.[97] This is not just the high school scene; much is started in the elementary schools. American history has been subverted to stress Native American culture, black culture, gay culture, Hispanic culture, or whatever the teacher thinks appropriate. Grades now reflect not actual subject knowledge but effort made in a subject. Students get credit if they are close to the correct answer.[98] In school the dress is "anything goes."[99] Girls wear the skimpiest of clothes, boys wear grungy T-shirts and jeans, and tattoos and body piercings are in, as well as bizarre hair colors and cuts. Smoking in school has been replaced by pot.[100] The teachers are afraid of the students and of course have lost control of the classroom. Many teachers are sexually involved with their students. The young adults graduating cannot even form a formal

---

[96] Anderson, Melinda D. "The Ongoing Battle over Ethnic Studies." *The Atlantic*. March 7, 2016.
http://www.theatlantic.com/education/archive/2016/03/the-ongoing-battle-over-ethnic-studies/472422/.
[97] "Start a GSA." GSA Network. Accessed June 22, 2016.
https://gsanetwork.org/get-involved/start-gsa.
[98] McKinney, Matt. "Virginia Beach parents voice concerns about lax grading practices." Pilot Online. *The Virginian-Pilot*. February 10, 2016.
http://pilotonline.com/news/local/education/public-schools/virginia-beach-parents-voice-concerns-about-lax-grading-practices/article_3d7dfd33-51c8-57c6-b85d-f56bec272dc9.html.
[99] Swan, Noelle. "High school dress code: The battle for keeping up appearances." *Christian Science Monitor*. September 11, 2013.
http://www.csmonitor.com/The-Culture/Family/2013/0911/High-school-dress-code-The-battle-for-keeping-up-appearances.
[100] Taylor, Marisa. "Teens more likely to smoke pot every day than cigarettes, study finds." *Aljazeera America*. December 16, 2015.
http://america.aljazeera.com/articles/2015/12/16/more-teens-smoke-marijuana-daily-than-cigarettes.html.

sentence and cannot spell.[101] Math is a joke. The cell phone has replaced communicating, and "sexting" is the favorite norm among students today. Sad to say, the girls are the most flagrant and aggressive. Insanity prevails. What norms in our education system are upheld in the private schools and charter schools? Of course, the educational ability of our students drops every year. The majority of colleges have remedial English and math courses in college. My question is this, among others: why is someone allowed to be admitted in college, heck, or even allowed to graduate from high school if they cannot even spell or form a sentence or do simple math?

Companies now look at states' rankings for educational achievement before locating there. The situation is even worse when comparing the US education with other countries. The USA now does not even rank in the top twenty nations in the quality of its educational system. By any standard, be it in reading, writing, mathematics, or science knowledge, the USA is a shell of what we in the past had achieved. Companies have left many states like Arizona because of the poor quality of potential employees in the state. The CEO of Intel—a large, multinational corporation—stated a while back that his company would have located elsewhere if they had known how bad the school system was in Arizona.[102] Arizona, by the way, still ranks at the bottom of scholastic achievements in the US.[103] Sad!

---

[101] "The U.S. Illiteracy Rate Hasn't Changed In 10 Years." *Huffington Post*. September 6, 2013. http://www.huffingtonpost.com/2013/09/06/illiteracy-rate_n_3880355.html.

[102] "Intel in Arizona." Intel's company website. Accessed June 22, 2016. http://www.intel.com/content/www/us/en/corporate-responsibility/intel-in-arizona.html.

[103] Ruf, Sarah. "Arizona ranks 47th in nation for education – again." *CopaMonitor*. January 16, 2015. http://www.copamonitor.com/kids_family/article_9e873346-9da5-11e4-8173-5f6e53a54578.html.

All this has occurred on the federal government's watch. Their answer is to spend more money on building schools, form more study groups, throw more money at the problems, and teach "Common Core" curricula or whatever the flavor of the month is. Looking back at these forty years of "federalism," if one is not laughing, one starts to cry. The Pledge of Allegiance is forbidden in schools,[104] and any prayer is also forbidden. I am surprised that they still allow "God bless you" after someone sneezes. Every year more and more students drop out or cannot find any jobs due to their intellectual ineptness.[105] Sad to say, in many instances, the parents and the local communities have brought on this insanity. By buying and accepting federal monies and thereby federal control, they have abdicated their responsibilities to themselves and their children. Again, the age-old adage is always the same; the government never makes anything better, only worse, from curricula to environment to health. Look at my predecessor. His wife even tried to control totally what children ate.[106] The schools and the students rebelled. Of course, she and her family did not follow what they sought for others.

I am sorry that I have been long-winded today and so shall stop here. Tomorrow I shall get into the details of my plans for the Department of Education. Until then,

"GOD BLESS AMERICA."

---

[104] CNN Library. "Pledge of Allegiance Fast Facts." CNN. April 12, 2016. http://www.cnn.com/2013/09/04/us/pledge-of-allegiance-fast-facts.

[105] "11 Facts About Dropping Out." DoSomething.org. Accessed June 22, 2016. https://www.dosomething.org/facts/11-facts-about-dropping-out. Also see "Employment and unemployment of recent high school graduates and dropouts." Career Outlook. Bureau of Labor Statistics, US Department of Labor. July 2015. http://www.bls.gov/careeroutlook/2015/data-on-display/dod_q4.htm.

[106] Username "Kosar." "Students in Full Revolt Against Michelle Obama's Horrible School Lunch Mandates!" The Political Insider. Accessed June 22, 2016. http://www.thepoliticalinsider.com/students-full-revolt-michelle-obamas-horrible-school-lunch/.

DAY 40: DEPARTMENT OF EDUCATION (PART 2)

Good morning, my fellow Americans. Today we continue our discussion on education in America and in particular the Department of Education, or DOE. If one looks historically at this department, the roots go back almost 150 years to when the department was only a data-collection agency with no additional functions or powers. All that changed for the worse in 1979 when the Department of Education was incorporated and started expanding its powers geometrically. As I stated before, up until 1979 the states and local government controlled the education of our children. Funding was primarily through property taxes, which kept the system solvent, so to speak. Parents were actively involved in the education process. Remember the parent-teacher meetings—the PTA—once a quarter? This local control led, in my belief, to an educational system that excelled by most standards.

However, excellence in education was not in the progressive dream of control, and so the federal government stepped in with the Department of Education and, of course, using the power of the purse, started the US on a horrendous pathway to governmental control. Every year in the past thirty-five years, control has been expanded and expanded, from curricula to "new standards," to civil rights, to teachers' qualifications, to immigrant schooling. There is not one aspect of education that the federal government does not have its hands in. The states to a very large degree have totally abdicated any positive role in the education process. NO MORE!

The most recent budget for the DOE is over $220 billion, in discretionary ($70B) and mandatory spending ($140B)![107] Think of the word "mandatory," folks. That is your government in control,

---

[107] DOE Press Office. "President Obama's 2017 Budget Seeks to Expand Educational Opportunity for All Students." US Department of Education. February 9, 2016. http://www.ed.gov/news/press-releases/president-obamas-2017-budget-seeks-expand-educational-opportunity-all-students.

not you; that is the government telling you what your children will learn, what they will eat, what they will wear, what they can say, and what activities, including sexual, are permissible. This will change.

I will be proposing legislation that will eliminate all of the discretionary spending and pare down the mandatory spending by 90 percent within the next fiscal year. I will propose that the department be disbanded within the next two fiscal years and that all agencies that are functional to any degree be reverted to state and local control.

Most of these funds, where applicable, will be returned to the states in proportion to the educational spending for that particular state. These funds will be the responsibility of and controlled at the state and local levels, not the federal. Federal grants will be eliminated, and programs such as "Teaching for Tomorrow" will be eliminated.

Pell Grants will be phased out over the next year. Funds will be distributed to the states for their own grant programs. The Pell Grant and other federal grant programs have been dismal failures and have served only to increase the cost of education over the past forty years.[108] The DOE has over \$1 trillion in IOUs for loans for education, most of which will probably not be collected.[109] I will propose that these assets be turned over to the Treasury for collections. We will be proposing several programs for those citizens who owe on their federal debt for early payments and forgiveness of portions of the debt. The federal government is not a banker and should not be in the business of making loans and

---

[108] Heller, Donald E. "Does Federal Financial Aid Drive Up College Prices?" American Council on Education. April 2013. https://www.acenet.edu/news-room/Documents/Heller-Monograph.pdf.

[109] Berman, Jillian. "America's growing student-loan-debt crisis." *MarketWatch.* January 19, 2016. http://www.marketwatch.com/story/americas-growing-student-loan-debt-crisis-2016-01-15.

loan collections to anyone or any entity. Our goal is to have this accumulated debt off the books within the next five years.

Continuing down my hit list for the DOE, the Elementary and Secondary Education Act (ESEA) will be defunded. The Individuals with Disabilities Education Act (IDEA) will be defunded. Funds allocated for civil rights issues will be defunded. America's College Promise—defunded. First in the World—defunded. The list goes on and on. Please log onto our website at WH2017.org to see a more complete list of the programs and agencies that will be getting the axe. Projects like the Native Youth Community programs will be defunded. I will be addressing the Native American issues in another speech. Today, let me make something clear. In this country, everyone pulls their own weight. The era of entitlement is quickly coming to an end. Funding for Native Americans is coming to an end. The NA need to come to the plate and start accepting responsibility for their state of affairs. This holds true for all other diverse ethnicities as well. Again, it bears repeating . . . NO MORE!

Lastly, federal personnel. In this regard the DOE does not have many employees, under five thousand. They will be getting their pink slips over the next six to nine months. Being well "educated," they should have no problem finding a job in the private sector. Thank you all for your attendance today. Until tomorrow,

"GOD BLESS AMERICA."

Day 41: Department of Energy (Part 1)

Good morning, my fellow Americans. Today our journey continues into another field that is near and dear to my heart, namely, energy. I have said it before, and it bears repeating, energy is the lifeblood of our economy, folks. A few years back, when gas prices fell by about half, our nation had a minor economic boom. The average family got the equivalent of a two-thousand-dollar tax break and what did they do? They spent it on trips, on travel, at the supermarket, and at the home-improvement store. The benefits extended even further. Fuel costs are one of the major determinants of the price of most goods and services in the US, from food to building supplies, lumber to farming. Much of what we produce is transported by truck, so fuel costs dropping immediately and positively affected the prices of a multitude of products. This positive stimulus on the economy is just a part of the picture because gas prices still are above what they were in 2008 when my predecessor took office. My goal is to have gas at the pump at a sensible $1.00 to $1.50 a gallon. That is the current price of the equivalent of natural gas per gallon. More about that later.

To continue, in the last seventy years the US has gone from the largest exporter of energy in the world, with petroleum, to a net importer of energy. Sad to say, this is not because of a lack of supply of petroleum products. Heck, estimates of oil and gas reserves in the US and Alaska range anywhere from five hundred up to a thousand years of supply beneath our soil. This does not even include our vast supplies of coal, which add another five hundred years of energy supply.[110] Why, then, this dismal outlook over energy and our failure to hold onto our leadership in the world of energy and energy resources?

Let me digress for a few moments and look back at these last seventy years and what has happened in these years since the Great War. In the '40s and '50s our reserves were vast, and our energy exports were above all. I am dating myself, but even in the '60s I remember learning to drive, and gas at the pump was twenty-five to fifty cents a gallon. That is right, twenty-five cents a gallon. You

---

[110] Coal Explained. "How Much Coal Is Left." US Energy Information Administration. June 17, 2016.
http://www.eia.gov/energyexplained/index.cfm?page=coal_reserves.

could fill the car up for under three dollars and drive all weekend on that three dollars. Those were the days of the Mustang, the GTO, and the Super Sport. The muscle-car era. A time of innocence and, most importantly, a time of value in our country, our churches, our institutions, and our economy. Inflation was a word used just in the business books; our coins actually had silver in them. Gold was thirty-five dollars an ounce.[111] The US was on the gold standard (more about that later).

What changed is that our government became active in the energy market and the disruption started big time. Instead of producing and continuing to produce and export energy, we starting importing more and more. Suddenly, we were no longer an exporter of energy; we were increasing dependence on foreign sources for our oil, namely the Middle East. Even back then the countries in the Middle East, except for Israel, were not our friends and to this day are not our friends (NOF). The boom ended in the 1970s with the oil embargo and the long lines at the pumps. I remember being stuck in the little town of Yuma, Arizona, because of the lack of gas at the pumps. I also remember being in Bakersfield, California, at that time and seeing thousands of oil pumps sitting idle. Kern County, California, had and still has one of the largest oil reserves in the world. Forty years later those oil rigs still stand idle in Kern County, collecting dust. The oil underneath the ground is still there waiting, waiting, waiting.

The progressives preached the end of oil; so-called scientists said that the world was running out of petroleum, that in twenty to thirty years, oil would be gone and we needed to import oil and gas

---

[111] "Historical Gold Prices- 1833 to Present." National Mining Association. Accessed June 22, 2016. http://www.nma.org/pdf/gold/his_gold_prices.pdf.

to conserve what little we had.[112] We had to go to solar, to wind, to geothermal power to fuel our nation. All lies and fiction, my fellow Americans, and we the people fell for the myths. Gas skyrocketed from cents to dollars, and mandatory federal regulations forced more fuel-efficient cars.[113] Suddenly we were held hostage by our own government telling us to conserve, conserve, conserve. The EPA came into being, initially to monitor pollution emissions from industrial uses, then expanding their reach into the auto industry, the utilities industry, and eventually all industries in the US. It never ends. Now the EPA is going after carbon emissions. Think of this, folks, a vital element for life on this planet, carbon dioxide, has suddenly become a toxin. Again, all fiction! Another myth fostered on the American public. Government monies are increasingly funneled into alternative-energy projects, many often blue-sky endeavors, even though the technology has not advanced and the economics are not feasible. Witness the debacle of Solyndra—over a billion dollars wasted on a solar project that never got off the ground. One of our greatest projects, the Alaskan Pipeline, luckily was completed in the 1970s despite being held up due to environmental impacts and other "studies." To this day I am amazed on how the pipeline ever got completed. Maybe it was because there was not a progressive in the White House. Of course, the progressives got their digs in. While the oil pipeline was completed, they did stop the gas pipeline for the last forty years.

It is ironic, looking back at those days. Every argument the progressives used to try and block the pipeline was false. The damage to the flora and fauna in Alaska—false; the damage to the

---

[112] Wuerthner, George. "The Myth of Oil Peak." Counterpunch. March 29, 2012. http://www.counterpunch.org/2012/03/29/the-myth-of-peak-oil/.
[113] "United States emission standards." *Wikipedia*. Accessed June 22, 2016. https://en.wikipedia.org/wiki/United_States_emission_standards.

air—false; the damage to the wildlife, particularly the caribou—false. The herds have increased vastly the last forty years.[114] I was in Alaska during those wild and heady years; unemployment was virtually nonexistent, the economy boomed, and people were coming from all over the lower forty-eight states because of the jobs, akin to what has been happening in North Dakota over the last five years. The pipeline brought Alaska into the twenty-first century, and its positive economic benefits still exist for Alaskans. Do you realize that Alaska has a negative income tax? Yes, the citizens receive a yearly check from the Alaskan treasury and have been receiving those checks for the last thirty years.[115] Tell me, does your state refund any of your taxes, or does it just take more?

Continuing on about Alaska, the proven natural gas reserves in Alaska are three times what the oil reserves are, and that is only from three fields. Congress has stopped any drilling in the Arctic National Wildlife Refuge (ANWR) wilderness in Alaska because of "environmental considerations." To anyone who has been to Alaska, this wilderness is like moonscape—not a blade of grass, no trees, no animal life, just dust and rock. Insanity!

I will be proposing legislation ASAP to start the gas pipeline in Alaska and to start drilling in the ANWR wilderness. It is time to move, and we shall move. I will also work with Congress to start the Keystone Pipeline. As I mentioned earlier, our goal as a nation is to once again be an exporter of petroleum products. We have the reserves; they are waiting under the ground, in the shale, and under the water offshore. My administration will be working with

---

[114] Anderson, Warren R. "Alaska Pipeline Doomsayings Revisited." MRC Business. April 19, 2006. http://www.mrc.org/news/alaska-pipeline-doomsayings-revisited.

[115] Uncategorized blog post. "Alaska – a "negative tax" state?" *One Man's Alaska*. July 17, 2010. http://www.onemansalaska.com/blog/2010/07/17/alaska-negative-tax-state-cost-living.

private industry to access these reserves and meet our energy needs. Here again, let me be perfectly clear: the role of government is not to produce energy. That is the role of private industry. Our role is to facilitate the production of energy and turn the private industry loose to achieve our nation's goals. Thank you for your attention. Next week I will continue our discussion on this subject and address the Department of Energy and its role in the expansion of energy sources and uses. Until then,

"GOD BLESS AMERICA."

DAY 42: REST

Our Father, Who art in heaven, hallowed be Thy name, Thy kingdom come, Thy will be done on earth as it is in heaven. Give us this day our daily bread and forgive us our trespasses as we forgive those who trespass against us. Lead us not into temptation but deliver us from evil. Amen.

DAY 43: DEPARTMENT OF ENERGY (PART 2)

Good morning, my fellow Americans. Today we continue our conversation on energy and how we can start to transform our country into a vibrant economy once again, especially, borrowing a medical phrase, by transfusing our nation with the energy we need to bolster a healthy economy. I know the word "transfuse" may have a pejorative meaning, but hopefully you will see it in a new light.

We left off yesterday with some ideas on how to jump-start the economic machine that moves our nation. Some of these ideas involve the Department of Energy, or DOE (pared down, of course). This department currently has a budget of over $28 billion, as well as employing some 106,000 personnel.[116] Both will drastically change over the next fiscal year. The departmental activities will be focused on only two main areas. The first has to do with nuclear issues. Currently the emphasis for the DOE is nuclear security. This mission will be transferred to the Federal Bureau of Investigation with coordination with the Department of Defense, or DOD. However, the increased use of nuclear power as a continuing source of energy for our nation will be the ongoing mission for the department. As I mentioned earlier, my goal is a minimum of six new nuclear plants started in the US by the end of my term in office. Our nation's long-term goal should be at least one nuclear power plant in each state within the next ten years. It's impossible, they will say, but they said that when Kennedy promised that we would land on the moon before 1970. France has over fifty-six nuclear plants meeting over 80 percent of their nation's power needs.[117] Nuclear energy is safe, economical, and especially long lasting. The major hang-ups and costs for nuclear power plants have been, of course, governmental regulations, EPA, and red tape. NO MORE! The DOE is charged with clearing away the debris and getting these plants built.

The science and research aspects of the DOE will be transferred to the state level, particularly colleges and universities where applicable. The mission of the DOE will be as a facilitator, not implementation. Federal grants will be available to these entities to continue enhancing the nuclear sciences. Clean energy projects will

---

[116] Press Release. "President's 2015 Budget Proposal Makes Critical Investments in All-of-the-Above Energy Strategy and National Security." Energy.gov. March 4, 2014. http://energy.gov/articles/president-s-2015-budget-proposal-makes-critical-investments-all-above-energy-strategy-and.

[117] "Nuclear Power in France." World Nuclear Association. June 2016. http://www.world-nuclear.org/information-library/country-profiles/countries-a-f/france.aspx.

be transferred to the state and local levels where applicable. We will be working with private industry in the areas of pollution control and emission standards for vehicles.

Speaking of transportation, the DOE will also be charged with working with the petroleum industry to facilitate the conversion of vehicles to run on natural gas and implementing the vertical industrial infrastructures to ensure that natural gas is as available to the American motorist, as is regular gasoline. As I mentioned before, Mr. T. Pickett will be my roving ambassador in getting this project off the ground.

Part of the problem, not only with gasoline production and natural gas production, is the availability of sufficient refineries to get the product ready to market. This office is committed to the completion of at least four additional oil refineries and an equal number of natural gas refineries within the next four years. Again an ambitious project, but we as a nation have always risen to challenges. With the additional refineries we can not only meet our continuing energy needs, but will be able to fulfill our role as a net exporter of energy to the world. No longer will we be held captive to other nations and international entities such as the Organization of the Petroleum Exporting Countries (OPEC).

This is probably a good place to reexamine further my earlier comments on alternative energy sources. We have already touched on the nuclear option. Now let us examine other sources of economically feasible energy sources. Again, the emphasis will be on private industry. A classic example of governmental failure, among others, is solar energy. The industry has been under the gun of government for the last fifty years. Solar energy has not seen any technological improvements in that time frame. We have gone to the moon and back, but solar power is still back in the '60s. NO MORE! I am urging private industry to step up to the plate and get solar power into the energy mainstream, more economical and more cost effective. Think about this, folks: the sun shines every day. The power is there; all we need is the technology to harness this power. My office will also be encouraging the utility companies to get behind this alternative power source and not impede its use, as I fear has been done in the past. An example of that impediment has been the Arizona Public Service Company, who has had a dismal record in encouraging the use of solar power. Many utility companies have been regulated on the state level, and I also encourage the states to become more active in enhancing and encouraging new sources of energy.

In conclusion, there are numerous sources of possible energy sources (wind, geothermal, ocean waves, water, and hydrogen, to name a few) for our nation, and it is in our interests, even with the petroleum reserves at our disposal, to research these alternative sources. Again, this is not a government function, it is private industry, which needs to be the leader in this regard and lead the way into the future. John D. Rockefeller did not rely on government when he created Standard Oil and brought oil into the mainstream of America. Henry Ford did not rely on government when he built the Ford Automobile Company, which utilized this oil in the form of gasoline to power his autos, creating a truly mobile America.

Needless to say with the mission of the DOE in transition, the budget will be decreased as will the number of federal employees. Many, I am sure, will be picked up by the states in their enhanced role in the energy fields. Many will be picked up by private industry with new facility production nationwide over the next ten years at the least. I wish them all well. Today is the dawn of new beginnings, my fellow Americans, a new dawn. Until tomorrow,

"GOD BLESS AMERICA."

DAY 44: TRANSPORTATION

Good morning, my fellow Americans. Today our journey will cover the vital aspects of moving goods and people in the US. Our nation has a vital interest in all aspects of transportation from roads to railroads, from air to ocean shipping. The goods and services that we produce as a nation depend on some form of transportation to get those items to the ultimate consumer. This also holds true for our nation's imports. From our earliest days as a nation, our government has been involved in the transportation industry. Back then it served as a facilitator, providing needed funds to complete many projects, from the first national road in 1803 that spanned the state of Pennsylvania to the Ohio River, opening up the Northwest territories, to the transcontinental railroad linking the eastern and western parts of our nation. It is interesting to note that the first national road was a toll road whose maintenance was paid for by the people using the road. While the government has been the facilitator, private industry has been the focus for the completion and continued use of the various forms of transportation.

It is important to remember that transportation is divided into two inherent parts; the first and most important are the vehicles used for transportation, from horses and buggies to trains, ships, trucks, and airplanes. These forms of transportation and others that are waiting to be imagined have always and will continue to be invented by private enterprise, often before any part of the second component of transportation comes into being, that is, the "infrastructure" that the progressives are so fondly enamored with. Folks, the auto was invented before the roads were designed for the auto; the airplane was invented before airports were developed; and the invention of the train decreed the building of railroad tracks, not the reverse. Government can facilitate the second aspect of transportation, but never the former.

However, like all else in America, what was a productive relationship in the past has become another totally government-run domain with the federal government getting into and controlling all aspects of transportation. What has happened is that the "infrastructure" harped on by my predecessor has and is continuing to decay daily. Funds that should continually be used wisely for repairing and updating roads, airports, bridges, and the like get diverted to whatever. How many of us have driven by roadwork and seen roads worked and then reworked, adding millions and billions in costs? Take a minute and compare the building of a road in your neighborhood with the building of a commercial venture, like a shopping mall. The mall seems to be built overnight, but the road project goes on and on and on, months, often years, before completion. Again, this illustrates the difference between private enterprise and government enterprise. Cost controls are almost nonexistent. This is not to mention the ugly delays while the roads are being built. The government knows it can raise highway and gasoline taxes ad nauseam and we will pay for any excesses. I was driving on a road a few years back that was being expanded to four lanes. The construction crew laid down the additional two lanes, then proceeded to tear up the original two lanes, lengthening the project for almost a year. By the way, the project to this day is still not complete. Funds that my predecessor earmarked for new road construction were diverted to on-and-off ramps. Turnabouts to nowhere abound on four-lane highways. Of course, in all these projects, efficiency of operation is not a very high criterion. The government is mainly interested in adequate union membership among construction crews, adequate minority representation, and, of course, protecting the "environment."

It is interesting to note that the interstate highway system, ambitiously started in the 1950s, linked the US as never before. However, after fifty years the highway system is not being upgraded properly and is degrading rapidly. Again, the problem is government interference. A decision was made in the '50s to favor the trucking industry over the railroads.[118] The long-term result has been the degradation of the railroads. Now the interstate roads are falling apart due to the extreme usage by the trucking industry. It is not unusual to be on an interstate highway and see 40, 50, or 60 percent of the vehicles being trucks towing not just single trailers, but often double trailers. The roads were not designed for the heavier weights of these vehicles and are disintegrating rapidly. The answer is better road materials, but there is no incentive to make better roads—or bridges, for that matter, not while the roads are still under the domain of the federal government.

At least with the railroads, private industry is still in charge somewhat and is gradually upgrading the railroads and equipment. It is amazing to see one-hundred-car and sometimes one-hundred-and-fifty-car trains heading down the tracks. The railroads are still the most efficient mode of transportation we have in the USA. However, as with any regulated industry, the emphasis is not on efficiency. I am reminded of Ayn Rand's famous book, *Atlas Shrugged,* in which one of the protagonists ran a railroad and tried to keep a regular schedule of delivery of goods but was hampered continually by governmental regulation. Think of this, folks, has any train in the US ever run on time? When I was in Europe, the train schedules were very exact. Trains ran on schedule. Last question, do you know of any commuter train

---

[118] "Keep On Trucking?" Video (23:52). Part of "Blueprint America" series featured on PBS. August 28, 2009. http://www.pbs.org/now/shows/535/.

system in the US that is profitable and not mostly subsidized by the government? A clear illustration is the light-rail system in Phoenix, Arizona, developed and built in 2008 when the State of Arizona had a surplus (you know how governments hate to have a surplus!). So with the help of federal governmental funds, over $3 billion dollars was spent on a system that started nowhere and ended nowhere and was functionally insolvent from day one. It continues to be insolvent, and what is the "government's" answer? Add more tracks and expand the system, sort of a "build it and they will come." The light rail has proven to be another government boondoggle but continues to grow at the expense of the taxpayer. This is insanity! The progressive governor ("Moonbeam" to his friends) of California wants to build a light-rail system from northern to southern California for $98 billion. Who pays? Of course the taxpayer! NO MORE! Tomorrow I will look at the Department of Transportation and how we will restrict and redirect the mission of the department. Until then,

"GOD BLESS AMERICA."

Day 45: Department of Transportation (DOT)

Today we will be continuing our journey down the road to a better and more vibrant America. As we mentioned yesterday, transportation is vital to the well-being of the US. I mentioned specifically the interstate road system developed over fifty years ago to link our nation in the twentieth century as did our railroads in the nineteenth century. To continually finance the maintenance and upkeep of the IRS, the federal government taxes every gallon of gas purchased in the US. Where are the roads, folks? "In each of the states" is always the answer. The federal government's job is long past on our road system. It is up to the states to take control of all the roads in their states, including the interstate. Therefore, I am directing the DOT to revert control over the interstate to the individual states. Funds gathered by the federal government for the interstate system will be directly apportioned to the states based on their portion of the interstate system. After sixty years it is time for the federal government to step aside and let the individual states take responsibility and control. The federal taxes on gasoline will be phased out over the next five years. The states will have to institute their own taxation on gasoline used in their state and will be answerable to the citizens for not only the taxes but the roads' maintenance.

Moving on, another agency under the DOT is the railroad agency. This too will be eliminated and control over the railroads will be the purview of the individual states. Right of ways, taxation, and maintenance will be under state control and responsibility.

The Port Authority agency will also be phased out over the next fiscal year and will revert to state control. Ports are located within the coastal states' borders and should be under their control. Port security will still be under federal control, namely, the FBI. Inspections of imports entering the US will still be under federal control and responsibility. Entry into the US will always be both a federal and a state issue, and coordination will be paramount. The security of our nation can never be compromised, and the various entry points, whether by land, sea, or air, will always be primarily a federal responsibility. The delineation to me is fairly simple; day-to-day operations of moving goods and whatever else is the responsibility of the state involved. Security will continue to be a federal purview. While the states may farm out day-to-day operations to private enterprise, under no circumstances will private enterprises not be totally American companies with no, I repeat, no ties to foreign governments.

This holds especially true for our nation's airports, large or small. The states will have control and responsibility for daily operations; security, whether at the airports or in flight, will be the responsibility of the federal government. Controllers will continue to be provided and be under the supervision of the federal government. Progressives still will wail and say that these acts will make our airports less secure. Well, our record—witness 9/11—is not that good. I have already addressed some of the security issues in prior speeches. This probably is a good time to address the security aspects of the airports in further detail. The most noticeable with the American people is, of course, the TSA, otherwise known as the "national goon squad." Here, again, the original idea had some merit but over the years has degenerated in a ludicrous, inefficient, and often harassing exhibition of how the federal government does not protect but works against the people. All of us have witnessed where a high-profile individual is allowed to pass though security at the airport and allowed to board a plane and a little grandmother is taken aside and probed everywhere. My mother is a prime example. She is in her nineties, a widow of a retired veteran—with military ID to boot—and she is taken aside and probed everywhere before being allowed to board. Insanity!

NO MORE! The TSA at each airport will be replaced by military police troops over the next year. These troops will be appropriately armed and will have clear orders as to checking, verifying, and detaining when needed personnel trying to fly into or out of the US. These troops will use any and all techniques to ascertain the legitimacy of travelers in the US. Profiling will be one of those techniques. Where the security of our nation is at risk, it is not the time for "political correctness." High-profile individuals will be detained and questioned. For those travelers who object to these actions, my answer is this: if you are from another country, DO NOT come here! If you are a citizen, take another mode of travel. Many of us have forgotten that we are still technically at war with Islam and the Islamic extremists, and as such they and their sympathizers are suspect and will continue to be suspect. The use of military police is needed. They protect our military bases worldwide and are specially trained in security procedures. Our nation will be secure, my fellow Americans. Until next time, may God be with you all.

"GOD BLESS AMERICA."

Day 46: Veterans Affairs

Good morning, America. I hope your week continues to be productive, those of you who are still working, peaceful, calm, and God-filled. Today is a good day to talk about the people who have defended our country over the past two-hundred-plus years and how we have honored or unfortunately dishonored them, past and present, namely our military veterans in the army, navy, air force, marines, and coast guard. Of all the wonderful aspects of being Americans, we should be especially proud of our veterans. Through every war in which the US has been involved, our veterans have put their lives at risk and, in many cases, have given up their lives in defense of our country. There have been times in our past when we have forgotten their sacrifices—like the Vietnam War—and that is sad.

My father, as I mentioned earlier, was career military. He served both in the US Navy and US Army, a career spanning twenty-five years of service. He was in the navy and was at Pearl Harbor on December 7, 1941. He served throughout WWII, seven major sea battles in the Pacific, and survived the war. He went on to serve in the US Army, raised a family with five children, and retired honorably in Arizona in 1959. I remember him not talking much about the war, but he had scads of books relating to the war. Much of my earlier reading was reading those books and looking at all the pictures of various battles both land, sea, and air. We would spend time talking about various aspects of the war: tactics, use of forces, strategies. It was a fascinating time in my life.

I think, looking back at my father's life, he was amazed, as were so many returning veterans, that they survived the war. It was such a horrific time; most who enlisted to fight figured it was a one-way ticket and that their return would be in a bag. For hundreds of thousands that was the way they returned, but for many like my father, God had other plans and he returned unscathed. Mentally, the return was in many ways as horrible as the war itself. What helped was that we were a different country then. Returning military had many strong support systems, such as their immediate and extended families, their churches, and their religious beliefs. Society itself was supportive, and returning military were intertwined back into society very quickly. The country was a vibrant one at that time; the economy was growing, the colleges were expanding, useful programs like the GI Bill allowed millions of military to advance their education and their horizons.

However, the past fifty years have not been kind to our veterans. The Vietnam veterans, and I am one, were not treated kindly or with any respect. I remember being at the San Francisco airport in my dress greens and having a number of the young "unwashed" give me the finger in the terminal. They knew better than to say something to my face, but the mockery was evident. I survived, as did many returning Vietnam veterans, but the sadness remained. I remember going to the Vietnam Memorial in DC and looking at the names of those lost—some friends, most not—over fifty thousand names. These names of veterans who gave their all were small in comparison to WWII but still significant. Like most veterans, I did seek government aid and made use of the VA loan process when I bought my house and for some job training. What was sad to me was not the VA, but that many of the supportive institutions, families, churches, and private counseling institutions in our country gave up their roles and support. Over the years since, as with any vacuum, support institutions relegated to the federal government the support roles for the veterans, and the Department of Veterans Affairs expanded geometrically. As with any government expansion, the emphasis became rapidly not service but perpetuation of the bureaucracy.

In fairness, when one looks at the turmoil this country has been through the past fifty years, from civil rights, to discrimination issues, to abortion rights, to separation of church and state, to immigration issues, to gay rights, to "whatever" rights, you can fill in the blanks; it is no wonder that the veterans have gotten far-less-than-adequate treatment from the government and, yes, society. To tell the truth, veterans affairs are just another example of government being involved in areas that were never envisioned in the Constitution and in areas in which the government is basically incompetent from the get-go. No amount of monies will change that basic premise. Of course, the progressives have had control over the government, and in their lexicon there is no area of the human experience that is not or should not be under some government influence and control.

War and the effects of war are part of the human experience. War is not kind, not endearing, but as long as we humans exist on this earth, there will be wars of some kind and of some intensity.

We as a country, in order to survive, must face this essential fact of life and always be prepared to fight and defend ourselves against all aggressors, foreign and domestic. I use the latter word on purpose, as I believe that many who reside here in the US, and are not true citizens of the US, do not wish us well and actively work to destroy this country. We as a people must continually be vigilant and prepared. Our weapon in this fight for survival is simply our military. We must support the military in every way possible, not only active duty but afterward with the veterans also. I will be addressing the military in greater detail when I address the Department of Defense. For now, let us look at the veterans, past and especially present, and how we can better support them after their service is completed. Tomorrow I will address the Department of Veterans Affairs and how to accomplish the above mission. Until then,

"GOD BLESS AMERICA."

DAY 47: DEPARTMENT OF VETERANS AFFAIRS (DVA)

Good morning, America. Today is a bright and sunny day, and a great day to address more positives in better handling of our government. Today, we will examine in detail the VA department, which has grown into a huge bureaucracy over $100 billion in yearly budgets, employing over 280,000 employees to serve the vets.[119] What are we getting for our monies? The ongoing scandals for the DVA points to an overstaffed, bloated, and increasingly

---

[119] "Department of Veterans Affairs Fiscal Year 2017 Budget Request Fact Sheet." Department of Veterans Affairs. Accessed June 22, 2016. http://www.va.gov/budget/docs/summary/Fy2017-VAsBudgetFactSheet.pdf.

inefficient agency whose main task is the perpetuation of the bureaucracy and not the aid of our veterans. While the department cannot be eliminated, we can pare down many of its activities and keep those activities that are beneficial.

The DVA currently operates over 1,700 hospitals and clinics nationwide, supposedly dedicated to treatment facilities for our vets.[120] As a doctor I have had to deal with these VA hospitals; the bureaucracy is overwhelming and always to the detriment of the vets. These facilities are the main albatross of the DVA. With this in mind, I am directing the VA chief to initiate the sale of each of these facilities to private enterprises over the next two fiscal years. The sales of the facilities will be with the proviso that veterans will still be treated at the facilities. However, it is time the private industry take over these facilities.

The monies generated from the sale of the facilities will be used twofold: one, to expand and provide for the care, expansion, and maintenance of national cemeteries for our veterans. These cemeteries are a national honor. There are currently one hundred and thirty-four national cemeteries in the USA;[121] this amount will be doubled within the next five years. My father is buried at one in Washington, and I have stipulated in my will that I be buried in that same cemetery. There should be at least one cemetery in each state, and in the populous states, at least two or three national cemeteries should be provided for our veterans. I would encourage any and all citizens to visit any of these national cemeteries often, maybe placing a wreath or flowers on some of the graves. It does

---

[120] *Ibid.*

[121] National Cemetery Administration. "Department of Veterans Affairs Cemetery Listing." US Department of Veterans Affairs. Accessed June 22, 2016. http://www.cem.va.gov/cems/listcem.asp.

us well as a nation to never forget the sacrifices these veterans made for our country.

Second, the monies will be set aside in a separate fund within Medicare to transition veterans under medical care for any reason. Veterans will be insured and become a separate part of the Medicare program and thus will have access to private medical doctors, clinics, and hospitals in the US. The access will be more efficient than that provided by the VA hospital. This access to Medicare insurance will be under the same requirements as regular Medicare patients, except that the 20 percent co-pay will be reduced to 10 percent. The overall benefit of this change will allow veterans access to private medical care whether or not the provider or facility is a part of the Medicare network.

Access to this private care will be tailored to length of military service. Provisions will be made for disabilities related to military service and such. Afterward, when the time limits have been reached for eligibility to veterans' medical benefits, the vets will be eligible for private insurance with their employment.

Speaking of employment, the DVA should and will always be a facilitator for transitioning vets back into the private sector. Training programs currently in effect will remain with the VA. Again, as in all transitions back to the private sector, training programs will be based on length of service and any military injuries that may have occurred. One of the most popular training programs has been the GI Bill, for those interested in continuing on to college or technical school. Provisions have been made for active-duty military to set aside monies for educational benefits. These provisions will be continued with the government matching up to $25,000 set aside for continuing education and training. The amounts of these funds will be adjusted by the person's length of service or disability.

Another useful program for the DVA has always been the VA mortgage program. This program will continue but will be transferred to the Department of Housing and Urban Development (HUD), to be monitored along with the Federal Housing Administration (FHA) mortgage loan programs. The VA program has been a great success in helping vets into housing for them and their families and will continue to serve the veterans and their families.

Many more changes will be made in the DVA in the upcoming year or two. Hopefully these changes will honor our vets and continue the tradition of helping veterans. With this in mind, in closing today's speech, I would strongly encourage the private sector to step up to the plate for our veterans. Churches are encouraged to reconnect with our vets by providing faith-based retreats, counseling, and, yes, some good old-fashioned hand-holding. Private companies are encouraged to hire vets whenever possible; the benefits are tremendous. Veterans with families should have access to private counseling and group therapies whenever possible. Alcoholic Anonymous (AA) is a private organization that has done a tremendous amount of good helping alcoholics since 1935. Other private organizations should be encouraged. Seventy years ago it was we the people, not the government, that helped our vets; it is time again to take the lead in transitioning our vets back into being a useful and productive part of our society. I wish you all a good day . . .

"GOD BLESS AMERICA."

DAY 48: DEPARTMENT OF COMMERCE (DOC)

Hello, my fellow Americans. Today's topic is commerce. It is somewhat of an irony since the very definition of commerce refers to the private sector and not the public. The governmental department, however, does exist and costs the American taxpayer almost $10 billion a year and employs over forty-five thousand federal personnel.[122] Doing what, you may ask. Why are so many people needed to promote business and commerce?

Analyzing the budget, several items and agencies jump out at us. The first and foremost is the Census Bureau. The US has been doing a census in the nation for the past two hundred years and is probably one of the most useful aspects of the federal government. Done every ten years, it does provide much-needed data on our population—demographics and such. However, like all data collection processes, at some point in time the data crosses over the norm and gets into areas that are none of the government's business. On the whole, though, the data is useful for many purposes, public and private, and needs to be continued.

However, the DOC has gone into many other areas: public safety, economic development, international trade, minority business development, and the largest, the National Oceanic and Atmospheric Administration, which alone takes almost 70 percent of the annual budget.[123] Now, one might question why and to what measure does oceanic/atmospheric conditions and research have to

---

[122] Office of Public Affairs. "Fact Sheet: FY 2017 U.S. Department of Commerce Budget." Commerce.gov. February 9, 2016. https://www.commerce.gov/news/fact-sheets/2016/02/fact-sheet-fy-2017-us-department-commerce-budget.

[123] *Ibid.*

do with commerce and the federal government. The answers will be forthcoming, and this agency will be pared down tremendously.

My goal for this department is to pare down the twelve agencies under the DOC down to three or four at the most. The Census Bureau and the Weather Service are notable and beneficial products. The Oceanic and Atmospheric Administration will be eliminated ASAP. The fisheries subagencies will be transferred to the Department of Agriculture for monitoring and control. Environmental agencies will revert to the states whose borders are on the ocean.

The DOC has a mission statement to make business more competitive and innovative at home and abroad. This, folks, is not—I repeat, *not*—the purview of the federal government. Government has absolutely no idea how business works and produces the goods and services needed by our nation. Every time the government intervenes into areas outside its inherent domain, no good comes of it; instead costs go up, and service and access to goods go down. The department does not hire business expertise to run the department; it hires lawyers, liberal arts majors, communications experts, and the like, all of whom have little or no business experience. But by having a government position of authority, they now have the means of controlling what they have no business controlling.

This insanity even extends into the private sector. The US Chamber of Commerce, the erstwhile organization for the promotion and expansion of US business interests in America, has in many ways become a tool of big government. Supporting government expansion programs such as Obamacare and amnesty for illegals, the organization has lost all objectivity and works against private enterprise instead of enhancing business. The chambers in most states get great donations from its members, but the return for those funds is miniscule at best. When I had my medical clinic, I belonged to the local chamber but never found any good arising from the organization. When I discovered their allegiance to the progressive agenda, I dropped all ties with the organization. I urge all business leaders to examine closely their membership in local and state Chambers of Commerce (COC) and elicit what their agendas are. Some local COC are independent and follow a true capitalistic philosophy, whereas many others do not. If your local COC does, support it; if it does not, disavow all membership. The only way individual businesses can make a difference is by fighting the liberal agenda.

On the international front, we will always be interacting with foreign countries regarding many issues, including trade. These issues will best be dealt with by the State Department, and much of those responsibilities will be transferred to the Department of State, or DOS, within the next year.

Before I leave this topic, I would like to relate two stories that illustrate, I think, the best of the entrepreneurial spirit of America. A few years back I was on a mini vacation and was traveling along the original path of the first national road, erected in 1803. I stopped at a museum that housed one of the hostels operating at that time along the road. This hostel was started by a widow with seven children. Her husband died and left her a small farm, which barely provided enough income for the family's needs. She was able to sell the farm and applied for a permit to start a hostel on the National Road. She was fortunate and was able to secure a permit. With scant funds, she and her family built a simple hostel and opened her doors for the travelers along the road. Her contract stated that she was to provide services seven days a week. So she did. Her children started a small farm for vegetables, and she bought daily produce from farmers bringing their produce along the road: meat, fish, chicken, vegetables. She served three meals a day for the travelers, as well as board in the evening. She had two bedrooms initially for the travelers; sometimes three or four were in a bedroom. Every morning she and her children arose at 4:00 a.m. to start preparing breakfast, baking bread and other foods for the day's travelers. Thirty years she ran the hostelry, providing a living for her and her extended family. At her prime she was making $40,000 a year, quite a sum for the early 1800s. As her business expanded, she plowed the profits back into the business. Due to her excellent reputation for food and service, her hostelry was always full. She added on to the basic foundation, enlarging the building to three stories, ten bedrooms, three kitchens, and two large living rooms. When she died, her family continued to run the business for many years. This, folks, is the American dream, the "can-do" spirit, that exemplifies our nation. No time off for good behavior, no welfare checks, no government handouts, no Medicare, no Social Security. They did what was necessary and succeeded admirably.

The second story is a personal one. As many politicians will tell you, they all grew up in impoverished circumstances. I was one of those. My dad was transitioning out of the military, and I was left with my aunt and uncle to finish my school year. There were no allowances then. Across the street was a little store. I used to go there, and if I had a few cents to my name, I would buy a little candy. One day I noticed a man bringing in a six-pack of empty Coke bottles and getting money back from the owner for the deposit. After he left I asked the owner about the refund. He told me that people who bought Cokes or other soft drinks paid a deposit on the bottles and that the deposit was refunded if the bottle was brought back unbroken. I thought of all the bottles I had seen in the fields next to my house. I asked if I could bring the bottles and get paid. He looked at me severely and said, "Okay, but I will check each bottle, and if there are any cracks, no money." I ran out the store, got out my Ryder cart, and lined it with pillows and blankets. Every day after school I would go along the road looking for bottles. I remember two cents for a twelve-ounce bottle and five cents for a sixteen-ounce bottle. It was a blast. Some days I would only find one bottle, some days none unbroken, some days two or three bottles. Suddenly, I was making twenty-five, sometimes fifty, cents a day. For a ten-year-old boy, that was riches beyond. Of course my aunt and uncle frowned on the endeavor, but I did not care. I was my own boss and making my own money. By the time my dad found out about my little business, I had almost twenty-five dollars saved. He was impressed. That money paid for my first savings bond to eventually go to college. Small beginnings, folks; small beginnings can lead to big careers.

Remember it is not government that built our great nation; it is that widow lady, it is the Rockefellers, the Gates, the Edisons, the Vanderbilts, the Mellons, to whom we owe our standard of living. This insanity of government bailouts because of the excuse of "too big to fail" must stop, and stop it will under this administration. Those of you in the US who increasingly look to governmental action for answers should start looking in the mirror and finding solutions within ourselves and our families. Until tomorrow,

"GOD BLESS AMERICA."

DAY 49: REST

Our Father, Who art in heaven, hallowed be Thy name, Thy kingdom come, Thy will be done on earth as it is in heaven. Give us this day our daily bread and forgive us our trespasses as we forgive those who trespass against us. Lead us not into temptation but deliver us from evil. Amen.

DAY 50: THE HALFWAY MARK

Good morning, my fellow Americans. Today is a momentous day. We have reached the halfway mark to my goal of one hundred days of problem solving for our nation. Already the cries among the progressives are loud and boisterous. Calls for impeachment resound in the halls of Congress each and every day. Judges everywhere are being mobilized to stop any and all executive orders that are forthcoming. The mailbags and the White House website are reaching mega proportions. As you can see to my rear, the bags are overflowing. On the WH website (WH2017.org), we have set up pages referring to each day's problems, solutions, and your responses to those issues. You can see how the responses are categorized, good, bad, or otherwise. I am proud to say the overwhelming responses are favorable, with some exceptions—say, California and New York—hotbeds of the progressives' rule. San Francisco is threatening to secede and become the first gay city-nation in the world. More power to them.

The country is very divided, but these past fifty days have mobilized the country in a way that has not been seen since 9/11. That is good. More and more states are getting on the bandwagon and endorsing the amendment convention. If all goes well, enough states will ratify resolutions for the convention by the end of this year. Think of how momentous this will be, my fellow Americans; next year, God willing, our nation will have a national convention to propose and pass amendments to our Constitution. This convention will be the first since 1787, the first in 230 years. Once again we as a people are standing up to tyranny and saying, "NO MORE." Those words effectively started our great nation, and those words will revitalize our country in ways as yet unimagined.

I can tell you all one thing for sure: those that hate this country near and abroad are very, very, very scared—akin to what the enemy felt in WWII. The progressives, the socialists, the PC crowd, the Marxists, all the special-interest crowds who have held sway with our government and nation for over sixty years, all are seeing the reversal of their horrible ideas and programs for our nation. They will fight you, the people, tooth and nail every inch of the way. We must be strong, reliant in God that we are on the right path, and awake every day and take the fight to the enemy. This is war, my fellow Americans, no different from the major wars we have fought in the past. As in the wars in the past there will be bloodshed; there will be riots by various special interest groups, such as the blacks, and murders of innocents such as witnessed by the Muslims against the Christians and Jews. We must not waiver. We must hold fast to our beliefs and principles. We are the God-fearing people; the other side is secular, atheistic, and, quite frankly, unholy. They will lose. They will not lose easily; they will vilify us, call us every name in the book: racist, homophobic, anti-gay, anti-women, anti-Hispanic, anti-black, anti-everything they can think of. Find your voice, my fellow Americans; do not be afraid to speak your mind. If they try to muzzle you, and they will, still speak out. Speak out in your churches, your local forums, your schools, your workplace, your council meetings. Write to your newspapers, to your state and federal representatives. Go down to your state capitol and speak with your representatives personally. Stand up for what you believe and do not back down. Teach your children what is right and true and, yes, God inspired. Be not afraid of the Pledge of Allegiance; repeat it at home. Sing the songs of our country ("God Bless America," "America the Beautiful") at home, in church, and, yes, in public. Demand that the American flag be present in all schools, public institutions, and even in the churches. Defend the flag if someone is desecrating it in public. Our military died in many places around the world defending our flag. Anyone desecrating the flag is not an American; the idea that burning the American flag is free speech is ludicrous. I am passing an executive order ASAP that deliberate flag desecration—burning, cutting up, defecation, or urination—will be a felony and punishable as such.

These are glorious and eventful days, my fellow Americans, for those who these many years have been frustrated by the progressive decline of our nation here and abroad. The tide is starting to turn. These next fifty days will be as significant as the first fifty days. We will tackle even more entrenched progressive insanity and address those issues. No more will the progressives be able to hide behind their regulations, their bureaucracies, their activist judges, their bullies in the schools, institutions, and the courts. The light of truth has started and will continue to shine on these many societal issues, and that light will show the way to a better country. After finishing up with the various cabinet and other agencies, we will tackle other issues: Social Security, Medicare, the racial issues of various ethnicities in America, the military, foreign affairs, and our involvement in the United Nations, a topic I am especially looking forward to. Our friends and enemies here and abroad will be addressed, and hard choices will be made. Our nation has had a glorious history, and we will not play second fiddle to any other nation. International economies will be analyzed. Our financial institutions will be analyzed—especially the Federal Reserve—as will our debt issues and the dollar as a continuous base for international trade; all will come under intense scrutiny. As I stated, the battle has just begun, and I, for one, look forward to the fight. So I shall sign off for today, eager to begin the new day and a new dawning for the US.

"GOD BLESS AMERICA."

SECTION 5

DOWNSIZING
THE GOVERNMENT

(PART 2)

Day 51: Housing in America (HUD)

Good morning, my fellow Americans. Today we will tackle another of the shibboleths in America and in our government, the Department of Housing and Urban Development (HUD). Created during the Great Depression in 1937 as another progressive solution to the economic problems of the day, it was raised to cabinet status in 1965, again under a progressive president and Congress. Have we noticed a pattern here, folks? It seems agency after agency is created under the progressive management of our government and always serves not the people, but to increase the power and scope of government. We have had four eras of rapid increase in government: the 1930s under FDR, the 1960s under Johnson, the 2000s under Bush, and of course my predecessor, Obama. Each had a special name, the New Deal under FDR, the Great Society under Johnson, Hope and Change under Obama. The names differ, but the programs always have the same purpose: increase the size and scope of government. They all sound good and well-meaning in the beginning, but they are all "wolves-in-sheep's-clothing" agencies.

HUD, like so many other agencies, has increased in scope over the years, getting involved in low-cost housing, Indian housing, FHA insurance, multifamily housing, Federal National Mortgage Association (FNMA), and Freddie Mac mortgages. HUD proudly announces the amount of home ownership in the US and proclaims it is under their tutelage. We know now about the horrors of FNMA and Freddie Mac mortgage scandals in the 1990s and 2000s. The real horror is that the American taxpayer has had to pay for the bailouts in the 1980s, the 1990s, and even into the new millennia. And we are still paying. Insanity!

Folks, housing is not a right for Americans, or anyone for that matter. Show me in the Constitution where it is even mentioned. Housing, the affordability, and the quality and quantity of housing have always been a part of the private sector, period. If there are any governmental regulations on housing, it is the responsibility of the states in which the housing is located, not the federal government. Here again, this is another example of government getting involved in matters that are not a concern of the government, many times creating or increasing the problem then making the government the solution. I remember hearing stories about my grandparents saving until they could afford to buy a house. They paid cash for the house, and it was a huge event in my family's life when they finally owned their own domicile. Back in those days, it was not uncommon for a family to pay 20, 30, 50 percent down on a house before a bank would finance the rest.[124] When my grandparents finally owned the house, their children and families also stayed there to help pay the overhead. Part of the reason the Great Depression lasted so long was that banks had eased up on lending and allowed people to purchase houses for very little money down. When the economy tanked, the homeowners just walked. This scenario was repeated in the 1980s, the late 1990s, and in the 2000s. One would think that after all these housing bubbles, aided and abetted by government interference and taking trillions of dollars of worth out of the economy, that we would wise up. Again the answer is "no." Failure to the progressive mind means that not enough money was thrown at the problem. Their solution is always to expand the agency, increase the budget, and never admit failure.

---

[124] Butkiewicz, James L. "Fixing the Housing Crisis." *Forbes.* April 30, 2009. http://www.forbes.com/2009/04/30/1930s-mortgage-reform-business-butkiewicz.html.

Currently HUD has a budget of $49.3 billion and employs over nine thousand federal workers. HUD administers almost one hundred and fifty different programs that are increasing yearly.[125] Programs from block grants, Hispanic housing, Indian housing, rural housing, multifamily housing, public housing, healthcare facility programs, housing counseling, fair housing . . . the list is almost endless. Now HUD has a new expanded goal of ending homelessness in America. Insanity!

Over the next year the budget for HUD will be reduced dramatically. The mission of HUD will focus on FHA mortgages and VA mortgage guarantees for those who are qualified. The actual mortgages will be made by the private sector. FNMA and Freddie Mac will be disbanded; their assets will be sold over the next few years in the private market and used as reserves to back the FHA and VA mortgage markets. No longer will the American taxpayer pay for the outrageous losses incurred by our government in these scandals over the last twenty years. Speaking of these scandals, I am directing the Department of Justice to immediately start the investigation of these scandals, especially FNMA and Freddie Mac from the 1990s and 2000s. Government personnel and private individuals who were actively involved in the malfeasance that occurred will be investigated and prosecuted to the full extent of the law. I am sure you, the people, are tired of those individuals getting wealthy at your expense and using these agencies as tools for their wealth, often flagrantly violating the laws of the land. I think it is time for some of them to be brought to trial, fined, and maybe spend some time in jail. There will be no pardons in this respect.

---

[125] Press release. "HUD Releases Proposed 2017 Budget." US Department of Housing and Urban Development. February 9, 2016. http://portal.hud.gov/hudportal/HUD?src=/press/press_releases_media_adviso ries/2016/HUDNo_16-016.

Here again while the budget will be reduced, I expect that many of HUD's programs will revert to state and local control and that much of the HUD money will be appropriated back to the states. Nevertheless, it will be the states' and local government' control and responsibility. I expect many of the states, especially those who have been at the federal watering hole for many years, to object to all these new responsibilities. It will be you the people and your representatives who will determine which if any of these programs will continue or permanently bite the dust. It is your money, folks; spend it wisely. Until tomorrow,

"GOD BLESS AMERICA."

DAY 52: DEPARTMENT OF AGRICULTURE (DOA)

Hello, my fellow Americans. As the week progresses to a close, the weekend will bring thoughts of food, backyard BBQ, grilling, and making cookies, pies, and the like with your children. This is a good time to talk about a huge department in the US government, the Department of Agriculture (DOA). Initially created in 1862, the department was for a different time and place in our nation. In the 1800s over half of our population lived on farms. Agriculture was the main feature of our society, and small family farms were the mainstay of the economy. Industrialization was confined to the urban areas.[126]

Fast-forward 150 years later, less than 2 percent of the population live on farms.[127] The small mom-and-pop farm operations have

---

[126] "Historical Timeline — Farmers & the Land." Growing a Nation: The Story of American Agriculture. Accessed June 22, 2016. https://www.agclassroom.org/gan/timeline/farmers_land.htm.
[127] "Farm Population Lowest Since 1850s." *New York Times.* July 20, 1988. http://www.nytimes.com/1988/07/20/us/farm-population-lowest-since-1850-s.html.

been replaced by large corporate concerns farming thousands of acres. Agriculture is now an industry spanning not only the national landscape but international also. The commodities markets provide open-market operations and instant information on pricing, quantities, and availability of agricultural crops, livestock, and other commodities. The private sector should be and is the sector that is in control of agriculture, not the federal government. The government system of price support for various commodities—paying farmers not to plant and regulating prices on commodities—is antiquated at best. The US maintains a two-tier pricing on sugar production, for example, and has for years been artificially propping up the prices of sugar nationally versus internationally. I am reminded of a former president who inherited a peanut farm in the South. For most of his adult life he was paid generously by the federal government not to plant peanuts. Insanity! As usual with our government, as the rational decreases for an agency, the governmental answer is to find new concerns and continue to expand the agency involved.

So it is with the DOA. Today the budget is over $200 billion and employs almost a hundred thousand federal workers.[128] The DOA touches almost every facet of our existence and oversees the vast amount of agriculture concerns in the US. Besides inspections of various food stuffs, commodities, and livestock in the US, the DOA has oversight of the Forest Service, with over 200 million acres of national forest, national parks, and grasslands. The federal government is the largest landowner in the US, controlling access to public lands for mineral exploration, forestry, livestock grazing, hunting and fishing, and, of course, government leases for oil and

---

[128] "United States Department of Agriculture (USDA) Fiscal Year 2017 Fact Sheet." US Department of Agriculture. Accessed June 22, 2016. http://www.usda.gov/documents/usda-fy17-budget-factsheet.pdf.

gas exploration. Under the past two administrations, oil and gas exploration have been virtually stopped on all public lands. The only exploration has been on private lands and has led to a phenomenal increase in our petroleum production. The government answer to any private usage of public lands is a resounding *no*, no matter what measures are taken to preserve the environment. Insanity!

The DOA has currently eighteen subagencies under its domain. Over the next year these agencies will be dwindled down by at least 75 percent. The agencies eliminated will revert in many respects to state oversight and control. Much of the budget will be allocated to the states. I am planning that federal employees in this department will be pared down to half by the end of this fiscal year. A simple question, folks, is, where are the farms? They are in the states, not in DC. If there is a need for intervention in the agriculture industry, it will be on a local level, not the federal level. Therefore, each state should have control and responsibility for their agriculture. The federal government will retain those agencies that provide research and data collection on the agriculture industry, such as the Agricultural Research Service, Economic Research Service, and National Agricultural Research Statistics Service. The DOA will continue to operate the Animal and Plant Health Inspection Service and Food Safety and Inspection Service.

The Forest Service will be transferred to the Department of the Interior at the earliest possible time, within six months. There its role will be limited. National parks and national forests located totally within the confines of a particular state will revert to that state's control and responsibility. Those that overlap states will still be under federal control. I will further address the public lands under the federal domain when I address the Department of the Interior. Suffice it to say, land ownership by government is in trust for the people. Public land belongs to the people, not the government. However, the government acts as if the land is its own and treats the land as its own private fiefdom. Again, insanity! Most public land should be under state and local control and responsibility. We can still preserve vast amounts of land for public use, just without federal control. Witness the state of Alaska, where 90 percent of the land is under government domain.[129] Insanity! This too will change. Until tomorrow,

"GOD BLESS AMERICA."

DAY 53: DEPARTMENT OF THE INTERIOR (DOI)

Good morning, America. We left off yesterday paring down the Department of Agriculture. Today we examine its counterpart, the Department of the Interior. Again, a huge department, totally unwieldy, and mostly out of touch with the needs of today. Originally created in 1849, the DOI is designed to address the needs and concerns of a very young, growing, and expanding nation with its problems on the restless frontier, the Indian wars, territorial governments (there were only thirty-one states in the Union at that time). The West was a wild frontier; the railroads were under construction, and the Civil War had not even been fought yet. The Mexican War had just finished, and vast new territories had been added to the US—the territories of California, New Mexico, and Arizona. Texas had just joined the USA. In all, it was a completely different picture of the USA. Fast-forward 160 years, those issues no longer exist; the states have grown to fifty. The country is not in

---

[129] Fact sheet. "Land Ownership In Alaska." Alaska Department of Natural Resources. March 2000.
http://dnr.alaska.gov/mlw/factsht/land_fs/land_own.pdf.

its adolescent stage but a full mature nation spanning the land from the Pacific Ocean to the Atlantic. The DOI, as with most governmental agencies, has never stopped growing. As the landscape changed, the DOI just changed its mission and has continued to grow. DOI now has a budget of over $18 billion and employs over seventy thousand federal employees.[130]

Here again, the numbers tend to be confusing. The government says the budget is only $11 billion, but when you read the fine print the budget has another $7 billion in "mandatory" funding. However, I am able to relay some good news for once. The DOI takes in almost $15 billion in user fees for offshore drilling, mineral rights, and other fees.[131] In essence the DOI is almost at a break-even point. That is good since with our reorganization of the DOI over the next fiscal years, the department should be "profitable," if I can use that word in a government setting.

Let us tackle the biggest agency with the DOI, and that is the Bureau of Indian Affairs. The bureau, after 150 years, still largely dictates the affairs of the Indian population in the US. The DOI is involved with all the schools on the reservations, social services, law enforcement, land management, and loan programs. INSANITY. The DOI states that its mission is promoting self-governance, but instead it perpetuates the entitlement mentality of the Indian population. I was on a hunting trip in New Mexico recently on the Zuni reservation. The Zuni tribe has some of the most spectacular land in New Mexico. However, when you go to any of the towns on the reservation, it is like going back to a third-world country. Vast acres that were once productive farms are now fallow and laid to waste, not because the land is not farmable, but

---

[130] "Interior Fact Sheet Budget 2017." US Department of the Interior. Accessed June 22, 2016. https://www.doi.gov/sites/doi.gov/files/uploads/Interior-Fact-Sheet-Budget-2017.pdf.
[131] *Ibid.*

because it is easier to get government aid than by farming or working the land. There are only a few shops in town. The Indians bring in their government checks to pay for their supplies. In order to hunt I had to hire a native guide. He was supposed to be experienced, but he was just lazy. We spent day after day just driving around looking for elk. We never did find any, but he was quick to charge me the full amount for the hunt and even demanded that I pay for his gas. I resolved never to hunt on any Indian land; they were not professional in the least.

In a way, it is not really their fault, as with all the entitlement programs that abound. If you are paid to sit on your duff, why should you work? With the Indians, all is paid for, the hospitals are free (courtesy of the US), the schools are free (courtesy of the US), they get full-ride scholarships if they want to go to college, and as such do not even have to qualify intellectually to go to college. They have some of the best hunting on their lands, but no Indian hunts. They instead go to the local supermarket and use their government checks to buy meat and the rest of their food. At one time the Indians farmed and produced much. No longer! Their homes are built by "Uncle Sugar," the US. The Indians, of course, treat their homes with no respect, and in a few years a new home looks fifty years old with trash in the front lawn and paint falling apart on the exterior. In essence the homes become hovels very quickly. I also remember in my medical training, I spent some time on the Apache reservation in Whitehorse, Arizona. The hospital had been erected by the US government and had the latest in solar arrays for power to the hospital. The arrays cost millions of taxpayer dollars. They were never used because the Indians did not know how to operate the grid, and besides, the electrical utilities were available. The grid stands today, rusting away for over twenty years.

This again is INSANITY, folks, and it needs to end. While I will be addressing the Indian problem in greater detail in a few weeks, it is sufficient to say now that all federal aid to the 567 native tribes nationwide will be decreased by 20 percent each year. The tribes have been on the federal dole long enough. It is time to stand on their own and be responsible for their own destinies. Over the past twenty years one of the biggest production industries for the Indian tribes has been the native casinos erected and operating nationwide on Indian reservations. These casinos bring in more than $30 billion each year for the Indian tribes. These monies have largely been shunted away and wasted, to my belief. NO MORE. The tribes have the means of self-support, whether it be the casinos, farming, mining, or jewelry making. It is time they learned to utilize their resources for their own self-sufficiency.

As I mentioned, the Forest Service will be transferred to the DOI and be managed along with the Bureau of Land Management (BLM). The federal government has not done very well in managing the public lands and has become very partisan with respect to land leases and usage for the public and private sectors. I am directing the secretary to immediately review and revise the policies regarding lease for farming, oil and gas exploration, and mining. The fear instilled by the progressives as to environmental hazards and destruction of the habitat have always been proven false.[132] The technology behind these industries is far in advance of any governmental research and does not need government interference in the use of these lands. Fears are driven by events that have happened fifty to a hundred and fifty years ago. That is not the scene today. Over the next four years of my term, the DOI

---

[132] Tracinski, Robert. "Seven Big Failed Environmentalist Predictions." April 24, 2015. The Federalist. http://thefederalist.com/2015/04/24/seven-big-failed-environmentalist-predictions/.

will be investigating the logistics of transferring of much of the public lands to state domain and responsibility.

The National Park Service will still remain with the DOI for the time being. The American public pays fees for use of these parks which by definition are held in trust for the American people. I am ordering that the fees for public usage of our national parks and forest services be reduced by 50 percent effective immediately. My goal is that the fees should be reduced by another 25 percent over the next four years. The parks should be opened to hunting and fishing by the public where possible. In many of these parks the animal population has grown to the point that the animals are going outside the park areas; witness the huge increase in the grizzly population in and around Yellowstone Park.

One last thought on the BLM—almost forty years ago, laws were passed by the progressives to protect the wild horses and burro population, particularly in the west. Folks, these animals were never endangered! This again is absurd. Millions of taxpayer dollars are spent each year transporting these animals from place to place because they are overpopulating the landscape. This will stop. I am today issuing an executive order stopping any further federal aid in this manner. The state where these animals reside will have control over their continued existence or protection. In my opinion they definitely do not need any federal protection.

Speaking of protection, the Bureau of Fish and Wildlife Service will be drastically reduced. Their mission will be pared down, and the wildlife refuges will be transferred to the Forest Service. The endangered species mission will be effectively eliminated. Folks, species have been coming in and out of existence since the world was created. It is not the government's responsibility to try and play God and keep every species imaginable alive. Responsibility for any endangered species will revert to the states were the species live. The state of Alaska, which harbors over 90 percent of all living bald eagles,[133] should be responsible for their maintenance and protection. There are number of funds within the DOI controlling many species—migratory birds, multinational species, wetlands, tropical birds, fisheries—in short, dozens of "funds" supporting areas that the federal government has no experience and no reason to be involved.

If I may digress for a minute, my fellow Americans, over these past weeks reading some of the information about all the cabinet posts and their inherent agencies, one at times has to shake one's head in amazement at how inculcated the federal government has become in the lives of all of us in the US. The other amazing part of this investigation is how many cubbyholes taxpayer money is funneled and hidden in. At times I feel I am part of the novel *Alice in Wonderland*. No wonder the government takes up to 30 percent of the nation's GDP.[134] Given the progressive nature of this humongous growth machine, it is amazing that the leviathan does not control even more of our hard-earned dollars. I am reminded how in the past a tally used to be done during the year on when the average taxpayer has finally paid all his taxes and can start earning monies for his own use. The tally used to be in April of each year; now it is way into June. Just think, folks, nearly half the year, your monies earned do not belong to you but to some government entity, federal, state, or local. That is not a definition of a free society or a capitalistic society. Hopefully, we can stop some of this insanity and steer away from the iceberg ahead. If we do not, we shall surely sink as the "unsinkable" *Titanic* did in 1912.

The last bureau in this DOI I wish to address is the US Geological Service. This service does provide some good in the

---

133 "Bald Eagle in Alaska." Environment Alaska. Accessed June 22, 2016. http://environmentalaska.us/bald-eagles.html.
134 "Total Spending Chart." US Government Spending. Accessed June 22, 2016. http://www.usgovernmentspending.com/total_spending_chart.

realm of scientific research and mapping services. This service shall be preserved; however, its mission, as with all other agencies, will be pared down and focused only on certain areas. This may be a good place to stress again this insanity of "climate change." Rampart in every aspect of every government agency is the insertion of research and control of the private sector in response to imagined threats of this change. Folks, the earth is roughly 4 billion years old. In these 4 billion years of life, the earth we live on has undergone continued climate change. That is the nature of life everywhere on this planet and the universe. To make a natural part of this process—the emission of carbon dioxide, an essential ingredient of life—a toxin needing to be controlled is ludicrous and inherently dangerous. I am directing all government agencies under my office to eliminate funding and involvement in any aspect of "climate change" immediately. This INSANITY will end now.

Finally, as I mentioned before, my speeches are on the WH website, WH2017.org. This website will also give more detail on changes within each agency and department. I encourage all of you to log on and look at the changes that are coming to your government. Think in the back of your mind that these changes will very soon be reflected in your increased paycheck, the gas pumps, in the grocery stores, and in many areas of your life. If those changes enhance your lives, I am doing my job as your president. Again, contact your representatives and let them know about these changes. Vocalize your thoughts and desires. This is your country, folks. Make your voice count.

"GOD BLESS AMERICA."

DAY 54: DEPARTMENT OF HOMELAND SECURITY (DHS)

Good morning, America. Today we will examine our nation's security and look at the cabinets responsible for our security. September 11, 2011, will always be remembered in our minds and hearts as the second time a nefarious foe has attacked us and lived to regret the attack. In the aftermath of 9/11, a new cabinet post was created, somewhat out of fear and necessity, but mostly as an overreaction to the horrendous events of 9/11. When this nation was attacked in 1941, we went to war; we did not create new government bureaucracy to help us defend our nation. Nevertheless, in 2001 the Department of Homeland Security was created, and as with the other agencies and cabinet posts we have looked at, it has grown into an enormous behemoth. Over the last sixteen years of its existence, it has steadily accomplished less and less in the defense of our country. Nonetheless, as with all government agencies, the answers to all is increased growth and power.

From the onset, the DHS was supposed to consolidate many disparate agencies under one roof and thereby achieve more efficiency of operation and also more enhanced defense mechanisms. Fast-forward fifteen years, our borders are more porous than ever before, and millions of illegals are flooding across and entering the US from God-knows-where. The southern border defenses are not complete and allow almost anyone to come across. Insanity! The department that was supposed to make us more secure has in effect made us less secure. My predecessor was more interested in getting more illegals into the country than not. Not only is our country less secure than at 9/11, we have opened our borders to more and more illegals, disease, and nefarious criminals and terrorists from other nations around the world, not only from Mexico and the like, but also the Middle East and Asia. NO MORE!

On day nine I talked with the nation on border issues, specifically the southern borders, where I have ordered and have in place four army divisions from California to Texas. I am able to say at this point the borders are becoming rapidly more secure. Illegals coming across has virtually been halted. There have been some firefights with our military and illegal terrorists, and they have learned very quickly that they are not welcome in the US. We have already seized in contraband over thirty thousand weapons of various sizes, makes, and lethality, as well as explosive devices—thankfully none of it is of a nuclear capability. We have seized and deported over ninety thousand illegals these past two months. You can look at our website to see the various nationalities that have been deported. I have asked Congress for $10 billion in funding to complete the full two thousand miles of border fence from California through Texas. Until the funding is approved, I have designated monies within the DHS budget to continue the completion of the border security. This, folks, will be ongoing, as our enemies are wily and will continue to try and get through the borders, either under, through, or even over. You have probably read that nineteen planes have been shot down in the last sixty days. All of these planes ignored the no-fly zones and have been found to harbor terrorists on board. Those terrorists, fortunately, are dead now and no longer a threat to the US. As I said before, enemies of the US beware, we will act with any means to defend ourselves, even to the point of warfare. Reports from our southern border states are unanimous in their praise of the military option and all have remarked in the decrease in various crimes, murder, drug running, and robbery in their respective states. Farmers and ranchers along the borders remark that for the first time in many years they feel secure with their lands and businesses.

As I also mentioned in the early days, the US Border Service and the US Citizenship and Immigration Service will be combined under one agency. The role of the border agents that I spoke about in the early days—where the border agents have fine tickets and will be charged with issuing fines to American businesses who knowingly hire and rehire illegals for whatever work—is finally bearing positive results. I realize that all illegal hiring cannot be stopped, but those companies who are being continually fined with the monies increasing with each infraction are learning quickly that flouting our laws is not the way to succeed. We are also publishing on our website, broken down by states, those companies who have been fined for hiring illegals and how much the fines were. I urge you, the consumer, to let those companies know what your thinking is on breaking the law. You as the consumer can do much by boycotting those companies who are engaged in illegal practices.

Until the borders are secure, the military option will prevail and will be under the Department of Defense and myself as commander in chief. The DHS will be pared down as appropriate. I have already mentioned the TSA, which is being disbanded as we speak. A unionized work force such as the TSA is ineffectual at best and is being replaced by military police. At those airports that have made the transition to the military police, the atmosphere is different these days. Travelers are no longer being harassed, and the security is significantly increased. We have also included in airport security the various companies and personnel that help run the airports. Companies that are lax in hiring US citizens for airport functions are having their contracts nullified. We need visibly to warn our enemies at home and abroad that we as a nation are serious about our security. Visas have been effectively halted for the time being and will be reissued as appropriate when the situation is more under control. Tens of thousands of illegals on expired visas remain in the US. They will all be found and deported without leniency. The student visa program has been radically curtailed and will also be suspended for the time being until matters are under control. Any institution of higher learning—high schools, colleges, and universities—that knowingly harbors illegals on expired visas will immediately have all federal funding halted until further notice. There will be no sanctuaries in the US, either public or private, for illegals in the US. As we discussed, cities and states that commit themselves to being "sanctuary" sites will immediately have all federal funding suspended indefinitely. If these locals persist in illegal behavior, drastic measures to include the National Guard will be on the table. This, folks, is the United States of America, not Mexico, not Saudi Arabia, not China, or whatever nation these peoples come from. We will act accordingly.

Continuing with the DHS, the US Coast Guard will be transferred to the Department of Defense and will continue their mission of securing our waterways and coastlines. I have ordered an enhanced role to the US Marines who will be deployed on all interdiction vessels in the Coast Guard. Foreign ships who do not conform to our search patterns will be stopped, searched, and, if need be, sent back to the nation of origin. The US Secret Service will revert to the Department of the Treasury and will remain there for the foreseeable future. The Nuclear Detection Office will also revert to the Department of Defense and will be under the military option. I will be reviewing the other aspects of the DHS and will be making appropriate reductions as warranted. Folks, this DHS has failed and will be replaced. Until tomorrow,

"GOD BLESS AMERICA."

DAY 55: HEALTH AND HUMAN SERVICES (HHS)

Today is another momentous day, my fellow Americans. Today and succeeding days we will go to the heart of entitlement programs, namely the HHS Department, the Social Security Administration, and the Medicare Administration. These agencies and their budgets comprise trillions of dollars each year in the federal budget and continue to grow out of control each and every year. As with all progressive actions, what started out as a manageable budget and agency has grown into a true federal leviathan. Every Congress and president in the past eighty years has tried to pare down these entitlements to little or no avail. Instead, you, the American taxpayer, continue to pay more and more in taxes to service these entitlements. Both the employer and the employees are mandated to pay the SS tax and the Medicare tax out of each and every paycheck. Every year or so Congress increases the tax rates for these entitlements, and more again goes into the federal coffers. SS has been especially egregious, since it was sold to the American public by that famous progressive FDR, that it was insurance for our old age and not a tax. "A rose by any other name is still a rose," as the saying goes. It is a tax, it is mandatory to pay, and we cannot even deduct it as a tax on our tax returns. It even gets worse, folks—it was sold as insurance, and the monies were supposedly put in trust accounts for the participants. Another big lie by the federal government. All the monies for SS since the 1930s have been going into the general fund for the federal government and spent on whatever. Those of you who get your SS statements each year and think those monies are somehow segregated and set aside and available for your use, as with private insurance, are laboring under a grand illusion. Folks, all the monies you have put in the SS fund over your working lifetime are gone; you have no equity at all. All that exists is a bunch of federal IOUs, which, like all government debt, is worthless in the general scheme of things.

I was going to save the following story for the day the topic will be the Social Security (SS) fund, but it is such a good story that I shall relate it here and now. When the Social Security Act was passed in the 1930s, the US was in a deep depression. FDR and his administration were trying a multitude of government programs to stimulate the economy. Nothing worked except to spend billions of dollars and increase the national debt. The SS Act was to provide "insurance for old age," to help keep Grandpa and Grandma from becoming destitute and having to rely on their families for support. The monies taxed were small, and the progressives toted the act as large in benefits to the elderly with little cost to the country. Never mind that the elderly in the US had survived the last 150 years on their own; now they all suddenly needed help. The progressives stated that one had to reach the age of sixty-five to collect the benefits, and of course the life expectancy at the time was only seventy-two. The first recipient of the SS monies was a sixty-five-year-old cleaning lady from Vermont. She had put in a grand total of twenty-five dollars into the SS fund, and she then started to receive benefits each and every month. The rest of the story is very illustrative. This lady beat the odds and lived to be a hundred and two years old. She received almost forty years of benefits to a tune of over twenty-five thousand dollars.[135] Not a bad return on a twenty-five-dollar investment, almost akin to the return a former First Lady received on a commodities investment. And so it goes. In the early years, there were one hundred workers paying into the fund for every recipient; now there are under two workers. The tax rate has to be increased virtually every year just to keep the fund partially afloat. Insanity!

---

[135] Research Notes and Special Studies by the Historian's Office. "Research Note #3: Details of Ida May Fuller's Payroll Tax Contributions." Social Security Administration. Accessed June 22, 2016.
https://www.ssa.gov/history/idapayroll.html.

So let us look into the Department of Health and Human Services (HHS). Created into cabinet position in the 1950s, it has a current budget of almost $1 trillion and has seventy-six thousand federal employees.[136] This budget includes Medicare but does not include Social Security. We shall treat both in our analysis. We shall also look at my predecessor's signature legislation, the Affordable Care Act, affectionately labeled Obamacare. HHS has a dozen major agencies under its wing covering areas like the Indian Health Service, Food and Drug Administration, National Institute of Health, the Center for Disease Control and Prevention, and on and on. I will save the analysis of the Medicare administration for another day and look at some of these other agencies that can be either pared down or eliminated.

Before I begin, let me preface my thoughts on these matters so that everyone listening will know what this administration is trying to achieve. Folks, this is—or was—a free country, and as such, our lives were meant to allow us the greatest freedom of choices in how to live our lives without government interference. Sadly, this is not the case today. I believe in personal freedom both for choice and also for responsibilities. For example, if one wants to smoke, knowing the dangers while continuing to smoke one, two, three packs a day, that is their freedom. It is not government's job to get involved in this freedom, either for advice or action. Putting warning labels on packs of cigarettes comes to mind. Everyone knows the hazards of smoking: cancer, heart problems, systemic degeneration. By the same token, if a person does smoke and gets a pathology from the smoking, they cannot complain and demand medical care because of their behavior. If they have private insurance and their medical conditions are covered, that is the

---

[136] "HHS FY 2017 Budget in Brief." US Department of Health and Human Services. February 8, 2016. http://www.hhs.gov/about/budget/fy2017/budget-in-brief/.

recourse. But for a person who smokes three packs of cigarettes a day for their adult life to demand medical aid for these ailments is not realistic or economically feasible. Our society now demands government entitlements for almost every aspect of our lives. If a person is morbidly obese, they want motorized carts to be supplied by the government. People who are infected with AIDS, a totally elective disease, want the government to sponsor research to help fight their disease. This is insanity! Folks, if you want the government off your back, you have to take more responsibility for your lives and the decisions you make in how to live your lives. Enough said!

On to agencies. I will start with the Indian Health Service, or IHS. As I mentioned a few days ago, it is time for the American Indians to control their own destinies, good, bad, or otherwise. The IHS will be pared down by 20 percent each year for the next five years. That will give the Indian tribes time enough to control their health issues, hospitals, and doctor availability. Over the next five years, all medical facilities for the IHS will be transferred to the Indian tribes. They will have the responsibility of running the facilities and staff, doctors, nurses, and the like for employment.

Other agencies, such as the Administration for Children and Families, or ACF, and the Administration for Community Living, ACL, will be transferred to state control and responsibility and will be eliminated on the federal level. The Health Resources and Services Administration, HRSA, will also be transferred to the states' control and responsibility. Substance abuse and mental health will also suffer the same fate. As each of these agencies are pared down, the personnel will be let go to return to the private sector.

The Food and Drug Administration will still be functional. However, I am ordering an in-depth investigation of the policies and procedures of the FDA. To take years to get any new medicine approved at a cost of hundreds of millions of dollars is insane. This is not the case in Europe or in other countries. The testing process should be months, not years. If there are dangers in any particular medicine, the drug should be shelved until the problem is resolved. I think it is insane that Americans have to go abroad to find medicines that are not available in the US. If there are products that go to market that are unsafe, then insurance and the courts can resolve the problems. Again, I am reminded of stories from my grandparents of going to a corner pharmacy and having various natural concoctions made up on the spot for a particular ailment.

The National Institute of Health, or NIH, is another major agency under Health and Human Services that purports to do needed research on biomedical and behavioral aspects of humanity. While for now the NIH will still be functional, the research facilities will be transferred to the private sector within the next fiscal year. States will also have the option of bidding on the research facilities within their state if they want to be involved in research. Within the next year, the NIH will be limited to an agency that acts as a clearing house for ongoing medical research, nationally and internationally.

The last agency I want to address today is the CDC, the Center for Disease Control and Prevention. I am sure most of you have seen movies about some epidemic hitting the US and the gurus from the CDC are called in to solve the problem and save humanity. Sad to say, this is not the real world. While the CDC will stay active, I am ordering another in-depth study as to the agency goals and mission in the coming years. To allow people into our country with ugly diseases such as Ebola virus, AIDS, medicine-resistant TB, and other infections is a sign of a dysfunctional organization, one more politically correct than functional. There are real dangers of pathologies that can get into our country and how to handle those situations. From where I sit, the CDC is not adequate to handle any of these emergencies. Medicine and politics do not make good bedfellows. By having open borders, no monitoring of aliens entering our country for diseases, and the like is another example of government nonfunctionality. This will stop, I assure you.

In conclusion, I would urge you all to examine the website for other details on this and other agencies that I have been analyzing over these past weeks. I know that many of you are, for whatever reason, on entitlements from the federal government and that many of these changes scare you tremendously. You need to analyze your lives and make positive changes that do not involve government largesse and handouts. Remember, folks, you may be getting these entitlements, but someone else is paying for those entitlements. The costs are now very prohibitive and endangering the future of our country. Think about that. Until tomorrow,

"GOD BLESS AMERICA."

Day 56: Rest

Our Father, Who art in heaven, hallowed be Thy name, Thy kingdom come, Thy will be done on earth as it is in heaven. Give us this day our daily bread and forgive us our trespasses as we forgive those who trespass against us. Lead us not into temptation but deliver us from evil. Amen.

Day 57: Social Security Administration (SSA)

Last week, my fellow Americans, we examined one of the largest departments in the federal government, HHS, and started the process of getting control of this leviathan. Today I will continue the examination and look at one of the oldest and most imbedded of the entitlement programs, the SSA. As I start on my talk today, let us remember, one of the favorite methods the progressives use to ensnare the people is by entitlements. Once someone is on the "dole," even the threat of a cutoff of benefits will make that person very, very afraid. Why? Because those people have relied on the federal trough and their once-a-month check for so long, the thought of having to fend for themselves—maybe actually get a job and be a functional member of society—is in many ways foreign to them. They have been bought off long ago and are "slaves" to the government. In many ways it is not that different from the slave society in the South before the Civil War. All we are talking about is the degree of slavery. It is still slavery. As Lincoln freed the Negro slaves in the US 150 years ago, hopefully this administration will start to free the slaves of progressivism and entitlements.

As we talked about yesterday, the SSA was instituted in the 1930s by that famous progressive, FDR. A firm believer in government control over the masses, FDR, his administration, and his party tried for over fourteen years to institute broad federal acts and regulations designed to increase government geometrically and move to a socialistic or communistic state. As I mentioned before, one of the mantras of progressivism is the concept of "incrementalism." That is, start any entitlement program on a very small scale and gradually increase until the control is total or "the government runs out of other people's money," to paraphrase Margaret Thatcher, a notable conservative.[137]

So it is with the SSA. The initial tax rate for SS or Federal Insurance Contributions Act, or FICA, as it is known, was 1 percent

---

[137] Mark R. Levin, *The Liberty Amendments: Restoring the American Republic* (New York City, NY: Simon & Schuster, 2013).

and only to $3,000.[138] The SSA also only covered a percentage of the population,[139] and of that, only US citizens. Fast-forward eighty years, FICA is the largest deduction for over 50 percent of the paychecks in the US.[140] It is the largest part of the federal budget. It is also one of the largest-expense items for businesses in the US because the employer has to match the employee's contribution. Those of us who were self-employed did not get off the hook either; our taxation rate is double that of someone who worked for someone else. In essence, no one gets off the hook. The progressives know that in order to control the people virtually everyone has to be taxed. Now of course you know who got off the hook, don't you—government employees. They got to opt out of the system and are under another plan much more solvent and beneficial to the employees. Witness even the latest in the government entitlement plans, the Affordable Healthcare Act—the federal government is exempt from the plan. It gets even worse, folks. The SSA started out small, then more and more provisions were added on to the ACT. People with "disabilities" and their families were allowed at any age to start on Social Security benefits, and once entitled they receive benefits for *the rest of their lives*. Their children were also allowed to receive benefits until the age of eighteen. Many of these, quote, "disabled" are getting five to ten thousand dollars monthly, covering them and their families. Of course, their "disabilities" now allow them to receive Medicare benefits, federal

---

[138] "Historical Social Security Tax Rates [1]." Tax Policy Center. Accessed June 22, 2016. Available for download at http://www.taxpolicycenter.org/file/60391/download?token=rxBb5nLq.
[139] "Social Security." Just Facts. Accessed June 22, 2016. http://www.justfacts.com/socialsecurity.asp#privacy.
[140] Hill, Catey. "45% of Americans pay no federal income tax." *MarketWatch*. April 18, 2016. http://www.marketwatch.com/story/45-of-americans-pay-no-federal-income-tax-2016-02-24.

subsidized housing, food stamps, and a multitude of other federal, state, and local handouts.

The SSA had also been expanded to include noncitizens and even illegal aliens.[141] The progressives know no bounds. Since it is not their money they are spending, the sky is the limit. Of course, the workers contributing into the fund are decreasing while the recipients are increasing, leading to dreaded forecasts of insolvency. You the people, many of you, still believe that your contributions are somewhere in that trust account with your name on it. Sorry, folks, your monies are gone. All that remains are accounting numbers identifying you and your Social Security number. You can buy on the open market fraudulent SS numbers for an average of five hundred dollars.[142] This is insane.

The most fraudulent aspect of all of this is that eighty years ago the American public was sold a bill of goods that the SS monies would support our retirement years. Even the concept of retirement is a fraud. Up until the mid-twentieth century, the concept of retirement did not exist. God made man to work and be productive for whatever amount of years that we each are allocated by God. To become financially secure is a worthy objective; to retire is not. So many retirees sit around doing nothing each day, waiting to die. The work ethic, the ability to provide for oneself and family and the future generations, has been taken away and replaced with government dependency. The happiest people I see on a daily basis are those in their sixties, their seventies, their eighties, still working, using their minds and bodies on an active basis and most importantly being productive members of society. I know a

---

[141] "Spotlight on SSI Benefits for Aliens – 2016 Edition." Social Security Administration. Accessed June 22, 2016. https://www.ssa.gov/ssi/spotlights/spot-non-citizens.htm.
[142] "Identity Theft and Your Social Security Number." Social Security Administration. February 2016. https://www.ssa.gov/pubs/EN-05-10064.pdf.

customer greeter at Walmart in Arizona in her eighties, healthy, vibrant, alive, and yes, working five days a week. Look at all the very wealthy—Gates, Buffet, Icahn, Pickens—who never retire, and if asked, plan on working until the good Lord calls them. The idea of retirement is then another progressive idea promulgated on the American public, for you see by retiring you get on the entitlement bandwagon and are now no longer independent but a slave to the government.

There have been many plans to try and restore the SS to long-term solvency, and I will be sending to Congress my detailed plan to save and restore financial stability to the SSA. First of all, the concept of "disability" as an entitlement to SS is false and will be eliminated over the next five years. All disabled will be off SS by that time, losing 20 percent of their benefits each year. All their families will be off SS by the end of this current fiscal year and no longer be entitled to benefits. All noncitizens, legal or illegal, will no longer receive SS benefits of any kind. This fund was meant for US citizens; those that are noncitizens and have paid into the system should consider it a tax for working in the US and nothing else. If they do not like the situation, they can always go back to their country of origin.

Moving on, SS deductions will henceforth be labelled as to what they are—taxes—and thus can be deducted on their tax returns, federal, state, and local. FICA will no longer be used to describe these taxes. Paychecks should say SS taxes, Medicare taxes, and the like.

Next, I want to reassure those who are on SS now, not for disability but as retirement, will continue to receive their benefits that the government has designed for them. The government will not abandon you. However, for all those who are still being taxed by the system, as the song goes, "The times they are a-changing . . ."

Major changes in the SS fund that I will be proposing will be deemed drastic but are needed not only for long-term financial stability, but for restoring the people's faith in the system. I will propose that all citizens sixty years or older shall receive benefits as to the current system and have all the options that the current system provides. However, I propose that these Americans who have the financial means and the solvency and are of the age of sixty or over can opt out of Social Security in total and donate whatever "funds" that are allocated to them back to the federal government. The remaining years of their working careers will be exempt from SS taxation. Those aged fifty-five to sixty shall have the option of continuing on with the current system or switching to a private equity plan which will be forthcoming. The State of Texas has been experimenting with these private plans; the benefits to the employees are quantum leaps from SSA. The added bonus with the private plans is that the employees have access to the monies and can will those retirement monies to their families. For those fifty-five or over who elect the private insurance route, the funds already paid into the SS will stay in the system and will earn interest of 4 percent per annum. At age sixty-five, those individuals will receive their monies plus accrued interest over a ten-year period.

Now to the bulk of the American workers under the age of fifty-five. Within the next year, all ongoing Social Security deductions will be placed into private insurance plans. Each American taxpayer shall have a minimum of three plans to choose from, depending on how fast they want their monies to grow. Monies already paid into the SS system will stay in the SS network and also accrue interest on said funds at a rate of 4 percent per annum. Each taxpayer will also have access to those funds upon reaching the age of sixty-five. These funds will be paid out over a ten-year period ending at age seventy-five. Monies accrued to private pension plans will be available to the individuals after age sixty. In the event of an untimely death, the pension monies will become the property of the estate to be distributed as seen fit.

Folks, these are drastic changes in this entitlement program, but the design is for you, the American public, to gain control of your monies and destiny. Many will be frugal, many will not. It is not the government's job to help define your personal future, financial or not. While personally I abhor the idea of forced deductions into any "entitlement" program, we also must deal with reality. Many of you have gotten used to the idea of a SS system in some manner. Hopefully the above changes shall right the train and allow the country to get on a better financial footing.

Lastly, let us look at the monies being collected by the government. As was explained, these monies get thrown into the general funds and spent who-knows-where. NO MORE! Starting in the next fiscal year, all monies for the SSA being collected on an ongoing basis will be placed in totally segregated funds only for use by SS recipients. Monies collected and already in the federal hopper will be accounted for by an independent auditing firm or firms. Whatever the SS debt is at the time of accounting will be paid into the SS segregated fund over a fifteen-year period. Hopefully by that time, SS will be financially stable and the vast amount of monies being paid into the funds and private insurance plans will be available for the taxpayers.

As I conclude today's speech, I wish to remind the American public that the above changes will have two very important benefits to the American taxpayer: one being that these monies are taken away from the progressives in government and not subject to their political whims, and two, these monies put into private insurance plans will be invested in the American economy and should provide a needed continuing stimulus for the businesses in America. Thank you for your support and your prayers. Tomorrow is a new day.

"GOD BLESS AMERICA."

DAY 58: MEDICARE ADMINISTRATION

Today marks a momentous day in the examination of another of the "sacred cows" of the progressive left in our country, Medicare. This legislation was inaugurated by a progressive Congress in the 1960s and signed by that other famous progressive, LBJ. He studied the actions of FDR and decided to continue the government's foray into the lives of Americans. Program after program under the banner of "the Great Society" were passed in those turbulent years, each program more expansive and egregious than the next. The progressives knew that by introducing the concept of "civil rights," something totally extraconstitutional, they could expand their control geometrically. Medicare was sold as an insurance plan for the elderly and the retired. The government went out of its way after the law was passed to sign up as many of the nation's elderly population over the age of sixty-five so that they would be "enslaved" into the system.

As with all progressive legislation, the insurance was sold as an adjunct to private health insurance and would provide a supplement to regular health insurance. Folks, I wish to reiterate that health insurance is not and never was a part of Constitution and is definitely not a "right" of anyone in the US. The progressives played down the cost to the American public. The initial cost for the first twenty-five years were placed at $3 billion per annum.[143] By 1990 the cost of Medicare was thirty times that amount, almost $107 billion.[144] Today the annual costs are approaching $1 trillion a

---

[143] De Rugy, Veronique. "The Facts about the Government's Medicare Cost Projections." *Reason* online. June 3, 2011. http://reason.com/archives/2011/06/03/the-facts-about-the-government.

[144] Hayward, Steven and Erik Peterson. "The Medicare Monster." *Reason* online. January 1993. http://reason.com/archives/1993/01/01/the-medicare-monster.

year and growing at an increasing rate each year.[145] Medicare is now the second-biggest expense item in the federal budget.[146] Again like SSA, it was touted as insurance, but in reality it is a tax, and as a tax is a mandatory deduction for all taxpayers in the US. Also as with SSA, each employer has to match the employee's contribution. The self-employed pay double the amount.

Medicare and SS are two sides of one coin. One enhances the other, and like SS, Medicare has been expanded over the last fifty years to include the "disabled," the indigent, noncitizens, and now even the illegals. The initial tax rate for Medicare was 0.35 percent on the first $6,600 of income earned.[147] That has ballooned to 1.45 percent on all income.[148] It even gets worse, folks. Under the new ACA, Medicare is mandatory for all Americans over the age of sixty-five, retired or working. If one has private insurance and is happy with that, too bad, you must switch over.

Medicare is a true federal leviathan; it is the largest provider of healthcare insurance in the US. As such, Medicare dictates healthcare decisions in the US. All private insurance companies have had to fall in line to conform to Medicare rules and

---

[145] "NHE Fact Sheet." Centers for Medicare and Medicaid Services." December 3, 2015. https://www.cms.gov/research-statistics-data-and-systems/statistics-trends-and-reports/nationalhealthexpenddata/nhe-fact-sheet.html.

[146] Jacobson, Louis. "Pie chart of 'federal spending' circulating on the Internet is misleading." Politifact. August 17, 2015. http://www.politifact.com/truth-o-meter/statements/2015/aug/17/facebook-posts/pie-chart-federal-spending-circulating-internet-mi/.

[147] Fleck, Pat. "A History of Medicare and Social Security Tax Increases." *The Raging Capitalist*. March 21, 2010. http://ragingcapitalist.blogspot.com/2010/03/history-of-medicare-and-social-security.html.

[148] EY staff. "US employment tax rates and limits for 2015." Ernst & Young LLP. December 18, 2015. http://www.ey.com/Publication/vwLUAssets/ey-employment-tax-rates-limits-for-2015/$FILE/ey-employment-tax-rates-limits-for-2015.pdf.

regulations. Compensation for medical services thirty years ago was under the concept of "fee for service." This simply means that the private marketplace determined the amounts paid for medical services for doctors, hospitals, medical equipment purveyors, pharmaceutical companies, and the like. Costs were kept down because of the competitive nature of the marketplace. Fast-forward to the new millennia: costs are skyrocketing because the private sector is no longer in control of the costs; the public now thinks that medicine and access to medicine is a right and that someone else should pay the costs involved. All this is under the federal watch. The progressives say that everyone should be under some form of health insurance irrespective to the ability to pay. Medicare has become a monopoly and, as you may have studied monopolies, prices go up when there are no alternatives to goods and or services. The federal government tries to hold down costs by, of course, decreasing reimbursements to the suppliers of medical care, doctors, hospitals, and the like. What happens is an overall decrease in the quality of medical care. Doctors are dropping out as providers for Medicare. Hospitals are going bankrupt because of the lack of adequate reimbursements. Almost every year Congress has to change the amounts that are reimbursed since everyone in the medical field is being slowly decimated. Imagine, folks, you have a government consisting of people, most of whom have no idea of medical care and its costs, dictating the pricing of medical care. The codes for billing have no bearing on the actual cost of a particular medical service, be it an office visit or a surgery. The federal bureaucrats determine the reimbursement codes, and there are no appeals.

Speaking of federal billing codes, in 2015 the federal government adopted the ICD10 coding system. This billing coding was formulated in Europe using a socialistic model for coding and reimbursing medical costs. The system magnified the billing codes by over 200 percent.[149] The purpose, of course, was to control the medical industry. There is absolutely no medical benefit to the new system. The costs for the private medical industry has been in the billions. Again, your government at work, increasing costs and decreasing benefits.

The situation has gotten noticeably worse these last few years with the implementation of the ACA. Many doctors no longer take Medicare patients; many hospitals also do not take Medicare patients. Cash is becoming the norm in the marketplace. Cash will buy you the care you may need. Many patients are also going out of country for various medical services, surgeries, and the like. The care is, in many cases, much more thorough than in the US. Think of this, folks: the average visit to a primary care doctor is ten minutes, a true assembly line. And even this assembly-line reality of seeing patients does not often work out. Patients are increasingly not even seeing a medical doctor; they are being seen by a nurse practitioner or a physician's assistant. If a patient wants to see a regular MD, the wait is often months. Welcome to the "brave new world" of socialized medicine.

The ripple effect is everywhere. Doctors used to be visited by pharmaceutical reps who left samples and informed the doctor of new products coming into the market. No more; doctors are going back to the older medicine of twenty, thirty years ago since those are the only pharmaceuticals that are reimbursed by Medicare and the private insurance companies.

---

[149] "ICD-10 Diagnosis Code Set." American Medical Association. Accessed June 22, 2016. http://www.ama-assn.org/ama/pub/physician-resources/solutions-managing-your-practice/coding-billing-insurance/hipaahealth-insurance-portability-accountability-act/transaction-code-set-standards/icd10-code-set.page.

As with SSA there have been numerous studies on how to control the increasing costs of Medicare and still provide adequate coverage. The studies all have been flawed since the assumption of the research is that it is government's inherent role to provide health insurance and care. That is a total progressive and socialistic viewpoint, and as long as the powers that be hold to that viewpoint, costs will continue to rise because there is no counterbalance to the government programs.

In order to even start on bringing this leviathan under control, we must ask ourselves the fundamental question, is it the government's job to provide me with healthcare? It is really an easy question, for nowhere in the Constitution or the subsequent amendments is healthcare mentioned either as a right or a governmental function. Now, those Americans that have been on the dole with Medicare will of course say yes, but, unfortunately, they have been bought off and are slaves of the system. They no longer can conceive of a life where they, and not the government, are in control of their destiny. The answer to the above question is a resounding "No!" I, as your president, will work to achieve a better healthcare world for our nation. It will not be easy, it will not be quick, and it will not be painless, but it must be done to preserve our nation and our way of life. I shall close for now. Tomorrow we will look at legislation that will start to change our healthcare for the better. Until then,

"GOD BLESS AMERICA."

Day 59: Dismantling the Healthcare Machine (Part 1)

Good morning, America. As our week progresses, let us continue our discussion on improving our healthcare and curbing the government's intrusion into all the private parts of our lives.

The task will not be easy, but it is not impossible. As the system grew in increments, so it will be dismantled in increments. I will be sending legislation to Congress detailing the initial steps in decreasing the Medicare influence in our lives. First of all, any federal healthcare benefits will immediately be available for US citizens only. Noncitizens can always access our healthcare facilities, but they will have to pay for the services by whatever means. People seeking emergency medical care will be financially responsible for their care given. This, folks, would hold true if you were anywhere else in the world. As someone said long ago, "There is no free lunch!" There are, as we all know, two types of noncitizens: those that are here legally and those that are not. Legal noncitizens will no longer be subsidized by government aid of any kind. They should either have their own private insurance or pay cash. The illegal situation is somewhat more difficult. Aliens not here legally will no longer have total access to our health system. ER facilities and the like will stabilize the patients, INS will be notified, and the patients will be deported back to their country of origin as quickly as possible. Children born of illegal parents will be immediately deported along with their parents. At the federal government level, the GAO will accumulate data on illegals' healthcare costs from the doctors, hospitals, and the like involved. These costs will be presented to the countries of origin for the illegals for repayment to the US and subsequent repayment to the medical facilities involved. If the country of origin refuses to pay, appropriate measures will be taken by the federal government to collect these costs. Our options are numerous: removal of favored-nation status, or decreasing any and all federal aid or grants to these countries by the amounts owed, as well as tariffs on goods entering the country. While it is our duty to be humanitarian, it is not our nation's job to be the world's doctor. The indigent of the world will always exist, and it is their government's responsibility to provide for their medical needs. Part of my legislation will be that ER care will no longer be mandatory for all who come through the doors. Some will be in fact true emergencies—accidents and the like—and should be seen; the vast majority treated in the ER use the medical facilities as their primary care provider. Hospitals will have the final say as to whether or not to treat those patients and not be penalized.

Medicaid, the ancillary program for the indigent, will be transferred to state control within the next six months. Federal funding will be apportioned to the states according to their needs. It will be up to the states to have the final say as to the amounts and applicability of medical services that will be provided. One last word about medical care, there is a wide array of needed and emergent medical care that may be appropriate. It will be up to the states to ration the medical care that is given to the indigent and the illegal population. Scripts for medical equipment, birth control, cancer treatment, and the like will be discontinued. Our nation's medical facilities are inundated with those seeking meds for the flu, vaccinations, and minor traumas to the body. These will gradually cease in the coming year. Again, any medical services to the indigent should be basic and not enhanced in any way. Of course the overriding factor will always be the ability to pay; if any patient from whatever circumstance can pay, medical care should be available.

As mentioned the previous day about SSA, the "disabled" part of SS will be gradually eliminated over the next five years. Those "disabled" have also had free rein to the government Medicare programs. That will also decrease over the next five years and be eliminated. Catastrophic insurance will be made available for these disabled in case of dire emergencies.

I will expand more of the following when the ACA debacle is addressed. Suffice to say, Medicare will no longer be mandatory to any class of citizen at any age. If someone who is a productive member of society is above the age of sixty-five and can obtain and wants private health insurance, then they should be allowed to. If said patient wants to use their Medicare benefits, either in total or in partial, they should also be allowed. The current payout for benefits of Medicare is the 80/20 rule. Medicare pays 80 percent of what they deem is covered charges, and the patient pays the other 20 percent. My legislation will reverse this equation over the next six years, from 80/20 to 70/30 to 60/40 to 50/50 to 40/60 to 30/70 to 20/80. Medicare will become the secondary insurance, and the private will be the primary. The current proportion will hold true for everyone over the age of sixty-five who is receiving Medicare benefits. Hopefully those numbers will decrease drastically in the coming years. If the citizen is financially stable in their later lives, the same ratio will hold. This reversal, folks, will change the game drastically. No longer will Medicare be the sole and final determinate of healthcare insurance in the US. Quite frankly, as mentioned in a prior day, our goal is to return to a healthcare system based on "fee for service." It is simple, cost effective, and competitive. If a doctor charges a hundred dollars for his services and insurance only pays fifty, the patient pays the difference. It will be up to the patient to either select that doctor or go to another doctor. It is not the government's job or the healthcare insurance industry's to dictate which doctor a patient can go to for medical care. If the patient wants Doctor X, he will be financially responsible for the difference in what is covered by insurance and what the doctor charges. Most doctors I know of have huge discounts for cash and are very competitive in the marketplace. That arrangement should be the basis of medical care.

I realize that many who are receiving Medicare insurance and are elderly will be very apprehensive about my talks for today. It is a well-known statistic that 90 percent of the lifetime cost of healthcare for an individual occurs in the last year of his life, and 90 percent of that is in the last month of that person's life. The question here is also simple: do the medical expenditures change the ultimate equation? Our time on earth is determined by God and, yes, in many respects by ourselves and our actions. The way we conduct our lives is a major determinant of our life-span. Those who smoke, as did my dear departed father, die very young; those that abuse their bodies with obesity, drugs, and whatever must realize that it is not society's duty to aid in that person's medical care. A classic example already mentioned is AIDS, an entirely elective disease. One does not get AIDS from a toilet seat. Those affected want society to pay for their care. NO MORE!

I know the industry has been following Medicare guidelines for many years on payment ratios. The list expands yearly and truly has no basis for reality. Some government statistician comes up with new formulas. There are no appeals and in most cases have no reference to the actual cost of a particular medical service. Take pregnancy care, for example; at one time, doctors were free to charge for the prenatal visits or bundle as appropriate. The prenatal charges differed depending on the complexity of the pregnancy. Now everything is bundled, including the birthing process. A high-risk pregnancy is the same as a normal one. A cesarean section is the same as a vaginal birth. Insane!

The fees for whatever medical care should be determined by those involved and not some nameless bureaucrat. If a person desires "Cadillac" medical care and can afford it, that is his business. On the other hand, if a person can only afford a "Volkswagen" medical care plan, that care should be had but will not equate with the "Cadillac" medical care. Equality of care is neither financially reasonable or sustainable in the real world. That is like equating a McDonald's with a four-star restaurant. When I was an OB/GYN physician in Ohio, I worked with the Amish, who believed in a cash world. They had birthing centers, where many gave birth to healthy and vibrant babies. Those facilities were basic facilities—no private rooms, no TV, no internet, no gourmet food. They were functional facilities designed to deliver excellent medical care at a no-frills cost. That should be our goal also.

Lastly, for Medicare to control doctors and the medical institutions, all had to become Medicare providers and were subject to the dictates and whims of the Medicare bureaucracy. For example, what Medicare pays for a patient's care is final; the medical facility cannot charge the patient for the difference in what was the actual charge and the Medicare insurance. On the average Medicare pays roughly 20 percent of actual charges. Insane! And every year the government wants to lessen the payments to doctors and the like in order to keep costs under control. That will also be another change in my legislation. Medicare will no longer dictate the provider status of the medical community. Speaking of restrictions, private insurance companies have followed the Medicare model and also restrict patients' access to only those doctors that are part of the insurance network. My legislation shall end this practice also. Finally, the industry should be brought back to the "fee for services" basis of medical care. This model is the basis for all other industries and should be for this industry. Those that see any insurance patients will be able to charge the differences back to the patients.

As I close now, pray for our country! God bless you all, and

"GOD BLESS AMERICA."

DAY 60: DISMANTLING THE HEALTHCARE MACHINE (PART 2)

Good morning, my fellow Americans. Today we will address the latest in the threats to the freedoms in our country, namely, the Affordable Care Act, known to all as "Obamacare." This act is not a new attempt to control our healthcare industry; other attempts have been ongoing for over eighty years. The SSA in the 1930s and the Medicare Act in the 1960s are all part of the progressive plan to control the citizens of the US. To control healthcare is a major step to the eventual socialistic takeover of the US. The ACA was strongly advocated during the Clinton presidency and fortunately was defeated in Congress at that time. The progressive mantra has always been "If you can't succeed the first time, try, try again." So they did when my predecessor was elected. By controlling all the branches of government, the ACA was passed in 2010. It is significant that not one member of the opposing party in both houses of Congress, namely the Republicans, voted in favor of the bill.[150] The American people in poll after poll opposed the bill. Over 75 percent of America said *no* to Obamacare.[151] Here again, the progressives did not really care about what the citizens wanted; it is the progressive agenda that matters. That agenda will be achieved by whatever means: laws, regulations, executive orders, or the judiciary.

Virtually everything the progressives touted to the American public about the act was a lie and a sham. They touted figures of 30

---

[150] Harsanyi, David. "No Republicans Voted for Obamacare, so It's Not Their Problem to Fix." *National Review*. June 5, 2015. http://www.nationalreview.com/article/419356/blame-democrats-obamacare-chaos-king-burwell.

[151] Benson, Guy. "Poll: Americans Still Oppose Obamacare, Uninsured Are Least Impressed." *Townhall*. November 17, 2015. http://townhall.com/tipsheet/guybenson/2015/11/17/poll-americans-still-oppose-obamacare-uninsured-least-impressed-n2081703.

to 50 million people without health insurance, pretending that these peoples were not receiving medical care. LIES. The figures mentioned were fabricated figures and included noncitizens, illegals, and those who paid for their medical care in cash. Many of the "uninsured" are young adults who are healthy and do not require medical insurance. When I was young I did not have medical insurance throughout most of my extended college days. They said noncitizens would not be covered under the act. LIES! They said that there would actually be a cost savings with the act. LIES! They said that the average family would save over $2,500 a year in medical insurance costs. LIES! Actually, the costs for American families have doubled, in some case tripled, versus what they had previously.[152] They touted that everyone could keep their doctors. LIES! They touted that families could keep their insurances. LIES! The government played great tunes about the people getting on the plans, but they made no mention of the over ten million American citizens who lost their insurance. The people enrolling on the plans have mainly been the indigent, and since they cannot pay for their insurance, the costs are being subsidized by the government. The GAO now estimates that the ACA will add over $1 trillion in new costs to the American public (here read "additional debt") and will be increasing each and every year.[153]

---

[152] Freedom Partners staff. "2016 Obamacare Premium Increase Tracker." *Freedom Partners*. January 10, 2016. http://freedompartners.org/latest-news/2016-obamacare-premium-increases/.

[153] Senger, Alyene. "Obamacare's Impact on Today's and Tomorrow's Taxpayers: An Update." The Heritage Foundation. August 21, 2013. http://www.heritage.org/research/reports/2013/08/obamacares-impact-on-todays-and-tomorrows-taxpayers-an-update.

They touted no new taxes,[154] when in fact at least fifteen additional taxes are part of the plan.[155] My fellow Americans, everything about this law is a lie and a sham. The icing on the cake is that the IRS, the most anti-American agency in the government, is overseeing the implementation of the law. Over sixteen thousand new IRS have been hired for this task.[156]

With the ACA, the progressives were clever. They noted the lessons of "incrementalism" and used it well in the law that was passed. First of all, virtually no one who voted for the bill actually read the bill, which totaled 2,700 pages. The Speaker of the House, a leading progressive, actually had the temerity to state that "We need to pass the bill in order to find out what is in the bill."[157] That person should have been impeached immediately. Many provisions of governmental control—government panels, additional taxes, increased medical overage, mandatory insurance requirement for virtually all Americans—were not made public and were carefully crafted to be put in place gradually over four to eight years, effectively hiding much of the socialistic nature of the act.

The initial implementation of the act turned out to be a disaster, as many of you experienced; billions of dollars were spent on setting up a website for enrollment into the various plans; foreign

---

[154] Ferrara, Peter. "Obama Promised He Wouldn't Raise Taxes On the Middle Class. He Lied." *Forbes.* July 19, 2012. http://www.forbes.com/sites/peterferrara/2012/07/19/obama-promised-he-wouldnt-raise-taxes-on-the-middle-class-he-lied/#16f5256a2f4c.

[155] "Full List of Obama Tax Hikes." Americans for Tax Reform. Accessed June 22, 2016. https://www.atr.org/full-list-ACA-tax-hikes-a6996.

[156] Willoughby, Mariano. "Price: 16,000 IRS agents will enforce Obama health care law." *Politifact.* July 10, 2012. http://www.politifact.com/georgia/statements/2012/jul/10/tom-price/price-16000-irs-agents-will-enforce-obama-health-c/.

[157] Roff, Peter. "Pelosi: Pass Health Reform So You Can Find Out What's In It." *US News.* March 9, 2010. http://www.usnews.com/opinion/blogs/peter-roff/2010/03/09/pelosi-pass-health-reform-so-you-can-find-out-whats-in-it.

companies were hired to produce the website, which was and still is a virtual fiasco, added to the fact that the websites were being worked on for over three years. Independent consultants in the private sector testified to Congress that given the parameters of the act, developing the websites for interface should have only taken six months, not three years, and should have cost under $100 million, not over $1 billion. As with the other previous entitlement legislation, government totally underestimates the cost, and when discovered, officials calmly shrug their shoulders and say, "What difference does it make?" as in the words of another famous progressive occupying government office. Progressives love to propose "feel good" legislation regardless of the consequences of said legislation. As another famous progressive recently stated, "It is no big deal; we can just keep on changing the law until we get it right." Thank you, Bill Clinton![158] Insanity!

Folks, I could spend the next month analyzing how bad this law is, but I shall spare you all since you have been living the law these past eight years. Therefore, my task is simple and direct. I shall immediately send legislation to Congress that repeals the ACA in total. This law shall take effect within thirty days of signing the bill into law. If Congress hesitates to repeal Obamacare in total, I will use what executive privilege I have to eviscerate the provisions of the law. As my predecessor willy-nilly changed aspects of the law when he was in office, I shall use the same privilege to negate any and all aspects of the law as it stands. I do not want to do this, but the American public has suffered long enough.

None of the above, folks, ignores the fact that as with any human endeavor, there are flaws in the healthcare industry. To destroy

---

[158] Cohn, Jonathan. "Bill Clinton Explains Obamacare." New Republic. September 4, 2013. https://newrepublic.com/article/114604/bill-clinton-explains-obamacare-better-barack-obama-does.

what once was the greatest healthcare delivery institution in the world is a black mark for us as a nation. It is also a black mark on our medical organizations—the AMA, the AOA, the ACA, and other medical associations that did not fight against this abominable act but literally gave in without a fight. Shame on you all. You are supposed to represent and support the doctors and other medical professionals who have to live under horrible laws such as this. I urge all medical personnel to voice your thoughts on this to your associations.

In 2008 the Republican Party proposed a very simple but highly effective bill in opposition to ACA that still addressed some of the major flaws in the healthcare industry then. Unbelievably, this legislation was under five pages. I ask Congress to resurrect this legislation, pass it through Congress, and I will sign it posthaste. We need legitimate reform, not socialism and more government control. I wish you all a very pleasant week. Keep us in your prayers; the journey is not over yet.

"GOD BLESS AMERICA."

DAY 61: ENVIRONMENTAL PROTECTION AGENCY (EPA)

Greetings, my fellow Americans. Today's topic concerns our nation's environment and the quality of our air, water, and other natural resources. The prime government regulator of our "environment" is, of course, the EPA, the Environmental Protection Agency. Created in 1970 to address pollution issues with water and air, the EPA has grown tremendously over the years and is involved in virtually every aspect of our lives, from controlling the emissions of our vehicles to factory air quality control and carbon emissions. Think of this, folks: every breath all of us take involves the exhalation of carbon dioxide, an essential ingredient of life on earth. It never was a toxic substance, no matter what the "scientific" data shows.

To analyze this agency, we need to go back to the turbulent 1960s when the progressives had free rein on the political direction of the US. Social legislation was the norm of the day, from civil rights and healthcare to clean air and disability. Nothing was beyond the reach of the progressives. If there was not a social problem, or a very minor one, the progressives would make one up or dramatically enhance a minor social ill to something very major. Of course, once pronounced to the public, legislation to control the problem had to be enacted. Scare tactics abounded and still abound today. Have you noticed when announcing any "social" problem in the media, very effective scare tactics are used to promote new and radical solutions to "said" problem? A black arrested for whatever reason is the cause of seemingly total racism against every black American in the US. A study showing an increase of less than 1 percent in the temperature on earth over a period leads to hysteria on the global warming of the earth and the extinction of the human race.[159] It is funny to remember that forty years ago the global scare was not warming, but global cooling; the new "Ice Age" was forecast by the year 2000. I still have the National Geographic magazine from the 1970s proclaiming the evidence of "global cooling" and the new Ice Age. I am still waiting!

One of the battle cries during the 1960s was, of course, "save the environment." Books and articles were incessantly written proclaiming the end times. One of the most influential books on

---

[159] Will, George F. "Dark Green Doomsayers." *Washington Post*. February 15, 2009. http://www.washingtonpost.com/wp-dyn/content/article/2009/02/13/AR2009021302514.html.

the environment was *Silent Spring* by Rachael Carson. This text used tons of false data to lambast the use of DDT around the world to control primarily mosquitos, which caused malaria, a major killer of humans particularly in the third world. No one questioned the reliability of the data but took all at face value when it was totally erroneous. DDT was and still is probably the least dangerous of pesticides and also the most effective. In Africa during the 1960s before DDT was banned, almost 90 percent of the continent had eradicated the mosquito population and decreased the incidence of malaria to virtually nil.[160] Projections then forecast the total eradication of malaria within ten years. It is sad to note that since DDT was banned, the mosquito has rebounded, and with this rise so has malaria. In Africa and other places around the world, malaria, far from being eradicated, is once again one of the deadliest diseases on the planet and, yes, on the rebound even in the US. In Africa, millions of children die each year from malaria, even with the medications available. The progressive propaganda has been so effective against the use of DDT that even today, with evidence to promote the use of the pesticide, no effort is made to reinstall the pesticide.[161] Rachael Carson ranks high along with Al Gore and his false documentary, *An Inconvenient Truth,* as leading purveyors of falsehood on our environment. Mr. Gore has made hundreds of millions of dollars proclaiming "the sky is falling; the sky is falling."

To continue, it was in this cataclysm of social events that the Clean Air Act was passed, and with the legislation came the creation of the EPA. No one asked the fundamental question that

---

[160] Zubrin, Roberet. "The Truth About DDT and *Silent Spring.*" The New Atlantis. September 27, 2012. http://www.thenewatlantis.com/publications/the-truth-about-ddt-and-silent-spring.
[161] *Ibid.*

our country survived very well for almost two hundred years without the EPA, so why now was it needed? As with all progressive legislation, the start is small, but through increasing regulations and other social legislation, the agency grew by leaps and bounds. From an initial budget of $1 billion and a staff of five thousand personnel, the EPA expanded quickly along with the social legislation giving it more and more power over the nation. By 1980, in a scant ten years, the budget had swelled to $5 billion. Today the budget is at $9 billion and growing.[162] The federal personnel have swelled threefold to sixteen thousand.[163]

The EPA has become an entity unto itself. Not content with waiting for legislation from Congress, it threatens to promulgate its own regulations concerning anything in the environment, especially with the new emphasis on "climate change" and greenhouse emissions. Insanity! Well, folks, it is time to rein in the EPA drastically. Any and all regulations pertaining to climate control will be terminated immediately. The budget for such regulations will be eliminated as well as the personnel. While there was some validity for early intervention on pollution, those reasons are long since passed. The EPA will revert to a clearing house for issues on pollution control. The NEPA Act passed in 1969, which started and established the government as the "protector of earth, air, land, and water,"[164] will no longer be in force and I urge Congress to pass legislation negating this act.

---

[162] "EPA's Budget and Spending." US Environmental Protection Agency." February 12, 2016. https://www.epa.gov/planandbudget/budget.

[163] "FY 2015 EPA Budget in Brief." US Environmental Protection Agency." March 2014. https://www.epa.gov/sites/production/files/2014-03/documents/fy15_bib.pdf.

[164] "National Environmental Policy Act." *Wikipedia*. Accessed June 22, 2016. https://en.wikipedia.org/wiki/National_Environmental_Policy_Act.

Again these powers for the federal government are extraconstitutional; if the people want or desire federal control over the environment, then an amendment should be passed to the Constitution. I am also urging Congress to nullify the myriad of laws passed in the 1970s (see WH2017.org for details), which established federal control over virtually every aspect of our environment. My administration's goals again are to pass control over these issues back to the states that may be having problems with pollution in any form. My specific goal is to reduce the EPA budget by 75 percent within the next fiscal year.

I think this a good place to sign off and prepare for my next speech tomorrow. My topic will be another favorite of everyone, the quasi-government agency called the Post Office. Until then, God bless you all, and

"GOD BLESS AMERICA."

DAY 62: POST OFFICE

Good morning, America. Many of you will relate to today's topic, the Post Office. My speech will be short but substantial. I am sure many of you have experienced the long lines waiting for PO services, mail misdelivered, mail lost. Today we begin to address this problem.

Of all the vast government agencies, the Post Office is probably the most nostalgic. The PO helped define our nation from its infancy and continues to define us as the years pass. You can remember tales of the Pony Express in the 1800s delivering the mail across the US, fighting the elements and hostiles to get the mail delivered. The PO symbolized adventure in a new and growing nation, the US. I can remember as a young boy getting my first stamp book. Collecting stamps was a very popular hobby when I was growing up, and stamps from ages past were put in the book. Stamp stores abounded, where one could buy and sell stamps of every kind. Most of the stamps were used but occasionally one would find early stamps with no PO mark. I vividly remember being in my grandmother's attic and finding letters written in the early 1900s with the stamps still on the letters. They gave me permission to take the stamps. It was a grand adventure. Alas, as with much in the US, stamp collecting has really become a hobby of the past. The nostalgia still remains, and on many of my family's trips we would pass through very small towns, and there would be a post office. I was always in awe. Stamps were cheap then—only four cents for a first-class stamp—and stayed that way for many years.

Today, stamps cost ten times that amount. It seems every year the postmaster general goes to Congress to increase the cost of stamps because of budget shortfalls. The equation "nothing is inevitable except death and taxes" now includes PO stamp increases. The stamps nowadays do not even have an amount printed on them, just the word "forever." Sad, because the word does not symbolize the PO at all.

When one analyzes the shortfalls and, of course, the endless increases in the prices of stamps and other services, the constant remains the same. The Post Office is tied inexorably to the federal government and is not a private organization. The PO is unionized, and the horrendous payrolls for PO employees take most to their budget and increases every year. I have mentioned the unions being an ugly influence on government workers and the steps we are taking to curtail their activities. The same should be true of the PO. If you look at private companies such as FedEx and UPS, their payrolls are at around 40 percent of total expenses;[165] the PO payroll is twice that.[166] I will propose legislation eliminating the union representation in the PO as a start. The PO will have the next fiscal year to balance their budget. If at the end of that year the budget is not balanced, I will then propose legislation to privatize the PO by the end of the following fiscal year. Whatever entity takes over, the PO will still provide the services and goods that the PO is noted for, will be the sole provider of US postage stamps, and still will have the placard of US Post Office. The sale will be major, as it will include all the physical assets and legal rights to issue US stamps. Hopefully the joys of stamp collecting will be revived. Since tomorrow is a day of rest, I encourage you all to attend the church of your choice and pray for your families, your nation, and if it is in your hearts, to pray for this presidency in its mission to restore America. Until next week,

"GOD BLESS AMERICA."

DAY 63: REST

Our Father, Who art in heaven, hallowed be Thy name, Thy kingdom come, Thy will be done on earth as it is in heaven. Give us this day our daily bread and forgive us our trespasses as we forgive those who trespass against us. Lead us not into temptation but deliver us from evil. Amen.

---

[165] "Pay Tables – Postal Positions in General." Postal Jobs Authority. Accessed June 22, 2016. http://www.postaljobsauthority.com/pay. Also see "Average Salary for Federal Express Corporation (FedEx) Employees." PayScale. Accessed June 22, 2016. http://www.payscale.com/research/US/Employer=Federal_Express_Corporatio n_(FedEx)/Salary.

[166] "Locality Pay." US Postal Service Office of Inspector General. February 7, 2014. https://www.uspsoig.gov/sites/default/files/document-library-files/2015/rarc-wp-14-008_0.pdf.

SECTION 6
ECONOMIC ISSUES

Day 64: State of the Economy

"Today is a fitting day, America, to delve further into the state of our economy and chart a different course for our nation with regards to the engine that drives our economy, capitalism. During the next days I will be addressing major issues with our economy, beginning with our monetary system and its control by the Federal Reserve, Department of the Treasury, and de facto the IRS, the collection arm of government. Also addressed in detail will be our currency, which defines not only our economy but also our economic dealings with the nations of the world. I will address our continued dealings with international forums, such as the IMF, the World Bank, Export-Import Bank, and the European Union. Lastly I will be looking at the oversight of the stock market and the various commodity exchanges. All in all, a lot to cover in several days. As usual the text of my speeches will be available on our website (WH2017.org) as well as more detailed aspects of our solutions to the various problems we have addressed these past two months. Hard to believe that a full two months have passed since my inauguration. Sometimes it feels like two years. Time does fly by when you are having fun . . .

"From the foundation of our nation in 1776, one of the defining aspects of our nation and our economy has been our currency. As any coin collector knows, our currency has changed over the years, with many coins becoming worth thousands, sometimes millions, of dollars due to their scarcity. The 1933 twenty-dollar gold piece sold for over $8 million at auction.[167] A nation's currency is the foundation of not only our economy but our trading with other nations. A strong currency goes a long way in defining the stability

---

[167] "1933 double eagle." *Wikipedia*. Accessed June 22, 2016. https://en.wikipedia.org/wiki/1933_double_eagle.

of a nation, any nation. For over 160 years our currency was backed by gold and silver at specific exchange rates." Here President M——— holds up a gold certificate and a silver certificate, a gold coin and a silver coin. "Citizens of the US could go into any bank nationwide and obtain gold and silver coins of the realm. During this time frame, our country, as with all countries, went through various stages of prosperity, cycles of recessions, and even depressions at times. Because of the capitalistic nature of our economy, we as a nation always bounced back, recovered, and became stronger.

"In 1916, after many attempts of trying to organize the nation's banking system, the Federal Reserve system was created to oversee the nation's banks. The purpose was to stabilize the dollar, or so they said. Charters would still be granted by the Treasury Department, but the Federal Reserve, or the Fed, and its system of 'reserve banks' would provide the liquidity to keep the banking system solvent in good times and bad. Few people realize the role banks play in the creation of money and the solvency of the money supply. It may be worth a few moments to discuss money supply and the banking system.

"When a person deposits money in a bank and is promised an interest rate on that money, the bank must be able to lend out that money at a higher rate in order to remain profitable. The Fed rules that 10 percent of the money must be kept in reserve and the other 90 percent can be lent out. The system works since monies lent out are often redeposited in the bank, which continually compensate for monies withdrawn from the system. This process is the basis for our money supply and our solvency. The Fed, since its creation, has tried with their 'economic specialists' to be able to control the economic ups and downs of the economy and have basically failed every time over the last hundred years. The Fed is adroit at monitoring an individual bank's solvency, but the money supply and the increasing variants of money supply—M1, M2, M3, ad nauseam—continually confound the Fed and their economists and are always beyond their grasp of control. More about that later. Banks remain solvent, balancing the duration of the deposits with the duration of the loans made. Problems arise when monies deposited in the short term are lent out in the long term. This situation can lead to shortfall in monies demanded by depositors, and hence 'runs on the banks' can occur. This situation occurred nationwide in the 1930s, forcing the government to have a 'banking holiday' to calm down the depositors. Again it is worthy to note that the Fed was unable to control the situation at that time.

"FDR, unfortunately, while calming the banking industry, passed an executive order eliminating the ability of US citizens to own gold in any form. Gold certificates would no longer be redeemed for gold. The people were told that the steps were needed because of the gold drain on the Treasury. This of course was bogus, and people did not realize that this was the government's first step in divorcing the currency from its backing of gold and silver. The protest was minimal since the country was still reeling under the elephant of the Great Depression, but the cracks in our currency foundation had started.

"Our nation bounced back in the 1940s with WWII, but the gold standard for citizens was gone. The next step taken in the 1960s was to debase our coinage and remove the silver content from all coins except for the penny. This was done in stages, but by the end of the '60s our coins were no longer made of silver and were instead made of base metals. That is the reason that 'pre-1964' coins today are worth ten or twenty times their face value and why they are hoarded and collected. Any coin in the last forty years is worth nothing, except for the fiat value as a coin of the US. I remember growing up, my grandmother would give me ten silver dollars on each birthday. Those coins are long gone, but today would be worth hundreds of dollars each.

"The situation and our currency continued to be debased, with the final divorce coming in the 1970s under President Nixon, when the US formally went off the gold and silver standards and our currency became a floating, or fiat, currency. It is interesting to note that in the forty-plus years since we have been off the gold standard, our dollar has continued to decrease in value and is currently worth only 10 percent of the value in the 1970s. Sad to say, this value continues to go down. The citizens in the US have been sold a con game in which all think their wealth is rising when in fact the increase in investments (cars, homes, stocks, whatever) over the years is virtually cancelled by the continuing decrease in the values of the dollar. My parents bought a house in San Diego, a nice 1,200 sq. ft. retirement house, for $14,000 in 1970. That home sold recently for almost $500,000. Is it worth that? Who knows, but the dollars needed to buy that house today is worth a tiny percentage of what it was in 1970. By inflating the money supply without restraint during these last forty years and also decreasing the value of the dollar, the economy has 'grown,' but the value of our economy has dramatically decreased. My father never earned more than $10,000 a year in his lifetime, but his purchasing power was vastly superior than college graduates in the current time.

"This is only part of the picture, my fellow Americans. Since the 1970s, the money supply has had no restraints and has grown geometrically. What was millions forty years ago had become billions by the 1980s and trillions by the year 2000. Has the economy become more stable in the last forty years? Not even! The savings and loan industry was destroyed in the 1980s, and the stock market crash in the 1990s was followed by the housing market crash in 2007. Trillions upon trillions of 'value' evaporated; millions of Americans who thought they would have a comfortable retirement have had to rethink their finances.

"The question is, is it getting any better? And the answer is a resounding no. The prior administration added over $10 trillion in new debt for our nation,[168] with absolutely no way of paying the debt or even the interest on the debt. The value supposedly bought by the new debt has evaporated, as has the most of the monies. The so-called improvement in 'infrastructures' hailed by the progressives has been a dismal failure. All in all, more debt for ourselves and especially for our children.

"To further compound the picture, up through the 1970s the banking industry was generally confined to lending for private and business entities. The banks quickly found ways of getting around the restraints of the banking laws and spread out into other areas in which they could make greater profits but also were highly risky. Suddenly, banks or their shell corporations were in the stock market, the commodities markets, derivative trading, and overseas investments, where the FED could not really oversee. The risks compounded. The bailouts in the 2008–2010 era did little to increase the solvency of the banking industry and other financial institutions.

"So here we are in the year 2017, over $20 trillion in debt, way past our GDP and still running around chasing our tails. The economic figures regurgitated by the government on a frequent basis are increasingly bogus. The government changes the basis for virtually every statistic at their whim if the data proves to not be positive. Look at the unemployment number given out each month

---

[168] Boyer, Dave. "$20 trillion man: National debt nearly doubles during Obama presidency." *Washington Times*. November 1, 2015. http://www.washingtontimes.com/news/2015/nov/1/obama-presidency-to-end-with-20-trillion-national-/.

by the government. Totally bogus, because if the number looks bad, the government just changes the basis for the math and then all looks good.[169] Tell me, how can our nation have an unemployment rate of 5.4 percent and have over 100 million people out of the work force, maybe permanently? By eliminating vast numbers of the population in the equation and including illegal employment, any equation can be made to look good. By this rationality, if everyone in the US stopped looking for work or was simply not working, our unemployment rate would be zero. Insane!

"Tomorrow we will continue the discourse on our economy and especially the currency situation and the debt situation. Until then,

"GOD BLESS AMERICA."

Day 65: The Gold Standard

"Today, America, we will continue our discussion of our nation's economy and especially on our devalued currency. Yesterday we had a short course on how much of the debasement has occurred over the last fifty years and how we got into this predicament. Unless we put the brakes on this runaway train called our dollar, we will end up like the German republic in the 1920s when their currency, the German mark, became virtually worthless in a short space of time." Here President M—— holds up a German mark note for a million marks. "At the height of their fiscal woes, a barrel full of marks was needed to buy a loaf of bread. People had to be paid twice daily so they could shop before the next devaluation. It was horrible; a classic situation of the government

---

[169] Matthews, Chris. "Donald Trump is right: America's real unemployment rate is 40%." *Fortune.* September 14, 2015.
http://fortune.com/2015/09/14/donald-trump-unemployment-rate-jobs/.

and its currency out of control. We cannot allow this to happen here. When our financial wizards state that it cannot happen here, it means the opposite—it can happen here!

"One good aspect of this situation over the last forty years is that our government reversed its decree and allowed US citizens to again own gold and silver. The government has resumed printing gold and silver coins in low denominations." Here President M——holds up a gold eagle coin. "This coin has an ounce of gold and is priced at the spot market price of the gold. Other gold and silver coins are readily available; however, they are not recognized as coins of the realm since they do not have a price on the coin. Of course, any coin is worth the value of its gold or silver content, not necessarily the price on the coin. The important takeaway message is that you the people can own gold and silver again without restriction. As a matter of fact, gold and silver again have become integral parts of the investment portfolios of many millions of Americans.

"Now is the time and the place to take bold steps to reverse the insanity of the last fifty years and to once again put our economy and our currency on a firm financial footing. Other countries have been following this course I will outline, albeit very surreptitiously, but still supporting their currency's value for their use in international trading. It would do us good to reflect on the Swiss franc, a currency which has been a bedrock currency for over a hundred years. Why is their currency stable? Well, the answer is simple. Their currency was backed by gold until 1999, and they have enough gold reserves to back up their currency.

"Well, folks, it is time for the USA to step up and once again stabilize our currency and, by default, our economy. You may have been reading in the papers about a new world order with baskets of currencies to be used in international trading and to be valued by some 'global' power, such as the International Money Fund, or IMF. This, folks, is bunk, and the US will not be a party to such tyranny—for that is just what it is. It will be another international power dictating the course and future of our country. The US has always been in control of our manifest destiny and will continue to be.

"So, without further ado, let us launch into a new vibrant economy. To achieve this goal, we will do something no other nation has had the temerity to do. Therefore, I am issuing an executive order that as of July 4, 2017, the US will return to the gold standard. Gold and silver will once again be the backing of the US dollar in all debts private and public. Yesterday, I held up gold and silver certificates used seventy years ago. These will be brought back into circulation. There will of course be changes in the denominations offered in the currency, but the important take-home message is that as of now the US will stand behind its money around the world.

"Now many soothsayers say it cannot be done, and that to go back to gold, we will need an exchange rate of $5,000 to $10,000 to an ounce of gold.[170] If that were true, folks, those values would have already been seen in the marketplace, since Americans have been able to buy or more properly exchange their dollars for gold during the past thirty years. The current exchange rate is $1,250 per ounce of gold.[171] As of the above date, the exchange rate for dollars to gold will be $1,500 and, for silver, $20 an ounce. There may be initial tendencies for a 'run' on gold and silver, but seeing that has not

---

[170] Moffatt, Mike. "What Was The Gold Standard? The Gold Standard vs. Fiat Money." Economics. About.com. October 17, 2015. http://economics.about.com/cs/money/a/gold_standard.htm.
[171] "Gold Price." Gold Price website. Accessed June 22, 2016. http://goldprice.org/.

happened in the last thirty years, such runs will be of short duration.

"I envision that other nations will follow our lead and also base their currencies on gold and silver. The more nations that follow, the more internationally the currencies will settle down. Folks, this will have drastic consequences for the dollar and other currencies. No longer will our government be able with the help of the Fed to arbitrarily increase the money supply and debase our currency. No longer will our government haphazardly increase our debt and not balance our budget as everyone else in America has to. Fiscal restraint will again be forced on the system. The progressives will shout that this will lead into another depression and totally disrupt our economy. Well, folks, the last forty years have seen vast disruptions in the economy. Their solution has gone completely against the basis of history and the value of money in general. Fiat money never works long term since it has no foundation except in the goodwill of the nation, and that never lasts.

"The process will be exciting, folks. Banks will have supplies of gold and silver coins and certificates. As the new certificates come in usage, the old Federal Reserve notes will be eliminated from circulation. The initial gold certificates will be higher denominations, $100, $200, $500, and $1,000. Each will be redeemable to the fractional weight of gold involved. Smaller dollar denominations will be in silver certificates—$5, $10, $20, $50, and $100, which will be redeemable of the appropriate weight of silver in coinage. Coins of the realm under a dollar will again have a certain amount of silver content appropriate to the price of the coin. Certain coins will be eliminated. The penny, the nickel, and the dime will be gone; the quarter and the half dollar will remain.

"Now, again, the progressives will shout about the lack of viable currency. Folks, think about the financial transactions currently in place. Cash is the least familiar. Most transactions are either by credit or debit card, checks, and the like. These are not affected by these changes. International credit charges will be at the current exchange rate existing between currencies involved. The fast food industry and other retail outlets will be accommodated since most items sold are not in the cents realm, but the dollar realm.

"As the dollar starts to stabilize, so will the twin specters of inflation and deflation. Monetary restraint will gradually come into being. The governments will be restrained by gold reserves available to back their currency. Value of goods, services, and investments will no longer be on an upward or downward spiral. Homes will revert to their historical standard, that of a dwelling place to grow a family, not as a spiraling investment.

"In addition to the gold standard, I wish to take this opportunity to introduce an additional standard with which the US will use to value our currency, that is, the PETRO dollar. Used from the 1970s as a means of international trading in the petroleum industry for oil and gas, the USA will now be issuing currency dominated as PETRO certificates. Mainly, these certificates will be used in commercial and international trades and will be backed by barrels of oil or British thermal units of natural gas. These certificates, issued in $500, $1,000, $5,000, and $10,000 certificates, will be exchanged as normal currency and backed by oil and or natural gas. The initial exchange rate will be $50 to a barrel of oil and $3 per million BTW of natural gas. We in the USA have some of the largest reserves of petroleum products on earth, and we will back our currency with such commodities. No longer will the US be under the thumb of OPEC and the like.

"It is highly probable that given the vagaries of the world, conflict will always be on the horizon. There will be fluctuation in prices of gold and silver and the like. The US Department of the

Treasury and the Fed will evaluate the exchange rates on a six-month interval and make appropriate changes if needed. Needless to say, any changes will be subject to congressional oversight.

"Lastly, I wish to remind any entities—domestic, foreign, or otherwise—that any efforts to disrupt our economy and our currency will be regarded as hostile in the extreme sense and dealt with as needed, even to the point of war. Individuals such as financiers, or SOROS, who get involved in disruptive activities will be regarded as enemies of the state and dealt with as such. For those entities who may think the US has become a 'paper tiger,' I would strongly advise that you consider long and hard what I have just said. President Roosevelt said one hundred years ago, 'Walk softly, but carry a big stick!' We will use the stick as necessary.

"That is enough for the day. God bless you all, and

"GOD BLESS AMERICA."

DAY 66: THE FEDERAL RESERVE

Today, folks, we will further our discussions into currency and our money supply by examining the two prime agencies involved in keeping the US solvent: the Department of the Treasury, or DOTR, and its companion agency, the Federal Reserve System, or the Fed. Each have overlapping spheres of influence, and especially the Fed has increased its power exponentially over the years. The DOTR directly affects the money supply, at least the amounts reflected in M1, cash in the system. The DOTR controls the mints and the printing of money and protecting the currency from counterfeiting, both domestic and foreign. The DOTR gets involved in other activities, which I will be addressing shortly. The new currency implementation, both certificates and coinage, will be the responsibility of the DOTR. This will be a phased-in change taking a number of months to change over to the new currency. In the meantime, current coinage and bills will still be legal tender, being removed as they are exchanged at banks. There will eventually come a time when the current currencies will effectively be out of circulation and no longer redeemable in the gold standard currencies. I anticipate that current coinage will be out of the public within one year. The reserve notes will be withdrawn beforehand. All currencies flowing though the banking system that are Federal Reserve notes and old currency will be eliminated from the system as appropriate. There will be those who will immediately want to hoard the new currencies; that has always been the case throughout our history. Collectors and the like are a part of the economy and will not be dissuaded. The DOTR will be working with the Fed for timely distribution and ample amounts of the new currencies and the replacement of the old. Given the inherent limited value of the current coins, the exchange to the new currency will be quick.

During this time the DOTR will be predominately focused on the currency transition. Its bureaus, that of the Bureau of Engraving and Printing and the Bureau of Public Debt, will be reinstated. The Crime Prevention Bureau will be transferred to the FBI within this fiscal year.

I want to talk about the Bureau of Alcohol, Tobacco, and Firearms and Explosives, BATFE. This bureau was implemented to collect excise taxes on the above commodities. The bureau has grown beyond its purpose. My administration will be proposing legislation to Congress to remove the excise taxes on all tobacco, firearms, ammo, and alcohol grown or manufactured in the US. Excise taxes are only applicable for foreign-made commodities. BATF will no longer be a controlling agent in the realm of these aforementioned products. I will be proposing legislation to further restrict this bureau. I have already discussed Second Amendment rights. Hopefully the BATF can be totally eliminated as an agency.

The big elephant under the DOTR tent is, of course, the IRS, which consumes over 90 percent of the DOTR budget and personnel.[172] The IRS was discussed on day twenty-three. There will be many changes forthcoming with the IRS. Hopefully with the passing of a flat tax for America, the IRS in its present form will be eliminated. Taxation and the IRS are topics that are convoluted but affect all of us as Americans.

Let us look at the Federal Reserve. As we learned, the Fed has been around for over a hundred years. Its original purpose—adding stability to the currency and money supply—has been marginally effective over the years, especially since what is defined as "money" has drastically changed, especially in the last fifty years. A hundred years ago money was cash, some checks, and loan instruments. Today the definition of money has expanded manyfold, way beyond the dollar bill in your wallet. The FED has not been able to keep up with even its basic purpose—solvency in the banking system. Witness the demise in the 1980s of the savings and loan industry. The additional missions of the Fed—management of federal debt, foreign banking interventions, and now even supposedly managing the inflation rate and unemployment—have all accomplished little in the realm of solvency of our currency. To those of you who have forgotten the horrendous interest rates during the Carter administration, those rates exceeded 20 percent. It was not until the Reagan administration that control and the lowering of the rates came about. Again, the Fed is great with the explanations of past events

---

[172] "United States Department of the Treasury." *Wikipedia.* Accessed June 22, 2016.
https://en.wikipedia.org/wiki/United_States_Department_of_the_Treasury.

but short on getting current events under control. To add fuel to the fire, since the Fed was created as an autonomous system, its actions and workings are mostly unsupervised by any branch of government. Except for appointment of the head of the Fed, the unknown rules the Fed. We the American people think that everything is working, but again, no one knows. Our system of government has inherent checks and balances provided by the Constitution. The Fed has no such checks and balances. The government even has agencies as the GAO and the CBO to oversee the government agencies in some degree. Nothing is available when dealing with the Fed, given their poor track record of any of their missions—currency valuation, solvency of the banking system, banking excursions into financial arenas not covered before and thus unregulated. Inflation control and foreign-banking intervention control must be established once again over the system, or if that cannot be done, implement an entirely new system for the banking industry.

Congress has passed legislation after legislation over the last fifty years, trying to curb in some way the various financial institutions that abound in the US: the banking industry, the financial services industry, the stock market, and the commodities markets. The various protective agencies, including the Federal Deposit Insurance Corporation, commonly called the FDIC, and the Securities and Exchange Commission, or SEC, have all proven ineffectual in either securing the safety of the institutions or the solvency of said institutions. If truth be told, all the above protective agencies are basically insolvent themselves and have very limited resources in case of emergencies.

I will propose a joint commission of both House and Senate to examine the Fed in detail and come up with sensible solutions to the instability of the system. This committee should include several members of the banking and financial service industry. This committee will be charged with finding viable solutions to the many inherent shortcomings of the Fed. I am not as concerned about the still-private financial institutions, such as the stock market, the commodities market, and the like. Cyclical movements in these markets will always be the case, and less rather than more government control should always be the norm. I am also directing the GAO to conduct the first comprehensive audit of the Fed system, its reserve banks, and any ancillary agencies that may be operating under the Fed. This audit should be implemented posthaste so that Congress will have its findings within the next twelve months. Of special concern will be the Fed's relationships with foreign banking systems, the IMF, the World Bank, the Export-Import Bank, and the like. International banking relations should not mean loss of control over our own banks and money supply. I will also propose that any financial agreements between the Fed and other international institutions must be approved by Congress. I consider such arrangements to be in the realm of treaties and covered by the Constitution, with Congress having the final say in such arrangements.

On that note, my fellow Americans, I will close; tomorrow is a new day.

"GOD BLESS AMERICA."

SECTION 7

FOREIGN AFFAIRS

DAY 67: THE MASTERS DOCTRINE (MD)

Good morning, America. Today we start to tackle the diverse issues of foreign affairs, our military, and our posture in the world. A short while ago, I went to the National Cemetery in Washington with my mother to visit my father's grave. The cemetery was a very beautiful, solemn, and serene place. Thousands upon thousands of gravestones neatly and orderly mark the service men and women who served to protect our country in various times of war and peace. The tombstones each highlight the person's service. My mom and I sat for a while, saying some prayers for my father and talking about times past. Since I also am a veteran, I have put it in my will to be buried at that cemetery so that when my time comes, I can be with my fellow veterans.

Our country, folks, has been defended by our military since our creation as a nation. Many thousands of men and women have given their lives in defense of our nation. They are the ultimate patriots; the price they paid with their blood has allowed this nation to endure and prosper. There have been many wars and conflicts in our nation's history; in all, we have stood firm and defended what was right and true. Two world wars in the twentieth century, horrors upon horrors, but throughout we not only stood up, we prevailed against the evils in the world. No other nation in history has done as much for the world and asked so little in return.

However, as with all in life, wars and conflicts are unfortunately reoccurring events. No matter what we do as a nation, no matter how much we help other nations in times of catastrophe and peril, there will be those nations and peoples who will hate and despise us for who and what we are. We have been called many names, the latest being "The Great Satan." Nothing could be further from the truth, but our enemies will always despise us. Be that what it may.

We will continue on our way, in the words of Teddy Roosevelt, as we mentioned before, to "walk softly and carry a big stick." Those who are our enemies are warned that we will not be cowed by the forces of evil and will respond in ways they will understand. The biblical admonishment of "eye for an eye" will be part of our nation's international policy.

With that thought in mind, now is probably a good time to outline what will eventually be known as the "Masters Doctrine." Every president from Monroe on has had a foreign policy, or doctrine, upon which that president dealt with the affairs of the world. Some doctrines were very encompassing; some were very specific. My predecessor, for example, pursued a policy of defeat and a withdrawal from the affairs of the world. The "apology" tour during his first term was a horrific example of a misguided view of the USA and what our role is in the world's affairs. My doctrine, as I will define in the coming days, will be far removed from the prior president's policies. I make no apologies for our nation's behavior, past, present, or future. We are who we are, and we will continue to stand for the principles upon which our nation was founded. "We hold these truths to be self-evident . . ."

It may be useful here to recap our history since WWII. We emerged as the greatest and most powerful nation in the world at that time. It is hard to imagine that the end of WWII was only a scant seventy years ago. Through the Marshall Plan, we helped many war-torn nations regain their economies and stability in the world. The peace, as with any peace, was short lived. Russia and China, through their communist regimes, became "not our friends" and swore to defeat us. Thus the Cold War started, and the policy of the US became one of containment. Starting with the Korean conflict and extending to the Gulf Wars, we changed—for the worse, I think. Our concept of war and conflict tried to get into the "ozone" of "nation building." As usual the progressives led the way with their "Pollyanna" view of the world. They imagined that with just the right amount of foreign aid, overlooking the evils of the world, all would be bright and the "sun would shine every day." This view, of course, is totally false and has led to a terrific distortion in our role in foreign affairs.

Quite frankly, America, throughout our history we have been in many conflicts and wars. Such is life on planet earth. In our history, we have had "friends" and "not our friends." Unfortunately, in the past seventy years we have forgotten which is which. NO MORE! One of the first precepts of the Masters Doctrine is highlighted on the board behind this podium. As you can see—and this delineation is also on our website—the categories are simple: "friends" and "not our friends." We have taken the liberty to categorize as many of the nations of the world into one of these categories. Why, you may ask?

Our foreign affairs will be made a little simpler. Our friends, abbreviated as FR, will enjoy the largesse of the USA as much as possible. As with our personal friends, if the need arises, either economically, politically, or whatever, the USA will be ready to lend a helping hand. Our history with England spans almost four centuries—sometimes turbulent, but as with any friendship, England and the US have remained close friends. This status can, I admit, change in the future. Friend nations can change governments and quite frankly transition to the not-our-friends, or NOF, category. I would warn even our friends that to get in the NOF category can have drastic changes in relations with the US.

On the NOF side, these nations will no longer have any or be eligible for any largesse from the US. While we may have certain trade agreements with some of these nations, no favorable status will be attained as long as they are NOF. The largesse will extend to any foreign aid, military aid, or any economic considerations. The State Department will be authorized to immediately suspend any and all aid programs to countries in the NOF category. No longer will the USA be seen as a "sugar daddy" to the world and especially to countries in the NOF category. As with any classification, there may be extraordinary situations where aid may be forthcoming, such as disaster aid. However, these countries will and can never rely on the US for immediate relief from disaster. It is stupid to give aid to countries who incessantly berate the USA and make it very clear that they despise us and wish us ill will. If disaster befalls any of these countries, the United Nations can render assistance. If private organizations such as the Red Cross wish to help the countries involved, that is their privilege. No direct assistance will be forthcoming from the USA.

As with the FR category, circumstances may change within any country in the NOF category, and we will be monitoring various countries' activities. If in a space of five years any country in the NOF zone has maintained a favorable relationship with the US, then consideration will be given for changing that country to the FR category. While this office will recommend such a change, it will be the Senate's responsibility under the "treaties provision" of the US Constitution to ratify such changes.

Speaking of treaties, this is another area where executive privilege has bypassed the Constitution. NO MORE! With this administration, any and probably all foreign agreements will be treated under the abovementioned "treaties" portion of the Constitution and will be ratified by the Senate as required by the Constitution. This office will, of course, be in regular contact with members of the Senate and House to assess the current state of affairs in the world scene.

Probably the biggest change initiated with the above categories is that the State Department will be directed over the next year to close our embassies in countries that are in the NOF category. Instead of a formal embassy, there will be a toned down, small delegation of diplomats in each of these countries. How large the delegation will be is a matter to be decided. It will be that country's responsibility for the safety of our diplomats. If that cannot be done, there will be no in-country delegation.

I wish to emphasize again, folks, countries in the NOF category, with very few exceptions, are just that—NOF. All relations will be on very arms-length terms. There will be no grants programs, no visas to the USA of any kind, no work visas, no immigrant visas, no student visas, no hardship visas. While there may be trade agreements, those will be scrutinized very closely by this office, the State Department, and Congress. Furthermore, any overt or covert acts of belligerency by any country in the NOF category will be looked at very harshly by the USA. We will determine whether any acts constitute an act of war. I warn again, those countries who contemplate such belligerency, you do not want to enter into any acts that the USA would consider as an act of war. You will rue the day if you choose such a course. The USA is not an aggressor nation, but we will not back down on any form of tyranny directed at us. Wanton killing of our citizens, desecration of our flag, or desecration or killing of our military will be responded to in the harshest terms. War and its ramifications will be addressed in the next few days.

With that, America, I shall close for the day. Tomorrow is a new dawn. Until then,

"GOD BLESS AMERICA."

DAY 68: "NOT OUR FRIENDS" (NOF NATIONS)

Good morning, America. Today I will continue our discussion on the Masters Doctrine, specifically with respect to the NOF category and the number of countries that are in that category. Two specific countries come behind Russia and China. Also, a block of Muslim nations (those ruled by Muslim theocracy, such as Iran) are in the NOF category.

As I mentioned earlier, we fought the Cold War for over forty years against Russia and China, and while it wasn't a "hot war," such as WWII, it was intense. I remember growing up having air-raid drills during the school year—the Cuban missile crisis. It seemed that war always loomed over the horizon. Yet it was in that time during college I got to spend an expanded summer touring Russia and practicing my Russian language. My major was Russian language and culture. Since the military was high on my list for career goals, I thought that learning Russian would be very helpful for my career. It was an exciting tour in Russia. The country itself was almost third world—shortages for everything, the people were poor, and the only ones who had any wealth were members of the communist party.

Thanks to Nixon, Kissinger, and finally Reagan, the thaw finally occurred; the Cold War was over and peace was at hand. Not! The animosity between these two countries and the US still stands and will continue to dominate our relations. Both Russia and China have hundreds to thousands of years of cultural history and are determined to eventually regain some of the grandeur of the past. Russia has expanded drastically since the 1980s with oil and gas production. China has become a financial and manufacturing juggernaut, rapidly becoming not just a first-world country but seeking to replace the USA as the number-one economic power in the world.

Sad to say during these past thirty years, the USA has acquiesced to their rise in power and has given up much of the economic, political, and cultural influence we once had. I remember the progressives pushing forth the agenda that it was a good thing that our manufacturing was moving abroad, that it was a natural course, since we were becoming a nation centered on the services industries and not basic manufacturing, except for agriculture, and even there the progressives were encouraging buying commodities from abroad. The trend was started even earlier when we encouraged imports from Japan, China, Korea, and Europe. Said imports gradually ate away at our manufacturing abilities in many ways. First and most insidious, while the imports were cheaper in price and quality, they rapidly become better in quality. As I mentioned in the past, I can remember when Walmart proudly announced that the vast majority of their products were made in the USA. Now the vast majority are made in China. The other Asian countries learned very quickly that price was as important as quality. The exception, not to our benefit, has been the goods made in China. It used to be that just the goods that had the label of "made in Mexico" were shoddy and not well made. Nowadays, any goods that are "made in China" are also known for their lack of quality. I would encourage businesses who still want to have their plants overseas to seek other nations known for high-quality manufacturing, such as Japan, Taiwan, South Korea, Thailand, or India. Goods produced in those countries will always be received well in the USA. For example, people very quickly learned that a Toyota had much more quality than a Ford and it was worth maybe paying a little extra for a quality-made car.

Here again, folks, much we did to ourselves. There is a dictum in physics: "Nature abhors a vacuum." If we do not compete, others will take our place. I remember long ago friends lambasting me for buying a Volkswagen bug and not an American car. I retorted that it was cheaper to purchase and run, better built, fewer repairs, and had a higher resale value than any comparable American car. Today, forty years later, I drive a Toyota, probably the number-one-selling car in the USA.

Our political policies, coupled with onerous regulations and taxes on businesses large and small, have helped encourage the business migration abroad. Even given the hazards of dealing with foreign government, it is easier to set up and accomplish a manufacturing facility overseas. The costs and the time involved are less than dealing with the regulatory tyranny of the US government. If you add the other major component in the equation, that of wages—and again including the influence of the federal government and, yes, the unions—the business of business in not pretty. Why are most manufacturing plants located in the South? Simply because the unions have little or no influence on the wage earners there. Every year you hear about the unions trying to get into the labor market down south and failing, thankfully. Lastly, look at Detroit—fifty years ago it was the powerhouse of cities in the USA, and the auto industry reigned supreme. Fast-forward fifty years, Detroit is a wasteland. The prices of homes have plummeted; as a matter of fact, you cannot even give a house away there. The population has moved elsewhere, and the auto industry verges on bankruptcy but never really got there due to government bailouts—more about that later. The eastern and midwestern states, formerly bastions of manufacturing industries, are also all wastelands. I was reading where a large former auto plant is now a movie studio where numbers of movies are made in the giant empty space on a regular basis. To top it off, in many instances over the past thirty years the federal government has even worked with big businesses and foreign countries to set up manufacturing plants abroad. Insanity!

Going back to the countries mentioned above, Russia has remained a not-so-friendly, or NOF, nation and our dealings with Russia will remain at a minimum. While, due to Russia's status in the world, we will still maintain an embassy there, I do not foresee any significant thaw in our relations with Russia. They have their interests and we have ours. There will be times when we agree on some foreign agenda, but most of the time not. Russia will stay in the NOF category for the foreseeable future. Russia's influence will more be felt in the European sphere and the Middle Eastern spheres. I will discuss those areas in greater detail later the next few weeks.

China remains a more significant problem due to many factors. Because of bumbling by our Federal Reserve, China has been allowed to accumulate trillions of dollars of our national debt and thus has much financial leverage against us. If that were not bad enough, by placing so much of our manufacturing in China, we have further abdicated our economic role in world affairs. I believe very strongly in the free enterprise system and am an advocate of free trade. Blackmail is another story. This office will be proposing significant economic incentives to any and all companies who relocate their manufacturing plants back to the USA. These incentives will include allowances for repatriation of funds now being kept overseas due to taxation and other financial considerations. Lastly, with respect to China, while we trade with China and have an embassy there and will continue to do so, the NOF status oversees all relations. As China builds up her military strength, the USA will closely monitor any belligerency on the part of China with respect to our friends. China holds a "most favored nation" status with respect to trade. This status is not sacrosanct and will be reviewed yearly. Freely given, it can very freely be taken away.

The third "nation" that was mentioned in the beginning of today's speech is the consortium of Islam nations, all ruled by Muslim theocracies and adhering to Sharia law. While these nations are individual entities, they commonly use the same rhetoric when lambasting the USA, even those who receive our aid on a regular basis. NO MORE! The Muslim nations on our NOF list will have all grants and aid from the USA suspended indefinitely. Visas to enter our country are rescinded immediately. All current visas, student, employment, or otherwise, will be revoked within sixty days. Any aliens who came into our country using those visas will need to be out of our country in sixty days. Any staying after the grace period will be labelled suspected terrorists, jailed, and deported as necessary. I will be addressing the Muslim question in much more detail in the next few weeks. Until then, suffice to say, this office is not friendly to the Muslim theocracy in any form. While we may have some trade agreements and may still continue to buy petroleum products from select Muslim nations, it is the goal of this administration to be completely free of dependency on petroleum produced by Muslim nations by the end of my term in office.

Here again, and even more important than with our other two adversaries, Russia and China, Muslim nations hostile to the USA that cross the bounds of belligerency will run the risk of a military response to such belligerency. The days of the velvet gloves when dealing with tyranny is over. The gloves will come off and those nations that continue to do ill will feel the iron fist of the USA. I will continue our discussion tomorrow. Until then,

"GOD BLESS AMERICA."

DAY 69: "FRIENDS" (FR NATIONS)

Good morning, America. Today I wish to continue our foreign-affairs discussion with a look at eight nations who we regard as our friends. This list is my no means complete or exclusive. I am highlighting these nations because they are the backbone of our foreign policy now and in the future. These friends have backed us in a multitude of affairs, often to their detriment. These nations are:

- Canada
- England
- Israel
- Japan
- Taiwan
- South Korea
- Germany
- India

As you can see from the list, our relations have been at times tumultuous—heck, we fought Japan and Germany only seventy years ago. We fought for our independence against England two hundred and forty years ago. The central concept of friendship is nevertheless demonstrated in our dealings with these nations. When one looks at one's friends, no relationship is steady at all times. There may be very "iffy" times; some may even lead to war. One of the beauties of life is that life is always evolving, if I may use that word. Enemies can become friends—not always, but sometimes. Of course, the opposite can come true also—friends can become NOF. Positive actions, though, can often produce good even from not good.

For now, I would like to take a few moments in which to acknowledge these friends and set the stage for even more cordial relations.

Canada shares our northern border and has been a friend for many years. They have their own set of political agendas; they have their own vibrant economy and their own brand of democracy. They are still part of the British Commonwealth. Nevertheless, they have been in our corner and continue to be in our corner. I trust that the relationship will continue to grow to be ever more fruitful in the future than in the past.

England has been with us since the pilgrim era, well before even the founding of our country. While we fought to gain our independence, in retrospect, the war was akin to a child growing up and demanding to be independent. England has a rich heritage, over a thousand years of recorded history, and is home to the most enduring language in the world, English. There have been many travails in the USA past, and England has stood by us in friendship through many of those travails. We owe much to England and will never be able to repay that debt. We will endeavor to continue a more enlarged relationship in the future. I do promise one thing: no gifts from England will ever be returned!

Israel deserves special mention. Since the founding of the USA, the Jewish immigrants have had a safe and prosperous haven here. These immigrants have contributed much to our heritage. When the nation of Israel came into being in 1948, the USA stood firmly behind the Jewish state and supported Israel through many good and many bad times. The Jewish people in Israel with courage, determination, and true grit have carved out for themselves a homeland. As in the Old Testament, this process has been fraught with difficulties. Israel has been strong in its dealing with the world, has the only democratic government in the Middle East, and has a vibrant economy. It also holds in trust for the Judeo-Christian world the Holy Land and its revered sites within. My administration pledges its continued support in every way possible for Israel's continued prosperity. Israel is one of our dearest friends and will always remain so.

Japan is one of the true economic miracles in the world. Defeated by the Allies in WWII and devastated physically, economically, socially, and politically, Japan has risen from the ashes to achieve great prosperity. Even though we were virulent enemies during WWII, both our countries have been able to set aside vast differences and grow and support a multifaceted relationship to the benefit of not only our two countries, but Asia and the world as well. My administration looks forward to working with the leaders of Japan to create the alliance mentioned in my prior speech and to protect such an alliance in Central Asia. I think the alliance will help revitalize Japan economically and socially.

Taiwan is another great example of a people who have risen from difficulties and even international scorn to achieve a vibrant nation and an economic miracle. Little hope was given to this small island nation after the communists took over mainland China, but the Taiwanese have proved everyone wrong. I look forward to helping create a Central Asian Alliance, or CAA, where Taiwan can continue to grow and power in their own right.

South Korea is another prime example of a nation split by political actions that can also rise from the ashes and achieve greatness. The Korean War was fought over sixty years ago to protect South Korea from the aggressions of both North Korea and China. Little hope was given to the then-fledgling nation of South Korea. Since then, however, SK has taken the lead and has created a dynamic country politically, economically, socially, and physically. We continue to pledge our support for South Korea. I think their presence in the CAA treaty organization will be crucial.

Germany shares a long heritage with the USA. Many of our immigrants came from Germany. Even though we fought two world wars against Germany, the relationship has been renewed and grown positively over the last seventy years. With our help, Germany is now an economic powerhouse in Europe and even the world. Germany has been able to reunite itself, east and west, and still continues to prosper. The EU, which many scoffed at and said to be unworkable, has also continued to evolve and grow and prosper. The euro, created as a new world's currency, has become one of the most stable currencies around. Germany and the EU are vital to the USA, and we will be working increasingly with Germany and the EU to foster peace and prosperity on the continent.

Lastly, I would like to mention India. Long regarded as just another third-world country, doomed because of population, religion, and political instability, India in the last thirty years has grown from a third-world to a first-world country. Little hope was given for this change since India has long been hampered by a burgeoning population, religious difficulties, and racial strife with the Muslim theology. India, though, has risen to the challenge. The economy has increased dramatically, and India is high on the technology forefront. The manufacturing industry is growing and hopefully will increase its presence in the world and compete directly with China. This administration will be working with the Indian leaders on the possibility of an alliance consisting of India, Singapore, Malaysia, and Burma. Such an alliance would be to the benefit of all concerned.

I know, my fellow Americans, that I have just touched on the possibilities with the above nations, but too often in the world we live in, scant recognition is given to friendships and acknowledgement, even brief, is a good thing. Good day! On Monday, I will conclude the foreign-affairs discussions with another very timely topic, sure to displease many of the progressives in the USA and around the world. In the meantime,

"GOD BLESS AMERICA."

DAY 70: REST

Our Father, Who art in heaven, hallowed be Thy name, Thy kingdom come, Thy will be done on earth as it is in heaven. Give us this day our daily bread and forgive us our trespasses as we forgive those who trespass against us. Lead us not into temptation but deliver us from evil. Amen.

DAY 71: DOCTRINE OF WAR

Good day, America, today we will tackle a very heavy topic, and not one addressed specifically—war, and its many manifestations in our nation's past and probable future. Up until WWII, our involvement in wars was fairly well-defined and consistent with our national philosophy. With WWII we fought two of the most formidable opponents on opposite sides of the globe and won the war. Many progressives lament—in hindsight, of course—the excesses we went through: internment of Japanese Americans during the war, devastation bombing of cities in Germany and Japan, followed by the dropping of nuclear bombs on Hiroshima and Nagasaki. These progressives forget the horrors this nation was going through at the time and that our survival was in question for some years. The war was all or nothing and, as with all wars, no quarter was given. Unconditional victory was the only possible way out. As a famous general once said, "You win a war not by dying for your country, but by making the other guy die for his country." In short, my fellow Americans, you do what is necessary to win completely, which is by killing as much of the enemy so that those remaining will surrender, or by killing and destroying the belligerent nation and its populace until those that are left surrender. This was done both in Germany and Japan. No quarter was given. The dropping of the nuclear bombs on Japan probably saved millions of American lives by not having to invade Japan. People forget that the Japanese were fanatical, akin to the Muslim terrorists today. Suicide was preferred to surrender. We did what was necessary and victory was achieved. The world was saved, at least for a short while.

As with any peace, the aftermath was followed by new aggression, and the Cold War started. Hot wars also arose. Our problem as a nation was that, through whatever circumstance, we changed our philosophy on conflicts and instead of victory we looked for "containment," we looked for nation building, we looked for negotiation. All the above goals were just different words for defeat. Korea started the "containment" wars. We had the means to defeat not only North Korea, but also China, and chose not to. President Truman chose not to listen to his military general, McArthur, and a military truce was negotiated. What did that truce achieve? Folks, sixty years later, North Korea is still a threat and now with nuclear capabilities is even more a threat. One of the truisms in life is that in life, there are some decisions that have to be made concerning ugly situations (divorce, death, job loss). If one delays the decision, the situation only gets worse, never better. Korea is that example. President after president has tried the PC route and nothing has worked. Clinton negotiated, and what happened? North Korea now has nuclear capabilities and is threatening not only South Korea, but Japan as well. Insanity!

It even gets worse, America. Korea was followed by Vietnam, the Middle East, the first and the second Gulf Wars, and Afghanistan. Every president from Truman to Obama has taken the PC route. What have we gained? Is there more stability in the world? Is the world safer? Look at Iran for that answer. What we have lost, folks, is thousands upon thousands of American lives in far-off places without giving them an explanation of why their lives were being taken. The infection of PC has even taken over our military academies—future leaders are not taught to win, but that "not to win," nation building, and diversity are good. Horrible stuff, and it continues to this day. NO MORE!

Today we step backward into a time where our goals as a people and nation were known and respected. War is a horrible experience, but one does not win a war by being PC or "mister nice guy." War is all or nothing. I am commander in chief of our armed forces, and as such I take my responsibility very seriously. Curtis LeMay, commanding general of the air force in the Pacific, spent countless nights writing to the families of airmen who died in combat. My question is this, do our generals do the same? I shudder to ask.

The Masters Doctrine will be much simpler than with prior presidents. We will not treat war lightly, but if we do go to war and that conflict is approved by Congress, then war will be fought as we fought WWII. We will fight and destroy the enemy, we will obliterate their military, we will obliterate their cities, their populace, their industries. When we go to war, we do not seek out "coalitions" to help us in our endeavors. If our FR want to join us in the fight, we will consider the offer. We will destroy and prevail until the enemy or whoever is left surrenders unconditionally. There will be no partial victories, there will be no appeasement. If our enemies combine with other nations, we will destroy them all. No quarter given. Once we have won unconditional victory, we will leave. The nation that was our enemy can rebuild itself; that is not our responsibility. If after the war is over, and the country involved becomes belligerent again, we will again declare war and obliterate the enemy as before. Again, no quarter will be given. We are not here to negotiate but to destroy. The idea of separating segments of a nation from the aggressive elements is a ridiculous notion. When we fought

Germany, there was no "good Nazis versus bad Nazis." All were open to destruction.

Speaking of destruction, the Geneva Convention was very specific with respect to combatants. These are uniformed soldiers who adhere to the Geneva Convention. Muslim terrorists are not subject to the conditions of the Geneva Convention at all. Any such personnel will be killed with no mercy. Any captured will ASAP be tried by military courts and executed where applicable. Since these personnel are not part of the Geneva Convention, those captured will be interrogated by whatever means available to gain information on their compatriots. Interrogation will be at the discretion of the military. As far as I am concerned, saving one American life overwhelms niceties.

In the engagement of war, there will be no safe places. If the enemy takes refuge in a mosque, church, hospital, or other public buildings, it and they will be destroyed with no quarter given. Terrorists who kill and dismember our troops will be sought out and killed. In the past certain citizens of the USA have joined the enemy. Those will be also treated as the enemy and killed. If captured they will be tried for treason and executed. Those citizens will automatically lose their citizenship and have no recourse with the USA. Any family member in the USA helping those who have chosen to go over to the enemy will be tried for treason and imprisoned or deported as appropriate.

During WWII we published not only our casualties but more importantly those of the enemy. Sad to say, we did away with that policy in the past fifty years. In the Gulf War, one and two, we killed tens of thousands of the enemy. Those statistics were never published. That policy will now change. You the American public, need to be updated on our casualties and more importantly those of the enemy. We need to let the enemy know how many we are destroying and how many we will continue to destroy. Because we do not publish these facts, the terrorist organizations around the world think we are a "paper tiger." One of the reasons why Japan surrendered was that they knew that we would never stop killing their population until they surrendered. The Muslims and other terrorist organizations need to know the same. Killing a leader here and there is totally ineffectual; killing thousands is effective. The pictures that will be published will be graphic, so that all will see the horrors of war and especially the horrors of making war against the USA.

Lastly, in the past, military personnel have been tried and in some cases imprisoned for not following the PC code of conduct. I am ordering the Joint Chiefs of Staff to immediately review all cases of officers and enlisted men who have been tried and or incarcerated for not following PC rules of behavior. Such military personnel will immediately be released from prison if such is the case. Those that have been blacklisted and dishonorably discharged shall have that stigma expunged ASAP wherever possible. These honorable military were treated very unfairly by the military. NO MORE!

I realize, my fellow Americans, that this has been a very heavy topic. I come from a military family, my father is buried in a national cemetery, and every year on Memorial Day I place flags on our fallen military. We as a nation owe these fallen a debt that we can never really repay. Let us honor their sacrifices with an honorable pathway in our dealings with the world. Tomorrow is a new day. Pray for our country and for me as your president.

"GOD BLESS AMERICA."

DAY 72: CONSOLIDATION OF INTELLIGENCE AGENCIES

Good morning, America. As this week progresses, the pace will continue to be fast and furious. We ended yesterday with the introduction of the Masters Doctrine and a revised concept of war. Today we will start off with analyzing our intelligence agencies. These agencies provide, hopefully, vital information that allows our nation to confront the many hazards in the world at large. These agencies, like all of the federal government, have grown so immense that much information that should be used in the defense of our country gets filtered out and we realize the hard way too late and thus fail to prevent a catastrophe. This is very evident in the events leading up to 9/11. The sad aspect of an attack like 9/11 is that we as a nation did not learn from our mistakes and thereby invited more horrible attacks. We created another agency—in this case, Homeland Security, which has been woefully inept in not only providing intelligence but also in increasing the safety of the American people. The TSA, under the auspices of Homeland Security, is such an example of ineptness.

Historically, intelligence gathering has been a part of our nation's security since our founding. Generally, the intelligence-gathering agencies were a part of various organizations in the federal government, namely, the Departments of State, Defense, Treasury, and the FBI. WWII demanded much broader intelligence capabilities and the Office of Strategic Services, or OSS, was created. After WWII this organization morphed into the Central Intelligence Agency—the CIA—which was to be the prime intelligence agency for the USA. For many years that was the case, but again, as the federal government has grown, so has the intelligence community. Far from consolidation, we have again a multiplicity of agencies, all gathering "intel" and often not providing any sort of facilitation for that information to other agencies to use in defending our country. For example, we have the aforementioned CIA, we also have NSA—the National Security Agency, we have the FBI, we have Homeland Security, and we have the intelligence arms of the Department of Defense, all the Armed Services, and the Department of State.

All of these agencies seemingly act independently of each other and have no obligation to work with or support other agencies. The aforementioned agencies are probably just the tip of the iceberg since there are many other agencies operating under the radar which also confuse the picture. You would think that with all these intelligence-gathering organizations, the USA would never be caught unprepared in dealings with the world. Sad to say, the answer is to the negative. Events like Benghazi, the fall of Gaddafi, the Arab Spring, the Iran nuclear buildup, and the Russian influence in the Middle East always point to the same question: Who would have figured? The last forty years of increased Muslim terrorism, every act has caught the USA unprepared and the question always is the same: Who would have figured? September 11 was the classic case of being unprepared again. Who would have figured? Who would have known that the terrorists would actually commandeer planes and use those planes as instruments of destruction? Who would have figured?

The list, folks, goes on and on; the sad aspect is that American innocents continue to die and our allies continue to shake their head at our ineptness. Insanity!

This must stop. To that end, I am requesting that Congress appoint an independent congressional committee to analyze the various aspects of the intelligence community and propose an overall consolidation of the disparate agencies under one roof. As an interim, I propose to elevate the CIA to a cabinet status, thereby creating the Department of Intelligence. The DIA will encompass initially the CIA, NSA, Homeland Security, and the FBI. The DIA will be charged with coordinating and directing not only these intelligence agencies but also directing and coordinating the other various intelligence agencies under, for example, the DOD and DOS.

This cabinet position will, hopefully, at last create some order out of the chaos that currently reigns in the intelligence community operating in the federal government. This cabinet will help immensely in providing this office, Congress, and the American people with the information needed to defend our country and respond forcefully to any enemies that are forthcoming. The world, folks, is a very dangerous place and is not getting any safer. We need to be able to stop any threats to our country and also to work with our allies in sharing information vital to everyone's security. Events like the Boston Marathon bombings a few years back, when Russian intelligence provided information on the bomber before the event and we, of course, ignored the information.

One last comment, my fellow Americans—the PC attitude of the progressive movement has definitely infiltrated our intelligence community. This is intolerable. Intelligence gathering is of utmost priority; any evidence of governmental PC attitude in this venture will be considered as a felony and possibly treason. Too long terrorist organizations like the Muslim Brotherhood and supporting organizations like Council on American-Islamic Relations, or CAIR, have been allowed special immunity from investigation. No longer will that be allowed or tolerated. Our country's future is at stake, and we will use any means at our disposal to discover, expose, and destroy the enemies of our nation. Speaking of terrorist organizations, I will be addressing the Muslim insurgency within the USA and without at a later date.

I shall close now. As a well-known TV character once said, "Live long and prosper!" Until tomorrow,

"GOD BLESS AMERICA."

DAY 73: THE MILITARY DILEMMA

Good morning, America. Today we continue to tackle the multitude of questions about the defense of our country and foreign affairs. I am going to focus on the military for the next few days and integrating the discussion into the Department of Defense and the Department of State.

As all are aware, I come from a military family. My father served honorably in both the US Army and Navy. I served a number of years in the US Army and my son also served in the US Army. The three generations spanned over eighty years of service in a multitude of wars and other conflicts. The military, thus, holds a special place in my heart, not only for my family's service but as a patriot. Without our military we could not exist as a nation and enjoy the freedoms we have. The military is vital to our nation's well-being, our security, our democracy, and even our religious freedoms.

Our military encompasses many areas of defense and can have many missions, but its primary mission since the founding of our country is simply the defense of our country in times of "peace" and in times of war. As such, the military is a tool, a weapon to be used as judiciously as possible, but when used should be used with enough force needed to accomplish its mission.

Sad to say, in the last sixty years our military has been forced to change its traditional mission, defending our country, and also forced to become something no military should be, that of an instrument of social change. A weapon is just that—a weapon— and if any nation allows a weapon such as the military to be tarnished and degraded, it loses rapidly its effectiveness. Those of you who have guns know the value of keeping your weapons cleaned and maintained at all times. If a weapon is not maintained, the weapon becomes useless. It is the same with nations. Those with better weapons will take advantage and eventually overcome. This has happened countless times in the past. Look at the Roman Empire, lasting over four hundred years, basically conquered from within then from without. When the empire became soft, the military became soft, and the infection spread throughout the empire.

We, America, are unfortunately allowing this to happen in our country. Our leaders have ignored the lessons of history and believe that global policies of "non-war" are as effective as war, that nation building is a vital mission of our nation and especially the military, and that the military should reflect the changing social mores that the country is going through. Insanity! Our soldiers are being forced not to defend our country, but more importantly be PC about its operations. Our military academies are churning out not war leaders, but leaders whose tasks are to be PC in an increasingly turbulent world.

When Russia essentially renounced communism in the 1990s, the progressives mistakenly believed that peace was at hand and the world would be, as the Beatles sang long ago, "The world will be as one . . ." The naiveté of this is astounding. Fast-forward twenty-five years, Islam is on the march again, nuclear proliferation is again on the rise, and even more dangerous, two-bit dictatorships are acquiring nuclear technology and, if allowed, have no reservations in using nuclear weapons to wipe out other nations, including attacking the USA. The "Pollyanna" progressives who say otherwise have already forgotten 9/11. Do you not think, folks, that if Bin Laden had had a nuclear device on hand that he would not have hesitated to attack the World Trade Center with such a device? Fortunately, at that time he did not, but now that possibility exists not only for another attack on the USA or its allies, but that the attack will be a nuclear device, capable of killing thousands if not millions of people. Many of you remember the successful TV series *24*, in which such a device was used against LA. Folks, this is no longer fiction.

We here in the USA have been increasingly ineffectual in stopping the proliferation of nuclear devices and technology. Witness the 1990s when North Korea gained the ability and built a nuclear device. The president at that time assured the American public that safeguards were in place. NOT! My predecessor with Iran is another example of supreme incompetence in the face of tyranny. The old adage of "balance of power" has never held sway and quite frankly has not stopped any war in the past. North Korea, while impoverished, has the means now for intercontinental missiles that can deliver such devices not only to South Korea, but to other Asian countries. Other nations, mostly on our NOF list, are going to great lengths to acquire nuclear technology. Most couch the desire, stating they are building power plants with the uranium for energy purposes. This rhetoric is false. Nuclear technology is desired to make nuclear weapons. I will talk more about this subject in the upcoming days.

Back to the military, the main topic of today's conversation. The degradation of our military has to stop if we as a nation can survive. Fortunately, as commander in chief, I have the authority and the means to affect much change in the military. My predecessors moved the military to the PC mode. I, as commander in chief, will start to reverse that PC mode.

First, as I addressed last week, the Masters Doctrine will revert to the traditional definition of war and preparation for war. The containment philosophy determining our foreign policies over the last fifty years will be stopped. Our military academies will be instructed to revert to the traditional aspects of military leadership training. PC instruction, diversity, and nation building will no longer be the dominate curriculum in our military. This does not mean that military tactics will not be continually updated for the changing realities in the world. That will always be vitally important.

As commander in chief, I want leadership in our military academies and in our branches of service. We need military personnel who are first, last, and foremost fighters and leaders. The current military, with its preponderance of yes-men and women, is not to be sustained. Combat experience will again be the mainstay of high-level leadership in all branches of the military—army, navy, air force, marines. Military promotion throughout the ranks for enlisted and officer will be focused on war missions and preparation for war. This office will be reviewing all officers recommended for generalship and will make the final determination on who will be recommended. To put it bluntly, we need more generals like Patton, like MacArthur, like LeMay, like Chesty Puller; we do not need military like Westmoreland, Petraeus, or Powell.

Next, the military will cease being a PC organization, and all indoctrination into the PC world will cease immediately. While the military may reflect the population at large, it is not the same, not in its organization or discipline or mission. The country is still reeling over the homosexual question and will continue to be divided on that question. The military has had particular problems with this, and all arrangements over the last thirty years have been unsuccessful. All this ends now. As for the military, the answer is simple. Homosexuals will no longer be allowed in the military in whatever branch of service. There will be no "kiss and not tell"; the military has had a tradition of no "fraternization" between members of the military. That will be strictly enforced. All openly gay servicemen and women will be discharged from the military within thirty days. Those that are within five years of retirement will be allowed to retire ASAP honorably. Those that are more than five years from retirement will be honorably discharged within the next thirty days. Appropriate severance pay will be given based on length of service. All gay servicemen and women will be removed from ranks of responsibility before discharge. No transgender individuals will be allowed in the military and will be discharged within the next thirty days.

Now there will always be that portion of the military that are gay, as in the world. As long as their proclivities are not known, they will continue to serve in the military. However, any personnel after the next thirty days who decide to stay in the military and "come out of the closet" will be discharged immediately with a general discharge and less than honorable. No tolerance will be shown. The military has enough problems with their missions without the extra hassles of PC events such as tolerating gays in their midst.

The next area that also has been a great problem with the military is the PC concept of a "co-ed" military. That concept is also terminated as of now. Women have always had a certain role in the military and that role will be reinstituted. Women will no longer be recruited into the military; no longer will they be allowed in any combat positions or combat support positions. Women will no longer be promoted to higher ranks or into any ranks that rely on combat experience. Folks, every nation that has experimented with a co-ed military has rued the day and reversed course.[173] I am a traditionalist. Men are suited for war, women are not. If nothing else, look at the body mass of a woman versus a man. Women in

---

[173] "Women in the military." *Wikipedia*. Accessed June 22, 2016. https://en.wikipedia.org/wiki/Women_in_the_military.

the special forces, Delta Force, Seals, and rangers are not to be allowed. Men in fighting units do not need to worry about women next to them. The sexual tensions by forcing this PC policy has been rampant in the military. Imagine how ridiculous this is, that on a carrier, 200 women are housed with 2,600 men. The incidence of sexual problems has grown geometrically. Every year, over 11 percent of the military are ushered out of service for getting pregnant.[174] Insanity!

Women in all branches of the military beyond the immediate need will be discharged within the next ninety days. Women within five years of retirement will be honorably retired early with appropriate benefits. Women with more than five years to retirement will be discharged honorably and given appropriate severance pay. Women in the military academies will be discharged from said academies and given credit of college courses completed and severance pay for years of service.

Women have assumed more important roles in our country's business, social, and government worlds. These roles have in many cases not been the best for our nation.[175] For these increased roles, our country now has a plunging birth rate, increased divorce rates, and yes, increased familial dysfunctionality.[176] The "feminazi"

---

[174] Pearson, Catherine. "Unplanned Pregnancies Among Women In Military High, Rising." *Huffington Post*. January 23, 2015.
http://www.huffingtonpost.com/2013/01/23/pregnant-military-unplanned-women_n_2534873.html.

[175] Quast, Lisa. "Causes and Consequences Of The Increasing Numbers of Women In The Workforce." *Forbes*. February 14, 2011.
http://www.forbes.com/sites/lisaquast/2011/02/14/causes-and-consequences-of-the-increasing-numbers-of-women-in-the-workforce/#2297e411c76d.

[176] Livingston, Gretchen. "Fewer than half of U.S. kids today live in a 'traditional' family." Pew Research Center. December 22, 2014.
http://www.pewresearch.org/fact-tank/2014/12/22/less-than-half-of-u-s-kids-today-live-in-a-traditional-family/.

movement has done much harm to our nation. While I cannot control the social mores of the USA, I can control its effects on our military. I honor the contribution that the gays and the women made to our military, but their time is past. End of story!

That is all for now. I will continue with changes in the Department of Defense tomorrow. Until then,

"GOD BLESS AMERICA."

DAY 74: DEPARTMENT OF DEFENSE (DOD)

Good morning, America. In the past few days we have been looking at our nation's foreign-affairs posture and especially our military and its capabilities to not only defend our country, but to protect our interests here and abroad. Yesterday we analyzed the PC military and the steps to be taken to stop the PC movement and to return to a more traditional aspect of the military. Our nation has had a very cyclical view of our military; we demand a large and effective military to defeat our enemies, such as in WWII, but thereafter we let our defenses down once more and decreased our military, often drastically, in the face of new oppression. Hopefully in the days ahead, this office will outline a more coherent policy for maintaining our military posture, which will do much to insure the continued well-being of our country. Folks, we have been attacked grievously twice now in the past seventy years and we should learn something from both of those sneak attacks. Our world is a dangerous place and, as time passes, is not getting any more peaceful. We have friends in the world, but we also have many more who are on the NOF list. The enemies of the USA are on the march and they avowed to destroy us by any means available. I have mentioned in the prior talk the renewed threat of a nuclear attack. This is very real, America, and the consequences can be disastrous for the US. Imagine 9/11 as a nuclear attack. Our enemies do not need missiles. They can simply hijack an airplane and put the bomb on board. Goodbye to a city or more.

Continuing on with our military and its mission to defend our country, we have and continue to have treaties and alliances with those whom we support, NATO being the most well known. We will be increasing these alliances in the near future, and I will devote a separate discussion on what this administration will term "spheres of influence" — alliances with group of nations friendly to the USA. Eight such alliances are envisioned. We will be working actively with these nations to facilitate such alliances and once created will continue to work actively to support and enhance such alliances. We envision having bases within each alliance territory and will use these bases to enhance the defense of these alliances. I wish to stress, the USA will not be the "shepherd" and these alliances the "sheep." We will facilitate the creation of military armament for these nations and alliances, which they will use to defend themselves. Case in point, and probably the most viable at this moment, NATO has been in existence for over sixty years. The countries in NATO are all advanced not only economically but politically with the EU. Their defense will increasingly be their providence and responsibility. This military defense can be implemented very rapidly, within three or four years, including army, navy, and air force. The details will again be the responsibility of the EU. While we actively support this military creation, we will not be the prime participant.

In conjunction with the aforementioned aspect of the Masters Doctrine, our military leaders will be formulating plans on how to meet aggression rapidly in the world. As the aforementioned alliances come into being and their military posture improves, we stand ready to help defend them against aggression from whatever source. With bases in each of these "spheres," rapid-deployment forces can be ready to stop and intercede in aggressive behavior from whatever source. While our military will still be relying on conventional forces to stop aggression, as in the Gulf Wars, we will have an equal reliance on armed military in the quick reaction mode. These forces—Army Special Forces, Delta Force, marines, SEALS—will be the quick reaction elements that will at times initiate combat conditions and also support conventional troops.

The above will entail a rethinking of "quick reaction" and "unconventional warfare" alternatives in the military. I remember being in the military during the Vietnam era and considering a military career. I wanted to stay in the special-forces arena, and was told emphatically that to stay in that arena meant small promotion opportunities. This also must end. The promotion of our enlisted personnel and officers must be based on combat experience and leadership whenever possible, not on PC attitudes.

DOD will be examining its protocol and its priorities with respect to the military, personnel versus equipment. While equipment is vital to a structured military, wars are won by boots on the ground, in the air, and on ships. With that is mind the DOD will be expanding our armed forces personnel significantly over the next four years. The USA has currently twenty-one divisions in the army and ten independent brigades. Total military personnel now number 1.3 million. Military personnel will be increased by 500,000 in the next three years. The US Army will be increased by at least five more divisions, combat ready. The navy has currently a total of 260 ships, down drastically from the Cold War era. This amount will also be doubled in the next three to four years. The number of planes, combat and otherwise, in the air force will be increased by 50 percent over the next three to four years.

I wish to emphasize that these increases will be not be blind and that costs will be examined closely. With that being said, functionality of armament, especially new armament, will be analyzed. New and costly hardware for the sake of new will not be the name of the game. We have all witnessed the billion-dollar overruns with expensive planes such as the F-35, the Seawolf submarine program, and even the F-22 plane program. The cost overruns are insane and will stop. Our military needs modern equipment, not space-age armament with no real applicability to the present and future missions of the military. First and foremost, though, our troops will have the needed equipment and armament to accomplish their missions.

The above increases in the military are, quite frankly, needed in the world we live in today. I am happy to report that our southern borders are virtually secure with the help of four divisions of army and marine personnel, enhanced by air-force planes flying surveillance. I have been meeting with the JCOS on the border issue and have been assured that by the summer, the borders will be locked down tight. Initially there have been some firefights as has been reported, but the enemy, and I use that word purposefully, has rapidly gotten the message that the USA borders are not friendly to them. Illegal immigration is down to a trickle and drug interdictions are still high, but very little is getting across the border. Deportations are in fact decreased over the past thirty days mainly due to the fact that fewer illegals are trying to get across the border. These four military divisions and support troops will remain on the border for the foreseeable future. The DOD will be building at least one permanent base in each state along that states border. Folks, our borders will be secure and remain as such.

The marines will also be expanded as to its military mission. Needless to say, the marines will again be searching for "a few good men." Of particular note will be the mission of defending our embassies worldwide from attack. In years past that was a marine role, but the DOS assumed responsibility for the embassy defense. Well, that has not worked out well at all. Witness Benghazi. The marines will now again be responsible for protection of our embassies and delegations. To accomplish this mission, the marines will be armed significantly to repel most attacks. This armament will include not only personal weapons but armored vehicles and warships close by. Our embassies have been sitting ducks for over twenty years. NO MORE!

Lastly, in this era of nuclear proliferation, the situation getting increasingly hostile and the threat of NOF countries acquiring nuclear capabilities is increasing daily. This situation will be a top priority of the DOD. Our nuclear arsenal, which for many years has been dismantled, will now be increased. We will continue to increase our arsenal to the levels in the Reagan era at the very least. In addition, we will continue to perfect our defense capabilities to stop any potential nuclear missiles from reaching the USA. Reagan started the Star Wars program to defend the USA against missile attack; it will be revived and expanded. The CIA will be charged with investigating hostile countries and their increased nuclear capabilities. As our ally Israel did a preemptive strike on Iraqi nuclear facilities, that option will be open to the USA also. Think of it this way, folks: if you had a gun in the house, would you use the gun to defend yourself and your family? The analogy is apt but even more pertinent with hostile nations. Look again at the NOF list on the website. Common sense will show how many are hostile and will remain so. Balance of power becomes irrelevant if a nation is run by fanatics not afraid of the consequences of nuclear war. This cannot be allowed to happen. The USA reserves the right for preemptive strikes in any of the above scenarios.

I wish to close today's talk with the admonition mentioned before. If the USA or any of our allies by treaty are attacked, especially with any nuclear devices, that enemy will suffer the full brunt of our military response, up to and including a nuclear response. If the enemy's country becomes a wasteland, so be it! Until tomorrow,

"GOD BLESS AMERICA."

DAY 75: MEETING WITH THE JOINT CHIEFS OF STAFF (JCOS)

The following takes place in the White House, early morning (9 a.m.), in the —— room. Breakfast is being served to the members of the JCOS and their assistant JCOS. The secretary of defense is also present for the meeting. All members are chatting when the door opens and President M—— enters the room. All stop talking and stand at attention.

"Please sit down," says the president. "Thank you for coming to this important breakfast. A lot has been happening these past two months and this meeting is definitely needed at this time. First of all, I wish to thank all of you for your rapid response to the request for the military divisions on our southern border states. The response has not only eased the intolerable situation with the illegal invasion on the borders, but has served to show other NOF groups that we as Americans mean what we say and that we have the means to accomplish swift military action when required and defend our borders. You are all to be commended on this mission. Our troops are also to be commended for their adherence to the mission and the thoroughness in sealing the border as swiftly as they have had to do. While other presidents have been reluctant to act, I am not. Again, thank you.

"If you will excuse me for a few moments, there is a matter I must attend to. While I am gone, the secretary of defense will review some of the mission statements I have been discussing these past days with the American public. When I return we will go over several of the topics in greater detail. Gentlemen and madams, for now, enjoy your breakfast."

The JCOS all sit down and start to eat, talking amongst themselves and the SOD on the tumultuous topics the president has relayed to the American public. Some of those present are extremely reticent on the ability of the military to accomplish this new Masters Doctrine. The makeup of the new military is also a big concern. The talks continue . . .

A knock on the door, and the orderly opens it for the president. All rise. The president says, "Please sit down. Let us get to work. Gentlemen and madams, you have all heard the speeches; lots of changes are in the works for our military."

As the president is talking, an orderly brings three folders and lays them on each of the JCOS tables. The folders are red, white, and blue.

"Gentlemen—if you will allow me to use that term even though there are women in uniform present—let us start with the folders in front of you. The first folder, the red, will be filled in today. The other two folders will be your homework assignments.

"It has been a tradition with cabinet members to hand in their resignations when a new term begins for the president. He is free to accept or reject said resignations. I am starting that tradition with the JCOS. In the red folder you will find a resignation form already filled out save for your name and date. If you will sign the form now.

"Now, there are those in this room that readily disagree with my policies and visions of the defense of our country. If you are one of those, please sign today's date in the space provided. You will be honorably discharged forthwith. For those of you who want to continue to serve, then leave the date blank for now.

"I wish to caution all of you, I value my military leaders and all your input into decisions that will be made in the upcoming term of office. I am commander in chief, though, and the buck stops with me, as President Truman used to say. If any of you cannot accept that, then fill in today's date and you will leave honorably. With that being said, if it comes to light that any JCOS still serving actively undermines our mission for the military, that person will be discharged and dropped in rank. Do I make myself clear?

"Now, on to the second folder, the white one. Please open the folder. You will see a recommendation sheet with three lines on it. I wish each of you to recommend three generals to replace you. These individuals will be combat experienced and will be leaders, not followers. They should not be politically correct. The future of our country is at stake.

"In addition to the three recommendations, you will also find on the next sheet another list divided into three sections. The first section will have the names of the top ten individuals in your branch of service, colonels and above, who are combat experienced and are skilled leaders. The next section is to be filled in with the names of five individuals who are skilled in strategic situations globally. In the last section are to be named five individuals who are adept in military operations, moving men and equipment globally on short notice. Some names will be on more than one list; that is good. All in all, twenty men who have the capabilities to lead each of your branches into whatever missions the world and our enemies will throw at us.

"The third folder, the blue—and just as important as the first two—will be your recommendations on the number of personnel, combat, and support that you will require to maintain your branch in the foreseeable future, three to four years. The armament list will consist of the top five armament programs that you need to accomplish your missions. As I stated before, these numbers and armament needs will be realistic and not blue sky as before. Too long have you all relied on technology to accomplish the military mission assigned. That will no longer be the case. Personnel, as I stated, will be top priority. Adequate armament and support for those personnel will be vital. To spell it out clear, drones are nice, but they are not the mainstay of our defense and offense.

"The recommendations given will follow the priorities I have been outlined in the last number of days. The first priority is, of course, the southern border situation. I envision that the military divisions assigned will be there for many years. Priority should be the construction of permanent bases along the southern borders to support these divisions. Luckily with the southern borders we have a number of bases there already: Fort Huachuca in Arizona and Fort Bliss in Texas, which should cover both that part of Texas and New Mexico. The marines at Camp Pendleton should be able to support the California border. We will probably need at least one more base in Texas. I look forward to your recommendations. The bases already established will be upgraded as needed.

"Another high priority will be the expanded role for the marines in defending our remaining embassies around the world. Our embassies have been targets for terrorists for too long. Not only will marines be guarding the embassies again, but we need contingency plans on how to support said embassies in case of grievous attack. I do not want a repeat of Benghazi ever again. We cannot rely on whatever host country to be our only defense. When was the last time a Russian or a Chinese embassy attacked? And why not? Because the enemy knows that retaliation will be swift and ugly.

"The next priority will be replacing the TSA at airports with military personnel. We have skilled personnel in the military police and they should be the forces at the airports. We need common sense precautions at the airports, not PC procedures. Whatever military takes over for the TSA, whether army or even marines, they will need to be in place as rapidly as possible. Shoring up our borders and entry points in the USA is vital not only to our security but also to send a message to the rest of the world that we are serious about these matters.

"The 'spheres of influence' alliances, which I will detail in a few days, will be the priority for the DOS over the next three to four years and beyond. Much will need to be planned as to adequate personnel in those bases located within the alliance and what amounts of assistance we will be rendering our allies in each alliance. Some of the alliances already exist and will need to be augmented. Again the emphasis will be the establishment of their own defenses—army, navy, and air forces. I would expect with many of these alliances, as they develop their own military expertise, new and better armament will be on the horizon. That is to the good.

"One last subject, gentlemen. My predecessor removed defensive missiles from NATO a number of years back. I would like those missiles reestablished within the NATO alliance. Coordinate with the SOD on how quickly this can be accomplished. I look forward to informing our allies ASAP.

"Thank you, gentlemen, for your attendance today. I will leave you with the SOD to continue the dialogue. I plan on having these sessions rather frequently, at least once a month. It is vital for our country that we stay close in contact. Have a good day!

"GOD BLESS AMERICA."

Day 76: Department of State (DOS)

Good morning, America. Today's topic continues in the realm of foreign affairs, namely the Department of State. This department has been with us since the founding of our country and will continue its vital mission in dealing with and interfacing with the nations of the world both friend and NOF. The department has probably been best known not for its experienced personnel, but for the various secretaries of state that have been heads of state for the past 240 years. Some SOS have been very notable, from Franklin to Jefferson to Kissinger, to name a few. Unfortunately, some have been deplorable, like Albright, Clinton, and Kerry. In the final analysis, it is probably not their fault as to their incompetence, but to the presidents that appointed them to this position knowing full well their capabilities and lack thereof.

The Department of State will be undergoing many changes throughout this presidency. Embassies will be closing down; new embassies will be created. The mission of helping to establish various alliances around the world and coordinating their amalgamation will be of prime importance. While these priorities will take precedence, I would like to look at the internal structure of the State Department, or SD, for a few moments and make some comments concerning those state-department functions that have been modified in the last number of years. First of all, I realize that the vast majority of the personnel in the SD are extremely dedicated and competent. The problem is, unfortunately, that agencies within the SD have become extremely PC like the rest of the federal bureaucracy. The foreign-service personnel should be continually trained in their areas of expertise and be promoted into slots that emphasize their areas of expertise. For example, if a Foreign Service Officer is an expert in the Asian sphere, their tours and specialties should reflect that expertise. Language proficiency should be paramount for FSO advancement in responsibility and rank.

Before I leave this topic, the aforementioned needs clarification. As I have already mentioned in prior talks, many organizations in the government do not lend themselves to the "co-ed" world. The SD is one such example. The SD deals with the rest of the world, and frankly, folks, in most of the rest of the world, women are not highly regarded, especially in the realm of government. The policies over the last thirty years of appointing women into roles of FSO and ambassadorship, even SOS, have been dismal failures. The countries have treated these representatives of the USA with little regard and respect. Of prime example are the Muslim countries. Like it or not, these countries, dominated by the Muslim religion, do not regard women as equals to men and never will. Most importantly, having women representing the USA weakens our influence much more than if a male were the representative. With this in mind, high levels of responsibility within the SD, especially when the responsibility involves international relations, will be a male domain, except under unique circumstances.

An ambassadorship is an extremely important role in today's world. The PC method of appointing ambassadorships as rewards for party and contributions will not be a function of this administration. Recommendations of ambassadors will be based where possible on international expertise, language ability, and foreign-affairs experience. Care will be given to all ambassadorships. Since the Senate has the responsibility of confirming ambassadors, I expect that they will be forceful in examining said candidates to make sure the most experienced get the slots. Again, as with many confirmations—judges, cabinet members, ambassadors—the Senate has been lax in such examinations. To this I wish to say, do not worry about hurting my feelings with the approval process. I want the best serving our government, not political appointees and party apparatchik. *not in dictionary*

We too soon have forgotten Benghazi and the horrors of losing an ambassador there. Mr. Stevens was not only an effective ambassador; he was highly skilled in his job. He spoke Arabic fluently, he had spent many years in the Middle East, and he knew many of the powerful and wealthy in the region. His loss was profound and virtually ignored in the media subsequent to the embassy attack. Even now, there is no one around who can fill his shoes. That situation must change. Our SD personnel must be protected at all costs. We need more ambassadors like Mr. Stevens.

I wish to elaborate, if I may, on the "spheres of influence" concept, which will be dialed over the next few days. Of these three alliances, one still exists, two are still as important. NATO is first and is well known to everyone. SEATO was an organization started in 1954 to protect the countries in Southeast Asia from communist intrusion. This treaty, sad to say, has been abandoned since 1977. Lastly, we envision a new Central Asian treaty encompassing Japan, Taiwan, and South Korea.

The first, NATO, has been in existence since 1949 and has served admirably to stabilize the European nations since WWII. Under this umbrella, Europe has grown and prospered enormously since the 1950s. Germany has been reunited, the EU has been formed with its own currency (the euro), and is the second largest economic force in the world. While NATO has continued to define the defensive strategies in Europe, as we stated before it is time for an even more active role to be played by NATO in the realm of military preparedness. The expansion of the army, naval forces, and air forces will be a great deterrent to aggression from whatever source. There are those who will say that their economies cannot stand additional spending on defense. The answer is simple; the

European countries cannot afford not to spend on military. A prepared NATO in all measures will do more to insure peace than any form of action. Again, it is the defenseless that are attacked, not so often the military-prepared. I will be scheduling a meeting in the near future with the NATO leaders to discuss this expanded role in more detail.

Looking at the SEATO treaty, which unfortunately is not in force as of this minute—this treaty needs to be revived and recast to meet the current political, economic, and military needs for that region of the world. The countries of Australia, New Zealand, the Philippines, Thailand, and Burma come to mind as necessary members of such a treaty organization. These countries are vital to the peace and security of that region. The SOS will be coordinating an exploratory meeting with the leaders of the above-mentioned countries for the creation of such an alliance, as was originally promulgated by the SEATO treaty. I will of course be attending such a gathering. It is a vital interest to the USA to have this area of the world stabilized to a greater degree. Not only is the area extremely rich in natural resources, the trade routes are also strategic to the economies of the world.

Lastly, an alliance that the USA will be fostering with great priority will be the Central Asian Treaty organization. The countries that are of great concern are Japan, South Korea, Taiwan, Okinawa, and possibly the Philippines. These countries are friends of the USA and rely on the USA for trade and, yes, military protection; both of which will continue. Our goals will be to expand an alliance with these countries, ultimately even forming somewhat of a "union" as Europe has done. Such an alliance affecting the economic, political, and definitely the military aspects of the above-named countries will bring great stability in this region of the world and help stem aggression from whatever sources.

With that, my fellow Americans, I will conclude today's speech. There is a lot to digest. Tomorrow is a day of rest. Please pray for our nation. Until next we speak, God bless, and

"GOD BLESS AMERICA."

DAY 77: REST

Our Father, Who art in heaven, hallowed be Thy name, Thy kingdom come, Thy will be done on earth as it is in heaven. Give us this day our daily bread and forgive us our trespasses as we forgive those who trespass against us. Lead us not into temptation but deliver us from evil. Amen.

DAY 78: GLOBAL SPHERES OF INFLUENCE

Greetings, my fellow Americans. Today is another exciting day in which we will further elaborate on the Masters Doctrine. Before starting, I would like to digress for a moment and talk about "gun rights" here in America. It may sound like an obtuse subject, but I will relate it hopefully to the main topic of today's speech. America holds the distinction of being virtually the only nation in which the citizenry is and has the right to be armed. The progressives have been trying for over one hundred years to overturn that "right," but have been unsuccessful. Some years back, many states—red states, that is—in the USA started allowing licensure of citizens to carry concealed weapons with a permit. Now all the states allow concealed-weapons permits. The progressives have wailed about this and continue to wail. However, their protests are hollow. Every statistic since concealed-weapons permits have been allowed has shown a dramatic reduction in violent crime in the states where the citizens are armed.[177] The statistics also show increasing violent crimes in those states that restrict gun ownership and usage, such as in Connecticut, New York, Michigan, California, and Illinois.[178] The message is quite clear, folks. A criminal will think twice about robbing or doing violence to someone if they think that person is armed. It is easier to do violence to someone who is not armed and cannot defend themselves. As an aside, I am encouraging all states, by the way, to honor other states' concealed-weapons permits. I myself have had a CWP for over twenty years, and even though I am in the White House and have the secret service for protection, I still carry, folks.

Why I digressed on the above story is because what happens within a nation directly affects its relations with other nations. Belligerency is not limited to the average citizen. Nations that cannot defend themselves are subject to violence from other nations just as its citizens are subjected to violence. Muslim terrorists in the Middle East commit horrible crimes against average citizens. Would that violence be as rampant if the citizens were armed and could defend themselves?

After WWII and as part of the containment policy against the spread of communism, the USA entered into a series of treaties with various nations around the world for mutual trade, defense, and aid. NATO in Europe, SEATO in South Asia, and treaties with Japan, Taiwan, and South Korea. These alliances proved their worth and were necessary given the poor state of the countries involved. Fast-forward sixty years; these countries around the

---

[177] Howell, Kellan. "Murder rates drop as concealed carry permits soar: report." *Washington Times.* July 14, 2015.
http://www.washingtontimes.com/news/2015/jul/14/murder-rates-drop-as-concealed-carry-permits-soar-/.

[178] Gillin, Joshua. "Is violent crime lower in states with open carry?" *Politifact.*
October 9, 2015. http://www.politifact.com/florida/statements/2015/oct/09/matt-gaetz/violent-crime-lower-states-open-carry/.

globe have grown and prospered. They no longer need to be sheltered as with children. It is time, as with our children, when they are grown for them to be on their own and responsible for their own lives and affairs. As with children, so it goes with countries. Around the globe, countries such as Japan, South Korea, Germany, England, and France have vibrant economies and need to step up to the plate and assume more responsibility for their destinies.

With this in mind, this office through our State Department will be reevaluating our treaty and alliance commitments worldwide. Let us look at NATO, for example. The European Union is a very vibrant economical union and should be responsible for not only its economy, but its own defense. It is time for the EU to increase its military, its army, its navy, and its air forces and assume responsibility for its survival. The USA will remain with the alliance, but our role will be secondary to the EU. Yes, this will mean an increasingly armed EU, but as in the USA, an armed EU capable of defending itself will deter much aggression from other nations such as Russia and the Muslim invasion. My predecessor removed many defensive capabilities from the EU. This office will be reversing that action.

This office will also be working on and helping to expand or implement at least six worldwide spheres of influence, each sphere to have its own armies, navies, and air forces capable of defending each alliance from aggression. Some of these spheres are as such:

1. NATO—EU mentioned above
2. Asian—Japan, Taiwan, South Korea
3. SEATO—Thailand, Australia, New Zealand, the Philippines
4. South America—Brazil, Chile, Venezuela, Argentina
5. Central America and the Caribbean
6. USA and Canada

The progressives around the world will look at the above as armed camps, and in a sense, they are. By forming protective alliances and building up their own defenses, their economies will grow, belligerency will decrease, and worldwide stability will, I think, increase. The citizens in the countries within each alliance will feel empowered by an increasing sense of safety and protection from the nations involved. Whether or not more nations will allow as with the USA, arming their citizens is up to the nations involved.

The USA stands ready with all the alliances mentioned above to aid all FR nations in increasing their economies and protective forces.

The above assumes that FR nations are forming these alliances. In a turbulent world, nations in the NOF category can and probably will form their own alliances. The USA has no control over that situation. But an armed FR alliance is still the best deterrent against aggression in whatever form, just as an armed citizen defending his or her home and family is the best deterrent against violence.

At this juncture, I would be remiss if I did not elaborate on the sixth sphere mentioned above. The USA is bordered by two nations and our relations with each vary greatly. There has been talk of an alliance between the USA, Canada, and Mexico. Unfortunately, that will never happen in the foreseeable future. Let me address our neighbor to the north first. Canada and the USA share much in tradition, language, culture, and economies. We trade freely with each other and should hope to continue to do so. Our citizens travel freely between our countries, many Canadians spending the entire winter months in the USA. Our relations are as equals and not dominant or submissive.

However, our relationship with Mexico, in some ways more intimate due to the fact that much of our illegal-immigrant problem has arisen in Mexico, has not been as friendly. Unfortunately, with internal turmoil in Mexico that seems to go on endlessly and a continuing stream of governments that cannot or will not correct problems such as immigration, drug cartels, currency, and the like, Mexico is on the NOF list and will remain so for the foreseeable future. Prior presidents have tried to stem the tide of illegals into the USA and have failed. Entreaties with the Mexican government have also failed. Mexico looks at the USA as a "sugar daddy" and continues to inject its abysmal economy, its citizenry, and its corruption into the USA. The placing of the US Army on the border states has eased immensely the flow of ugliness from the south. Mexico will stay on the NOF list until they, the Mexican people, change their country.

On that note, I shall close for the day. Tomorrow will be another heavy topic that will be of much interest to all Americans; namely, the United Nations organization. Until then,

"GOD BLESS AMERICA."

Day 79: The United Nations Debacle

Good morning, America. Today's conversation will deal with, to me at least, a persistent thorn in the side of the USA for the last seventy years, namely, the United Nations organization. Originally conceived as a utopian dream called the League of Nations, or LON, by a very ill President Wilson at the end of WWI, it was fortunately rejected at that time and died in the real world. As with many progressive ideas, as harebrained as they may be, concepts like the LON are kept on the back burner to be resurrected at a more opportune moment in time and history. The names may change, but the progressive idea is still the same.

After WWII, the resurrection of the LON became real, though the name was changed to United Nations. New York was designated the site for the UN, and everyone clamored on board to join this *munificent* organization. The time was especially appropriate. The world had just experienced the second of two devastating world wars, communism was spreading rapidly around the globe, and the UN was seen as a balancing mechanism to the threat of communism. The UN would assure some sort of peace and tranquility in a troubled world. The USA signed on board and, being the most powerful nation at that time, was charged exorbitant membership fees. The UN charter allowed for a five permanent member Security Council (US, Russia, China, France, England) to decide the important issues. However, the vote had to be unanimous, thereby negating whatever positive measures that could have been passed. A UN military force was enacted, composed of contingents from different countries. This force was supposed to insure peace throughout the world.

As the member nations multiplied, especially in the post-colonial world after WWII, the membership became more and more divisive and more and more despotic. The UN became rapidly a forum for disparaging the USA and the allies of WWII, while, of course, relying more and more on economic aid from said first-world countries. The heads of the UN, when elected, represented increasingly the third world more than any of the first-world countries. Far from being a forum for peace, the UN became a propaganda tool for the progressive, the fanatical (Muslims), the tyrannical (Castro's Cuba), and the communistic (Russia and China). Any wars the UN participated in were general failures as with any attempts on foreign aid to any disaster. The economic support, of course, for all of the above was laid on the shoulders of the USA.

Meanwhile, the member nations of the UN sent their delegates to New York, where they were regarded as diplomats and enjoyed all the largesse that was given. Currently there are 193 members of the UN.[179] As can be seen, the vast majority of the UN members are on the NOF list that I talked about a little while back. (Check our website for a current list of NOF nations around the world.)

Sad to say, seventy years after the creation of the UN it remains a total failure in all measures. Wars have not been stopped, and peace has not grown around the world; as a matter of fact, the current situation in Iran with nuclear facilities has been exacerbated by the incompetence of the UN monitoring force. Remember this is the same organization that was supposed to monitor the North Koreans during the 1990s. Who has the nuclear arsenal now?

For seventy years the USA has sent ambassador after ambassador to the UN with hopes of better outcomes. Nothing has been achieved. The one democracy in the Middle East, Israel, is continually being vilified. Israel has had to defend itself in five major wars over the last sixty years with absolutely no support from the UN. Israel is now treated as a pariah in the UN, especially by the multitude of Muslim nations that comprise the UN.

Unfortunately, the past few presidents have tried to accommodate this incompetence and work with UN forces to achieve whatever. All results generally have been futile, from Bosnia to the first and second Gulf Wars to Afghanistan. The tales of graft and corruption within the UN forces are rampant. UN forces sent to protect civilian populations have often participated in the atrocities.[180]

---

[179] "Member states of the United Nations." *Wikipedia.* Accessed June 23, 2016. https://en.wikipedia.org/wiki/Member_states_of_the_United_Nations.

[180] Freedman, Rosa. "When UN peacekeepers commit atrocities, someone has to act." *The Conversation.* November 17, 2014. http://theconversation.com/when-un-peacekeepers-commit-atrocities-someone-has-to-act-34317.

Someone once said that insanity is repeating the same thing over and over and expecting a different result. NO MORE! This experiment in progressive utopianism must end.

Therefore, I am issuing an executive order that as of July 4, 2017, the USA is withdrawing from the UN organization. All USA support will end as of that date also. This support will involve financial, economic, military, and political. Humanitarian aid will need to be elicited from the member nations remaining. I would advise the UN heads to look for another headquarters for the UN. By the end of this year, all diplomatic status will be withdrawn for UN delegates. All visas for foreign delegates will be subject to review and will be issued for short-term periods, six months or less. Any delegates remaining in our country after the first of the year will have no immunity to the laws of the USA. I will be sending to Congress legislation accomplishing the above and hope that it will be passed by Congress posthaste. This nightmare must come to an end, and so it shall.

One last comment with respect to humanitarian aid worldwide. The USA is a generous country and where appropriate will continue to render aid globally where and when needed. The USA will make any and all decisions regarding such aid. That is not to say that the multitude of private organizations that exist to aid in disaster relief cannot continue to do their relief efforts. Where appropriate we will support such efforts. The days of unlimited support, however, are over.

My fellow Americans, this speech ends our discussions on foreign affairs. It has been a demanding agenda, as can be seen in the media reaction to my speeches. As usual, I encourage all of you to write, phone, or whatever; communicate to your elected representatives as to your thinking on the many aspects of my speeches. It is only through you, the people, speaking your mind that change can result and this great country of ours can continue to grow and prosper. Tomorrow is another new day and a whole new series of speeches, now dealing with our American culture. Pray for our country and, if you can, please pray for your president.

"GOD BLESS AMERICA."

SECTION 8

AMERICAN CULTURE

Day 80: Overview

Good morning, America. A new day and a brand-new set of challenges for America. I hope this week is peaceful and calm, unlike the White House, where turmoil is the byword. I also hope that you, the faithful, had a chance to attend services in the church of your choice this past weekend and that your prayers are answered. Today we start on the final countdown to the magic number of the first hundred days to a new revitalized America. To give you an idea of these final few weeks, I would like to mention an individual, a true patriot, the man who coined the phrase "Borders, Language, Culture"—Michael Savage. Those conservatives will know him by his daily radio show, *The Savage Nation*. While in prior days' discussions, I borrowed many of his ideas on the travails in the USA, I will be referring to him in the next few weeks. The topics to be discussed will expand on a few main themes that need to be addressed here in the USA: American culture, personal issues such as religion, personal values and morals, and finally the civil rights issues that have led to the promulgation of horrendous laws, all extraconstitutional, and redefined citizens' rights and the devaluation of these rights.

Each day, I will review a particular part of the many problems in these areas and, of course, solutions to those problems will be given. I guarantee the liberal progressives will be rioting in the streets daily when faced with the solutions that will be provided. To elaborate even further, many so-called conservatives will also be against many of the solutions that will be offered. The problem, folks, is that many of these special interest "groups" have gained much power in our country in the last fifty years at the expense of you, the citizenry of the USA. These groups have had their way because of a very liberal educational system that no longer teaches values and truth, a very liberal media that only focuses on one side of the equation and totally ignores the traditional side, and finally, a political party—the DSP—totally immersed and dedicated to the destruction of the USA and our way of life. They are all formidable "enemies of the state" and as such need to be publicly exposed for the horrendous acts they have achieved against the USA. Each day more and more of the darkness will be revealed and exposed. The light will come, but it will be a battle. It will be a battle for the hearts, minds, and soul of our great nation. These problems are the main inspiration for this book and for my analyses these past two months.

What is the American culture? For many, that is a difficult question. When you look at various nations in the world—Germany, England, China, Japan, wherever—their cultures have been around for many hundreds, maybe thousands, of years and encompass not only language but race, borders, customs, and the like. All go into the making of a nation's "culture." America is somewhat unique because our culture stemmed mainly from various European nationalities coming to America from the 1600s and establishing themselves in this country. From the pilgrims to the Germans, Italians, English, Dutch, and Spanish, all played a part in the definition of American "culture." English was always the main language, both in speech and formal documentation. Our laws, our way of government, was heavily influenced by England. We fought a revolution against England, and the thirteen colonies became the thirteen states in the USA.

From the beginning, our roots have been the European, white Caucasian stock. Yes, there have always been certain minority groups, but those groups did not define our culture and our heritage. From the 1600s we fought the various Indian tribes for territorial expansion. The Indians were and never have been part of the American culture. Most of the time the relationship has been adversarial and in many cases still is. The Indians have their place in the USA and probably will always be in the category of "separate but equal." I was in Japan many years ago and talked with a native Japanese. In Japan there is a large minority of people from Korean stock who have lived in Japan for many generations. Most speak fluent Japanese, their children go to Japanese schools, they are totally immersed in the Japanese culture, but they are not and never will be "Japanese." They will always be separate. It is the same if I went to Japan and lived there all my life and raised my family there. We may be assimilated into the Japanese way of life, but we would never be "Japanese."

We, like many countries, imported slaves from Africa for many hundreds of years. Those minorities were never meant to be assimilated into the culture and were never meant to be a part of the culture. We as a nation have been fighting the "black" problem for over four hundred years now and are no closer to a solution than when the problem started four hundred years ago. I will be addressing this minority in a few days.

The third major minority group that has been a terrific social issue has been the Mexican (Hispanic) immigration to the USA for the past two hundred years. The problem increased after the Mexican American War in the 1840s. We won the war, and Mexico ceded what is now California and the southwest USA to us. Mexico and its population have never come to grips with the war loss. They never realized that as victors, we should have taken over all of Mexico and made it a part of the USA. In hindsight, that may have been the preferable solution. From its inception as a Spanish colony, Mexico has not been a stable nation in any sense of the word; governments come and go, but the third-world nature of Mexico stays the same. Be that as it may, the problem with the

Mexican illegals entering the USA is a constant thorn that must be finally pulled out so that some healing can come about. This problem will also be addressed in the next few days.

To continue on our original vein, namely, the formation of our American culture, let us look at the growth of our country. As our country grew, so did our heritage and culture. Various groups of immigrants, mostly of European stock, settled in our country and rapidly, over one or two generations, assimilated into the American way of life and culture. As our culture grew, people became Americans—not Polish Americans, not Irish Americans, not German Americans—just Americans. Our country expanded from the Atlantic to the Pacific Oceans and all points in between. Wars were fought, new states were added, and America was becoming America. Alexis de Tocqueville, a French political writer in the 1800s touring the USA from Europe, eulogized the USA and the new America arising from the unknown. He praised the industry, the inventiveness, the energy of this new land and people. One of his quotes from his well-known treatise, *Democracy in America*, was "Among a democratic people, where there is no hereditary wealth, and every man works to earn a living . . . labor is held in honor. The prejudice is not against but in its favor."[181] Amazing times and an amazing nation!

We almost made the grade up until about seventy or eighty years ago. Looking at our nation then and at our nation now, the changes are not evolving but devolving. Let us try and relate to what has happened in the interim. Then our nation was fighting for its very existence against formidable foes seeking very readily to destroy us and our culture. At that time, we were very much a God-fearing nation; prayer was a mainstay of daily life, in schools, in the

---

[181] Alexis de Tocqueville, *Democracy in America* (New York: J. and H. G. Langley, 1840), page 162.

workplace, and definitely in the home. The Pledge of Allegiance was said daily in our schools. The flag was honored and displayed everywhere. The family unit was sacrosanct. Children grew up knowing a mother and father. Families were larger—three, four, five children or more in a family was the norm. Respect was shown everywhere.

After World War II as we in the USA resumed our daily lives, we continued our traditions and expanded our families, our nation, and our culture. The country's demographics reflected our culture that had been in place since the nation's founding. The nation was 85 percent white Caucasian, European descent. Nine percent was of black descent. Five percent was of Hispanic descent. One percent was of various minorities.[182] Immigration had been stopped for over twenty-five years at this point and the demographics in the USA were stabilized.

Our immigration laws had changed little since the founding. Priority was in keeping the demographics unchanged and thus European immigrants always had priority. Ellis Island and the Statue of Liberty symbolized not only America, but our heritage. While we encouraged a cross section of society, we were very careful as to the quality and health of the immigrants. The third-world population was not encouraged or solicited.

English was the spoken language in schools, in the workplace, in our churches, and in our government. Respect for our country was paramount. Our history was taught unabridged in our schools. George Washington was familiar to all schoolchildren, as President George Washington's birthday was a national holiday.

---

[182] "A Look at the 1940 Census." United States Census Bureau. Accessed June 23, 2016.
https://www.census.gov/newsroom/cspan/1940census/CSPAN_1940slides.pdf.

The economy boomed after WWII, and inflation was under control. The average house sold for under $10,000. The average car was under $2,500.[183] Our currency was backed by gold and silver. Inflation was something for the textbooks and not a factor in the real world. The churches were filled on Sundays; as one watched the parishioners going into church, the vast majority were families with children and all dressed in their Sunday best. Civility was everywhere; honor and respect were a part of the everyday life. The country sang every day with the energy, with the industry, with the vitality, and with the culture. It was a time when everything was possible in the USA. Dreams, any dream, could be achieved with hard work and ambition.

Fast-forward to the new millennia. If one had not grown up in the era described above, that world is as foreign as living on another planet. In the 1960s the population was about 200 million people in the USA. The basic stock (European descent) of the US citizenry numbered about 170 million.[184] In the past fifty years, with the progressives in control and the immigration laws changed for the worse, the demographics have changed dramatically. The European Caucasian stock still numbers 170 million, but the US population has grown to almost 350 million; the vast amount of the increased numbers, another 150 million people, had come from third-world countries and,[185] of course, vast amounts of illegals, accounted for by some estimates almost a third of the above 150

---

[183] "1950s News, Events, Popular Culture and Prices." The People History. Accessed June 23, 2016. http://www.thepeoplehistory.com/1950s.html.

[184] "A Look at the 1940 Census." United States Census Bureau. Accessed June 23, 2016.
https://www.census.gov/newsroom/cspan/1940census/CSPAN_1940slides.pdf.

[185] "2010 United States Census." *Wikipedia*. Accessed June 23, 2016.
https://en.wikipedia.org/wiki/2010_United_States_Census.

million additions to the US in the past fifty years.[186] Aided, as mentioned before, by an immigration bill authored by a profligate Democratic senator named Ted Kennedy and signed into law in 1965 by another progressive president, LB Johnson, the immigration laws have changed the demographics of America and, if left unchecked, will forever change what is known as America, and with it, the "American culture."

I have talked about the immigration problem both for constitutional amendments and executive actions. But it's you the people who will have to make the final decision on what and who will make up America. It is relatively easy to tear down a house and exceedingly hard to erect one that can withstand the ravages of nature. Unless you the people finally say "NO MORE," this country will fall, and what comes afterward will not be to your liking.

Tomorrow I will begin addressing aspects of our demographics that have contributed to our current insanity. Each speech will address a particular minority group who has influenced greatly the insane direction this country has taken the last fifty years. I can promise you all eventful speeches and solutions to problems that will not be to the liberals' liking. No matter; you all did not elect me to be popular, you elected me to produce results. That is what I am doing. Until tomorrow,

"GOD BLESS AMERICA."

---

[186] Zeigler, Karen. "Immigrant Population Hits Record 42.1 Million in Second Quarter of 2015." Center for Immigration Studies. August 2015. http://cis.org/Immigrant-Population-Hits-Record-Second-Quarter-2015.

Day 81: Dismantling the Civil Rights Legislation

Hello, my fellow Americans. Today we again review a topic I had mentioned on day twelve of my talks, the civil rights debacle and the proposed amendments to correct this legislative nightmare. This speech will be somewhat abbreviated since much was stated already on day twelve. Today will serve to introduce the following series of speeches regarding the rights and privileges of various groups in the USA that have had free rein in their involvement with our society. Of course, they have been aided by fifty years of progressivism and legislation that have totally bypassed the Constitution and effectively destroyed our rights as defined in the Constitution. I realize that it will take much time in order to pass amendments to right these crazy laws, but in the meantime it will be necessary to use the power of the presidency to at least halt some of the legislative forces that have been unleashed in the last fifty years. These laws are myriad, as can be seen on our website, WH2017.org. The first steps were outlined on day thirty-four when I was discussing the future roles of the Department of Justice. These steps have been initiated and are slowly stopping the progress of civil rights legislation. By redefining the priorities of the DOJ and placing *no* priority on civil rights legislation and infractions connected with these laws, much of the legislation has and is slowly dissolving. Of course, many states have passed their own CR laws and have the option to still prosecute supposed "violations" of these various acts. They are also free to appeal to the SCOTUS for continued support of these laws. I wish them luck. Many of the states' laws in this regard were passed based on their interpretation of the legislation, federal regulations, or executive orders. The constitutionality of these laws are very much in question. The Supreme Court is still reeling from the plethora of laws that have been passed these last ninety days, so I do not think that aid for the progressives will be forthcoming from the High Court. SCOTUS, I think, is finally understanding its role in government and how far it has overstepped its bounds as defined by the Constitution.

To reiterate, the concept of "incrementalism" can creep into our society and, like incipient infections, gradually gain strength and eventually start to destroy the host. It is the same with the civil rights movement. Supposedly implemented to protect the minorities, it is destroying the fabric of our country in favor of every kind of minority: gays, Muslims, Latinos, blacks, Indians, illegals. It seems "they" have all these new "rights" and the white Caucasian citizens of America have no rights. Discrimination abounds everywhere nowadays. We are not a "God-fearing" nation anymore, we are just a "fearful nation." Free speech is gone in most facets of our society. The last refuge of free speech is in the home, and even there, the progressive attack is increasing. Children are taught to speak out against their parents, not to obey their parents, that "their" rights are more important than the family rights.[187] Insanity reigns. In the public sector, all evidence of free speech is rapidly dissolving. Every day you hear of some media personage being fired for saying something controversial and therefore "discriminatory." Even such bastions as radio talk shows are being assaulted and in many cases have to tone down their messages to stay under the wire, so to speak. Our last president used the race card to silence any and all opposition to his malfeasance in office. Every offense he and his administration

---

[187] Goldsmith, Edward. "Social disintegration: effects." Edward Goldsmith's blog. Accessed June 23, 2016. http://www.edwardgoldsmith.org/1073/social-disintegration-effects/. Original excerpt from Tom Stacey, *Can Britain Survive?* (London: Sphere Books, 1971), chapter 21.

committed, from fast and furious gunrunning, to the Benghazi murder, to the Middle East debacle arming Iran, was effectively allowed because of the race card. The horrors unleashed, especially in the last eight years, will be felt by generations of Americans to come.

To further get back on track with the Constitution, I will be reversing every executive order relating to civil rights since 1965. Our website will highlight each of these executive orders initiated since LBJ.

We will start with my immediate predecessor and his horrific executive orders over the past eight years. We will then be going back president by president to remove as many of these executive orders that also deal with civil rights and that are, in the judgment of this office, totally unconstitutional. Many of these executive orders should have been overturned by the SCOTUS over the years; however, the judiciary and Congress have failed the American public in this regard. This administration shall endeavor to correct some of these horrors. I encourage public and private institutions to challenge these laws in the state and federal courts. The assault to regain our freedoms must come from all angles.

Lastly, as outlined in a number of my speeches, all "civil rights" provisions in federal agencies will no longer be enforced except under very unusual circumstances. A federal committee will be set up to examine any of these "unusual circumstances." I can tell you from the get-go that the bias of the committee will not be for "civil rights."

With that I will close for this day. Tomorrow we will start the discussion on the first of the minority issues that are plaguing this nation, namely, the "black" conundrum. Until then,

"GOD BLESS AMERICA."

DAY 82: THE BLACK DILEMMA—HISTORICAL

Good morning, America. Today we will start the analysis and propose political and social directions for various ethnicities that have influenced our social mores, especially these last fifty years. None of these ethnic problems are easy to solve, but these people are here to stay, and we must as a nation confront the problems and propose pathways to getting past the difficulties. I would like to say at the onset that my analysis of various social and ethnic problems is not in any way an apology to anyone or any ethnicity. Life is life. We are and still are a great nation, maybe the greatest the world has ever known. No nation is perfect in any respect. Pathways are chosen, some good, some bad, some ugly. History is what it is.

So, America, we start our journey into the first of the inflammatory social issues that plague the USA and have continued to plague us for over four hundred years—the Negro race issue in the USA. A highly emotionally charged issue, which even if mentioned by a non-black person, that person is often labeled by the epithet "racist." When I was preparing this speech, I had a long debate with myself on what label to use in describing the "black race." There have been many monikers over the years, some good, some bad. I will choose the term "black race," knowing full well many will be offended even at that label. So be it! Now back to the discussion. Perhaps like our other journeys, it is instructive to look back at history past.

First of all, let us examine the human phenomenon called "slavery." This human behavior has existed for thousands of years and is still common, especially in Muslim countries.[188] Slavery was

---

[188] "Muslim Statistics (Slavery)." WikiIslam. Accessed June 23, 2016. https://wikiislam.net/wiki/Muslim_Statistics_-_Slavery.

practiced by most nations and tribes. As with wars, slavery is a byproduct of conquest. When a nation or tribe conquered another, slaves were made of the people conquered. When one examines the major theological books—Koran, Torah, Bible—all mention and refer to slavery as being a part of the customs of nations. Many myths have evolved about slavery, especially in the US. One myth is that slavery only occurred in the USA. Totally false! As a matter of fact, the vast amount of slavery in the past four hundred years were into countries outside the USA, for example, Central and South America. While Africa is always toted as the slavery capital of the world, in truth many nations in the last five thousand years were either enslaved or had slaves. Another myth about slavery in USA is that the blacks only became slaves when they were brought to the USA. False! Africa then and still is largely a tribal and aboriginal continent. These tribes were ruled by chieftains who had absolute control over their tribes. They sold their people into slavery, and when they conquered other tribes, sold those people into slavery. The idea that all the blacks in Africa were free spirits is another myth. As aboriginal people they had no written language, lived in the forests, ate with their hands, had no toilet facilities—or homes for that matter—and had very limited life-spans.[189] The middle men, the agents in many of these sales over the years, were the Arab Muslims, who believe and still believe that the black races are aboriginal and not human. Probably that is why my predecessor had little success in dealing with this issue.

Another myth is that the blacks were incessantly abused while slaves in the USA. That may have been true for black slaves in other

---

[189] Username "Brain Glutton." "Why did most pre-colonial nations of sub-Saharan Africa have no written language?" Straight Dope Message Board, Great Debates. July 3, 2004.
http://boards.straightdope.com/sdmb/archive/index.php/t-264698.html.

countries, but in the USA the blacks had a better existence than where they originated.[190] First of all, a slave on the auction block brought somewhere between $600 and $1,500 per person.[191] Three hundred years ago, that was a phenomenal amount—more than a year's wage. Only the wealthy could afford slaves. A slave was bought to work and be productive, as with a farm implement, like a plow. The last thing a slave owner wanted was to abuse the slave since a slave that could not work was a wasted asset. The same holds true for lynching. The very last thing an owner wanted was to kill a slave, since it meant that the whole investment in the slave was lost and another slave had to be bought to replace the one dead.

The slaves in the USA lived in homes, had decent clothes, were treated by doctors, ate well, eventually assimilated a formal language, and became somewhat civilized. Black churches evolved and the slaves became religious to a large degree. What one cannot ignore is that these people were slaves, brought over as slaves, and most importantly were not ever to be considered citizens of the country in which they were enslaved, especially the USA. The same could be said about the Chinese brought over to work the railroads in the 1800s, or the Hispanic migrants brought into the Southwest to help out on the farms. Being citizens of the USA was never an option.

---

[190] Mintz, Steven. "American Slavery in Comparative Perspective." The Gilder Lehrman Institute of American History. Accessed June 23, 2016. http://www.gilderlehrman.org/history-by-era/origins-slavery/resources/american-slavery-comparative-perspective (subscription required for full access).
[191] Williamson, Samuel H. and Louis P. Cain. "Measuring Slavery in 2011 Dollars." Measuring Worth. Accessed June 23, 2016. https://www.measuringworth.com/slavery.php.

With the above in mind, let us further examine the race relations between the blacks in the USA and the rest of the population. The last four hundred years can actually be divided into three large segments of history. During the first 250 years, the situation was very stratified; the blacks were slaves and were property of their respective owners. An interesting sidelight was that there always was a segment of the black population in the USA who were never slaves, and many of these "free blacks" were also slave owners. The slavery issue continued to foment in all parts of the USA and eventually brought about the horrendous Civil War in 1860, after which slavery was abolished. The blacks forget very often that the vast majority of blood spilled during the Civil War freeing the slaves was shed by the Caucasian race, not the black race.

After the Civil War, the USA entered into the second segment of historical relations with the black race. Yes, there were no more slaves, but the black population, though free, was largely segregated from the rest of the population in the USA. These hundred years were actually very beneficial to the black race. Family life was paramount, and children actually grew up with a father and mother. Black families were very stable; over 75 percent of black children grew up in such families. Amazing, they actually knew their fathers! Contrast that to the current day where only 30 percent of black children grow up in stable, married families.[192] The black population then economically was very well off. Not to the degree as the white population, but compared to other minorities, very well off indeed. Segregation was institutionalized in all parts of the USA but not enforced everywhere. The South, of course, was

---

[192] Lloyd, Maria. "The Black Family Is Worse Off Today Than In the 1960's, Report Shows." Your Black World. March 2, 2016.
http://yourblackworld.net/2013/03/02/the-black-family-is-worse-off-today-than-in-the-1960s-report-shows/.

the most rigid, but the North, the Midwest, and the West had very little rigidity in race relations. It is interesting to note that the Democratic Party was strongest in the South and supported segregation the most vehemently. What again is forgotten is that while blacks had their own schools, their own neighborhoods, their own churches, their own shops, and their own industries, these segments of black society reflected the society in the USA at large. Ghettos were not the norm, black children had to learn in schools, black neighborhoods were neat and tidy, and the people had standards. Yes, they lived among themselves, but their values reflected the society at large, and they thrived.

While the progressives are totally reviled by this segregation, they forget that this separation of races was probably necessary given the historical aspect of slavery and the Civil War. What is also forgotten is that during this time, the black society contributed much to the American society at large. Jazz, for example, was created by the blacks during this period. Today jazz is almost gone, replaced by *rap*. Horrors! This time also produced Diana Ross and the Supremes, Nat King Cole, Jackie Robinson, Motown, the Four Tops, and Cassius Clay, the heavyweight boxer. The list goes on and on. Howard University produced many black scholars. One has to ask oneself, what has the black race produced in the last fifty years? The answer, sadly, is often the negative. This is probably a good place to stop for today. Tomorrow we will examine the last fifty years of race relations and offer some solutions to the black dilemma. Until then,

"GOD BLESS AMERICA."

DAY 83: THE BLACK QUAGMIRE—SOLUTIONS

Today continues our look at a very volatile relationship with the black race in America. The relative calm of the hundred years of segregation was broken in the 1960s with the civil rights movement. Interesting to note that the black race did not instigate the civil rights movement but was led on by the liberal progressives of that time.[193] New information has come to light that many of the agitators were funded and inspired by communist Russia.[194] The progressive mantra, though, has always stayed the same: never waste a good calamity; if there is not a problem, create one, and then provide the means of "solving" the imagined problem. Thus America entered into the third segment of race relations with the blacks, the civil rights era, in which we are still embroiled. Now ongoing for over fifty years, we see that America has decayed into a chaotic national situation in which everything and everyone not black is labelled "racist." America is no closer to an answer to the black question and in many ways has allowed the situation to deteriorate steadily to the point where it again threatens to destroy the fabric of our society. The last president, elected by the progressive left to heal the racial divide, was a dismal failure and in fact used the race card to foment even more discord.

Let us look at the social scene that has evolved since the civil rights years in the 1960s. Yes, there was a separation of races up to the civil rights era, or CRE, but the standards of America were

---

[193] Martin, Michael. Tell Me More. "How 'Communism' Brought Racial Equality To The South." Interview with Robin Kelley on NPR News, 17:12. February 16, 2010. http://www.npr.org/templates/story/story.php?storyId=123771194.
[194] Massie, Mychal. "How Communists Co-Opted Black America." WND. February 6, 2012. http://www.wnd.com/2012/02/how-communists-co-opted-black-america/#!.

upheld by all, especially the blacks. In their efforts to succeed, they strove to improve themselves, in schools, in their jobs, in their neighborhoods. While poorer than the rest of the population, they moved forward. This all ended with the CRE. Now affirmative action replaced incentive; no longer did a person of color need to excel or even meet job requirements. They got into the work environment, into the government, into college, not by virtue of their abilities, but by their color alone. They graduated from prestigious universities, not with ability but with grades given because of their color. The quota system within a very few years, upheld by the SCOTUS, became prevalent in the USA. Suddenly every workplace had to have a certain number of blacks, later expanded to women and other minorities.[195] Discrimination became the hated word in the American lexicon. Even the mention of "discrimination" caused leaders in the business world, in the university, and in the government to bow down in compliance. Those accused of "discrimination" were automatically guilty unless proven innocent. The full weight of the federal government was placed against any and all who did not comply with the various CR dicta. Legislation after legislation came about and expanded the CR of virtually all groups of peoples in the USA except for the white race, the founders of our country. Even the illegals found sanctuary in the CR world.

How have the black communities nationwide fared? Unfortunately, the answers are dismal at best. The blacks have increasingly separated themselves into their own communities, now mostly ghettos, from LA, to Chicago, to Detroit, to Baltimore, to Ferguson. All urban areas in which these ghettos exist—and that covers vast numbers of cities and towns—are characterized by poverty, gangs,

---

[195] "Racial quota." *Wikipedia.* Accessed June 23, 2016.
https://en.wikipedia.org/wiki/Racial_quota.

drug dealers, and riots on a frequent basis. The federal government tried to force communities to integrate and accept black families into the communities during the '80s and '90s.[196] All such forced entries ultimately failed, and the communities involved deteriorated into ghettos. I remember thirty years ago visiting my aunt who lived in Dearborn, Michigan, a part of Detroit. It was a nice, middle-class, white neighborhood. When she wanted to sell and move in with her children, she was forced to sell to a black family who, frankly, did not qualify for the home loan. The feds stepped in and the family entered this community. When I visited four years later, the community had totally disintegrated for the worse. Gangs roamed the streets, and graffiti was everywhere. Nobody except the criminal element went out at night. Many of the homes were vacant hulls with windows broken, unkempt lawns, and smells everywhere. Urban change at its worst. Detroit today is an urban wasteland. Seventy percent of the population has vacated the city. Urban blight is everywhere. One can buy a house for under twenty thousand dollars, but who wants to live there? Of course, all these cities are controlled by the DSP who dispense social programs galore in order to keep the "rabble" calm. Ask yourself, folks: in the last fifty years, every decade has been marred by riots for whatever reason. The riots are uniformly comprised of the black population. Nobody gets arrested, nobody goes to jail, the city rebuilds with federal funds. The excuses are always the same. "They" are poor, "they" are the downtrodden, "they" are oppressed. The riots let them let off a little steam, then all will calm down for a while. Folks, there is never progress in this matter, only the calm before another storm.

---

[196] "Integration: The 1964 Civil Rights Act to the Present." Info Please. Accessed June 23, 2016. http://www.infoplease.com/encyclopedia/history/integration-the-civil-rights-act-to-present.html.

The attitude of the black society has all deteriorated. Instead of improving their lot in life, they blame the rest of society for their ills and that the rest of society "owes" them. When questioned, they rattle off the "owes" for the last four hundred years. Every few years the question of "reparations" comes into being. The federal government tried that with various Indian tribes in Alaska and failed miserably. Look at the aftermath of Hurricane Katrina. New Orleans, which is overwhelmingly black in population, received tens of billions of dollars for their losses real and imagined. It has been estimated that almost seventy-five percent of federal funds to New Orleans were misused.[197] Have any of these funds helped the black society in New Orleans? The answer is no. I am sure everyone remembers the black lady in Detroit during the Obama campaign who was joyful, for she was going to get tons of "Obama" bucks to pay for her house, her car, her phone. Insanity!

Continuing on, fifty years ago, as I mentioned before, black children were born into stable families. Now 70 percent are born out of wedlock.[198] A black child may know who his mother is but rarely will he know the father. In the 1960s, 27 percent of black families were in poverty.[199] Fifty years later, after $13 trillion spent on poverty elimination, 27 percent of black families are still in

---

[197] Lipton, Eric. "'Breathtaking' Waste and Fraud in Hurricane Aid." *New York Times*. June 27, 2006.
http://www.nytimes.com/2006/06/27/washington/27katrina.html?_r=1.
[198] Lloyd, Maria. "The Black Family Is Worse Off Today Than In the 1960's, Report Shows." Your Black World. March 2, 2016.
http://yourblackworld.net/2013/03/02/the-black-family-is-worse-off-today-than-in-the-1960s-report-shows/.
[199] "Poverty in the United States: Frequently Asked Questions." National Poverty Center. Accessed June 23, 2016. http://www.npc.umich.edu/poverty/.

poverty, depending on the area of the country.[200] Black unemployment is over 12 percent, twice the rate for white.[201] Black unemployment for teenagers hovers around 40 to 50 percent.[202] Black illiteracy is the highest in the last fifty years. Why do employers not want to hire blacks for work? Simply, they have no skills, no work skills, no intellectual skills, and in most cases cannot spell, cannot do math, or formulate a coherent sentence. If those are not enough reasons, these individuals all have "attitudes." They expect to get paid for essentially little or no work. Insanity!

We could go on and on about this chaotic situation, which as we all know has been made much worse by the most racially divisive president in the last fifty years, my predecessor. Today, however, I will spend some time elaborating on a solution to this social issue. It focuses on how we dealt with the Indians and their separate-nation status and also the segregation issue.

As I mentioned earlier, segregation was just a term for separation of races. Of the three major historical times in our relations with the blacks, the segregation time was still probably the best of the worlds for the reasons elaborated. There is a word in chemistry—immiscible. It refers to a state of basic incompatibility between two disparate elements. Water and oil come to mind; you

---

[200] Rector, Robert and Rachel Sheffield. "The War on Poverty After 50 Years." The Heritage Foundation. September 15, 2014. http://www.heritage.org/research/reports/2014/09/the-war-on-poverty-after-50-years.
[201] Morrison, Aaron. "Black Unemployment Rate 2015: In Better Economy, African-Americans See Minimal Gains." *International Business Times*. March 8, 2015. http://www.ibtimes.com/black-unemployment-rate-2015-better-economy-african-americans-see-minimal-gains-1837870.
[202] May, Caroline. "Obama Economy: Black Unemployment For Teens 6xs National Unemployment Rate." *Breitbart*. October 2, 2015. http://www.breitbart.com/big-government/2015/10/02/obama-economy-black-unemployment-teens-6xs-national-unemployment-rate/.

can mix the two elements, shake the bottle for a while, and it looks like the two elements have blended, but set the bottle down and the two elements always separate. So it is with our nation. There will always be a separation of races.

What this administration will propose can be traced back to the post-Civil War era when the country of Liberia was created in Africa for the black population in the USA, who were invited to return to Africa. Few did take advantage of the offer, I think, because even then the black race knew that as bad as life was in the USA, it was immeasurably better than Africa. I realize that this will not be the solution. Therefore, we will purpose legislation to Congress, as with the Indians, to set up land, cities, even parts of states as "black reservations." Looking across the USA, there are many urban and rural areas that the blacks even now are the predominate inhabitants of. Once the reservations are established, other races living there will be paid for their properties and will move. Areas such as Detroit, St. Louis, New Orleans, Baltimore, Ferguson, parts of Chicago, all are viable places to establish these reservations. Granted, the cost of the establishment will be in the billions, but folks, we have spent trillions of dollars and still the problem exists.

Once the blacks are established on their reservations, they will have the same separate-nation status as the Indian population. They will have their own local government, their own laws, their own police, their own justice system, their own schools, their own medical facilities, their own industries. In short they will have their own separate society, culture, and individuality. While they will have dual citizenship as the Indians have, those living on the reservations will not have their own federal elected officials. While the Indians can work off the reservations, where land is available, the blacks will be encouraged to establish industries to accommodate their population.

The blacks can also choose to live off the reservations. However, those that choose to do so will have no special privileges in any environment, work, government, school, or private enterprise. In all social settings they will compete with the rest of society on skill levels excluding all government privilege. Discrimination will no longer be a part of the American lexicon, as with diversity, affirmative action, and the like.

While I know the progressives are really howling right about now, this separation of races is the only solution that has a chance of calming the situation in America and allowing the USA to move forward. Folks, as a faithful man, I read the Bible a lot. God made the different races for a purpose. He could just as easily have made only one race of man, but He did not. The races were meant to be separate and most countries are structured along those lines. Race is a structural part of humanity and the nations worldwide. The Chinese do not blend with the Japanese, or the Koreans and vice versa. Even the various tribal nations in Africa rely and cherish their individual identities. So it shall be in the USA. While there will always be crossovers between different races in America and the world, the majority will stay with their own. Diversity is a killer for any society and has been killing our society. It must stop. NO MORE!

With these thoughts I shall close today and wish you all God's blessings. Until tomorrow,

"GOD BLESS AMERICA."

DAY 84: REST

Our Father, Who art in heaven, hallowed be Thy name, Thy kingdom come, Thy will be done on earth as it is in heaven. Give us this day our daily bread and forgive us our trespasses as we forgive those who trespass against us. Lead us not into temptation but deliver us from evil. Amen.

DAY 85: THE INDIAN QUESTION

Good morning, America. Today will continue the examination of another ethnic problem that has haunted our nation since its founding, that is, the Indian question. For over four hundred years we have been dealing with the various Indian tribes in America. Most of our relations have been adversarial and in many ways still are. As with many relationships, myths have arisen as to the goodness, the worthiness, of the Indian opponents and how our side is totally at fault. It is useful to remember historically what transpired, starting from the original colonists in the 1600s. There were many Indian tribes in America at that time. All were adversarial and were constantly at war with each other. The Indian tribes were frankly aboriginal in all ways. None had a written language,[203] eating was done with one's fingers, toilet facilities were unknown, everyone all slept on the ground, and the concept of a house in which to live was foreign to them.[204] The tribes increased mainly by raiding other tribes, killing the men, and taking the women away, making them part of the winning tribe,

---

[203] Rehling, John. "Native American Languages." Indiana University Bloomington Center for Research on Concepts and Cognition. April 5, 1999. http://www.cogsci.indiana.edu/farg/rehling/nativeAm/ling.html.
[204] "Native Americans." English Online. Accessed June 23, 2016. http://www.english-online.at/people/native-americans/native-americans-introduction.htm.

and of course bearing children for the winning tribe. Small children were enslaved and raised as new tribal members. Many of these tribes were cannibalistic. Eating the heart of one's opponent was a warrior's gesture. Scalping was an Indian custom; counting "coup" and hanging the enemy's hair on one's person was a symbol of manhood. The Indian tribes were nomads. They moved from place to place as the weather or game dictated. Their genetic stock was renewed by the tribal wars. All in all, the Indian's genetic stock was primitive, which is why so many died when exposed to the colonists, whose autoimmune systems were vastly superior to the Indians.[205]

The USA and the Indian tribes have fought for hundreds of years. Finally, the US forces won, and the Indian tribes settled on reservations and achieved "separate nation" status. This status has continued to the present day and in many ways has served both the US and the Indian nations well. The Indians have kept their culture—good, bad, or otherwise—they have their own schools, their own laws and government, their own lands, and in many cases their own language. They also have had much access to the US government largesse over the years, in social aids, grants, housing, and other benefits. In the last twenty years, the Indian tribes have even been able to establish casinos nationwide, which have brought tens of billions of dollars annually to the reservations.[206]

---

[205] Adams, Cecil. "Why did so many Native Americans die of European disease but not vice versa?" The Straight Dope, Ask the Master column. July 29, 1994. http://www.straightdope.com/columns/read/995/why-did-so-many-native-americans-die-of-european-diseases-but-not-vice-versa.
[206] Stutz, Howard. "Indian casinos set new revenue record, topping $28.13 billion." *Las Vegas Review Journal.* March 26, 2014. http://www.reviewjournal.com/business/indian-casinos-set-new-revenue-record-topping-2813-billion.

However, life on the reservations has progressed very little in the past hundred years. There was a time up to WWII when the tribes were essentially self-sufficient with farming, industry, and the like. All that has evaporated in the last fifty years. Traveling through most reservations now is like traveling to a third-world country like Mexico. Vast areas of farmland once productive lay fallow. The farm equipment is in the fields, all rusting hulks. The houses on the reservations are generally squalor; the people themselves are unkempt. The Indians at one time valued their hunting prowess, and indeed on most reservations wild game abounds, but the Indians would rather buy their meat at the local grocer. Sad, very sad! Even with the monies coming from all the gambling casinos nationwide, life on the "res" still is third world. Where does the money go? Graft and corruption, I think, are rampant, just as in most third-world countries.

The solution will be, of course, another example of "tough love." The Indian nations will continue to have their hands out for monies unless they are set out on their own. With that in mind, I will be proposing legislation to Congress to decrease all federal largesse to the Indian tribes by 20 percent per year from all government sources. I will also propose legislation for Congress to update the overall treaty provisions that have been in existence over the past 150 years. The separate-nation status is still paramount, but the dependency on the federal government needs to be stopped. The Indian nations have five years to become self-sufficient. The structures are in place, their government entities are there, the social structures are there, even the vast amounts of monies from the casinos are there. What is required is the will of the Indian people to do more for themselves than just exist. Waiting for the government checks at the beginning of each month is not a way of life. The Indian tribes need to revive their agriculture, their industry. The reservations nationwide comprise some of the most fertile land in the USA. They need to attract other industry besides casinos. They need to attract private enterprise unto the reservations. They need to rid themselves of the sloth that has accumulated over the past hundred years. They incessantly talk about the "Indian" culture and their traditions. They need to modernize that culture and move into the twenty-first century. In the final analysis, this is not the USA's responsibility to support the Indian nations, it is the Indian tribes who must control their own destiny.

In the 1970s the federal government gave billions of dollars to Indian tribes in Alaska in compensation for tribal lands taken for use in the petroleum exploration. What happened to the billions? The vast majority was wasted by graft and corruption.[207] Forty years later the tribes in Alaska are little better off. Money is never the answer unless it is earned by industry and hard work. It is the Indians' responsibility to either adapt to the environment and survive or fall by the wayside. The USA will help in the transition but will no longer continue the insanity of endless governmental bailout. Other nations have risen from a much worse environment and have succeeded. I hope the Indian nations will do likewise.

Until tomorrow,

"GOD BLESS AMERICA."

---

[207] Poverty & Race Research Action Council. "Native Americans and Alaska Natives: The Forgotten Minority." *Poverty & Race* 17, no 6. November/December 2008. http://www.prrac.org/newsletters/novdec2008.pdf.

Day 86: The Hispanic Question

Today continues our journey into more elements of the American culture with the focus on another very large social issue, the Hispanic population, especially those migrants who have flooded over our borders in the last fifty years. The blur between legal and illegal is enlarging. Sponsored by extreme progressive legislation and a total neglect of constitutional laws and border security, the Hispanic question threatens the very foundation of these United States.

I choose to use the term "Hispanic" as a global term, pertaining not only to the vast people from Mexico coming across the borders, but also to the rest of Central and South America and the Caribbean. The migrant problem, illegal and legal, has been addressed in prior discussions and the situation is improving, I am pleased to say. The military on the borders, especially the southern border states, has increased our security immensely and will continue to be based on our borders. For today, however, I will limit my discussion to the "Hispanic" question.

The Hispanic question became more and more evident as the US expanded westward in the early 1800s. Many factors led to our expansion; the gold fever was high then, and land for farming and industry abounded. The Louisiana Purchase led to vast areas of what is now the West to become a part of the US. Americans moved westward in droves. These frontier Americans could build a future for themselves with very few restraints (as compared to today). While the Indian nations were a constant threat, another significant factor was the nation to our south, Mexico. Mexico at that time had control over most of what is now the southwestern part of the USA. The closer the US got to the Pacific Ocean, the more acute the problem with Mexico became. We eventually fought the Mexican War and those lands were ceded to the USA.

Historically, most of the countries south of the US were colonies of Spain. Many of the inhabitants of these countries are blends of Spanish blood, Indian blood, and other native stock. Mexico was granted independence in 1821 and has been unstable since. As a matter of fact, in the last two hundred years all these nations south of the USA have remained "third world" and continue to do so today.[208] Other nations in various parts of the world have overcome immense social and political difficulties and emerged as first world. Look, for example, at Japan, which was totally devastated by WWII but has rebuilt to a major economic power in the world. However, that is not so with Mexico and Central and South America. When you visit these countries, the settings are all the same: a small elite class, a very small middle class, and a vast lower class. Governments come and go, tyrants come and go, the currencies rise and fall, and the economies stay the same. Graft and corruption are paramount, and the countries stagnate.

One can, of course, blame the Spaniards and colonization, but that was long since passed, and these nations still are not in the mainstream. I mention this history because for whatever reason, some peoples and some nations never get the picture and improve themselves. What is worse, these peoples get tired of dire straits in their countries and seek to emigrate, in our case, many to the USA. Herein lies the problem, folks: these people flooding our shores are not the best and the brightest. What is worse is that they are bringing their backward cultural norms to this country and infecting our society with these norms. Many,

---

[208] "Countries of the Third World." Nations Online. Accessed June 23, 2016. http://www.nationsonline.org/oneworld/third_world.htm.

especially from Mexico, have been here for generations. They are here for economic reasons only. They have no loyalty to the USA; their allegiance is to Mexico or whatever hellhole they came from. Go to many cities on the US border. You will see people who have been here from Mexico for many generations and are still totally tied to Mexico. English is not the spoken language in these cities and towns. Look around at how many cars there have the Mexican flag on their license plates. Every month billions of dollars are exported back to the families of those living here. Ask any inhabitant of the border towns where they go for vacation; it will not be the USA. I lived in a little town in Florence, Arizona. Originally a very agricultural locale, Florence has had five Mexican families who have lived there over a hundred years — all, by the way, were illegals when they came to the USA. These families still have most of their cultural ties to Mexico, not to the USA. Their children are taught Spanish as a first language.

This migrant issue was generally under control until the 1960s. The USA stopped all immigration for almost forty years. Even with the cessation of immigration, millions of illegals again primarily from Mexico came into the USA after WWII. In 1955 President Eisenhower ordered the mass deportation of over 3 million illegals. This was accomplished in under a year and cooled the situation for another ten years. Those in the progressive world say we cannot deport these illegals today; there are too many and it would disrupt our economy. Well, folks, our economy has been disrupted for almost four decades now. Do you realize that over 25 million jobs in the USA are in the hands of non-US citizens?[209] INSANITY!

---

[209] Greenberg, Jon. "Economist: Immigrants have taken all new jobs since 2000." *Politifact*. December 2, 2014.
http://www.politifact.com/punditfact/statements/2014/dec/02/peter-morici/economist-immigrants-have-taken-all-new-jobs-creat/.

As we discussed before, progressive legislation, primarily the 1965 immigration legislation sponsored by Senator Ted Kennedy, totally opened the floodgates to the USA. In the late 1980s President Reagan was persuaded to sign legislation granting amnesty to over 3 million illegals with the promise that the borders would be closed and that employers would be constrained from hiring illegals. Neither promise became fact, and the floodgates have become a tsunami in the last thirty years. The estimates of illegals in the USA now range from 10 to 40 million.[210] These illegals take over $200 billion a year out of the economy in federal aid programs, from welfare to housing, to unemployment, to schooling, to healthcare access, to whatever.[211]

Folks, the dam has burst and now we must stem the tide and hopefully reverse this insanity. The solutions proposed already, especially the amendments, will do much to stem the craziness. In the interim, let us review the steps we have taken and what actions still are needed. The military is now on the border. The border patrol is now giving out "migrant" tickets to employers who knowingly hire illegals. The deportations at the borders are working. The federal government is currently building four major prison facilities to house the immigrant illegals in this country. As I mentioned before, the first deportation is gratis, the second is a mandatory prison sentence of six months. The third is prison for two years; the fourth is prison for ten years.

---

[210] "Illegal immigrant population of the United States." *Wikipedia*. Accessed June 23, 2016.
https://en.wikipedia.org/wiki/Illegal_immigrant_population_of_the_United_Stat es.

[211] Wooldridge, Frosty. "Staggering Cost Of Illegal Aliens In America: Taxpayers Taken To The Cleaners." Rense.com. April 10, 2008.
http://rense.com/general81/dtli.htm.

I wish to emphasize again that with our military on the borders, any armed illegal will be regarded as a terrorist. The military will use whatever force is necessary to prevent their coming across the border up to and including lethal force. We are at war, folks; we are being invaded daily, except these invaders do not wear uniforms. Their goals are the same, however—infiltrate and destroy the USA. This will be stopped by whatever means are necessary.

The cost of this increased vigilance will be high, but many times less than the economic burdens these migrants are costing the USA. How to contain these costs? We will attack this problem on many fronts. First, I will propose legislation to stop immediately any and all federal largesse to people who are not citizens of the USA. These people can still obtain many benefits of living in the USA but they will pay for these benefits. There will also be costs to house illegals before deportation and prison expenses. Starting in thirty days, the government of Mexico will be presented with a monthly bill for the costs of handling these illegals. If Mexico refuses to pay, various measures will be initiated. For example, effective immediately, all foreign nationals visiting the USA will pay a tariff of ten dollars per person per visit to the USA.

I mentioned that over $200 billion flows back in to Mexico from illegals in the USA. Effective immediately, there will be an excise tax on all monies transferred to parties outside the USA. The tax on noncitizens will be 20 percent of monies transferred; the tax on citizens will be 10 percent. The various private agencies and public—Western Union, US Post Office, CVS—will collect the tax at time of transfer and deposit said monies into the Federal Reserve. Monies in the form of checks and money orders will also be subject to the tax with on the issuance or when cashed.

The above steps will be just the start of various programs that will address the migrant issues. I would recommend logging on to the WH website for further information. I will close by focusing your attention at the banner behind me. It is very explicit as to the situation of migrants into the USA. This is the United States of America, not the United States of Mexico, Guatemala, Saudi Arabia, or whatever. The free ride is over, and we will work to see that it not be reenacted again. Until tomorrow,

"GOD BLESS AMERICA."

DAY 87: THE MUSLIM INSURGENCY

Good morning, America. Today continues our dialogue with you, the American people. This week has been eventful with the politically sensitive topics we have discussed. Today's topic is another highly charged social issue, namely, the Muslim invasion. This topic is sensitive for a number of reasons, not the least of which is that Muslim adherents are the ones who attacked us on 9/11 and are the ones with whom we continually wage war. Again, to start this discussion it is instructive to look at the history of the Muslim movement and get an historical perspective on who these people are and why the Christian world has been in conflict with them for over 1,400 years. The PC crowd does not want to recognize the longevity of this conflict and the fact that here again the adherents to the Muslim belief system are incompatible with all who are not Muslim.

As we start, let us look first at semantics. As a scholar once stated, words have meaning and can be distorted in many ways.[212] The word "gay" used to mean "happy, carefree." Now the meaning is quite different. In the USA and in Europe, freedom of religion is very much a bedrock of society. But we have to be careful in what movements or philosophies we label as "religion." The Muslim movement has made much political gain about being just a "religion" and therefore wanting to be treated with the same tolerance as other, say, "Christian" religions. With the Muslim movement, nothing could be further from the truth. The Muslim movement was never just a religion, it is at the very least a theocracy, believing that all other forms of government and religion are false and should either be subverted to the Muslim way of life or eradicated. Sharia law is paramount to the Muslim adherents; all Muslims, wherever they reside, show allegiance to Sharia,[213] not to any form of other law like our Constitution. Let me make one thing perfectly clear: Sharia law and our Constitution are incompatible.

The Muslims are very cagy in this respect; when confronted with any bias against them, they put on the "religious" garb. When they move to conquer peoples and land, like ISIS, they are the conquering vengeance of Allah, their erstwhile God figure. Many Christian peoples have been propagandized to believe that the Muslim "Allah" is the same as our Christian God. Nothing could be farther from the truth. The Muslim Allah is a piece of rock in Mecca that was worshiped by the pagan tribes before converting to

---

[212] Anonymous. Thinkexist.com. Accessed June 23, 2016. http://quotes.thinkexist.com/quotation/words_have_meaning_and_names_have/177176.html.

[213] "Sharia Law." Billion Bibles. Accessed June 23, 2016. http://www.billionbibles.org/sharia/sharia-law.html.

Muslim. The Muslims claim kinship to the Judeo-Christian origins, and here again nothing could be further from the truth. The Koran, their holy book, is replete with passages about killing the infidels—the Jews and the Christians—wherever you find them. For example, the Muslims do not believe Jesus Christ is the son of God. They believe that he was just a prophet, but Mohammad was a greater prophet.

Historically, Mohammad was a brigand living near Mecca; in other words, he was a highway robber, preying on the caravans that crossed the desert at that time. He began to have visions, probably from drugs ingested, and as his band of cutthroats enlarged, he started conquering areas of the Middle East. He confronted two powerful religions in the area, the Jewish faith and the Christian faith. Being a very practical individual, he decided to add a religious component to his tyranny and conquering armies.[214] Armies guided by a religious aspect tend to be more passionate and bloodthirsty in their approaches. From 632 AD, the Muslim armies branched out and started conquering all the neighboring tribes and nations. They invaded Europe and conquered Spain. Turkey was a very Christian nation at that time, but after the Muslims conquered the nation, they destroyed the Christian churches and built mosques over them. The Christians were either killed or forcibly converted to Muslim. This has been the standard for the Muslims from the beginning; once peoples are conquered, they are forced to either convert to the Muslim "religion," be killed, or submit to slave status in the nation. There is absolutely no tolerance in a Muslim country for any other religion or philosophy.

---

[214] Heiser, James. "A Review of 'Did Muhammad Exist?'" *The New American.* July 13, 2012. http://www.thenewamerican.com/reviews/books/item/12074-a-review-of-did-muhammad-exist.

Much has been made about the Crusades, which were a number of wars fought against the Muslim regimes in the Middle East to free the nations there and the Holy Land from Muslim tyranny. The Muslims had conquered these countries prior and immediately suppressed the people. The fight lasted centuries, and the Muslim onslaught was finally stopped in the fourteenth century. The various caliphates continued their conquering ways, however, branching out eventually into India. They tried to continue into China, but the Mongols stopped them. During these centuries, tens of millions of "infidels"—that is, people who did not believe in Allah—were slaughtered wholesale. This slaughter has continued on to modern times. Almost 2 million Armenians were slaughtered by the Turkish caliphate one hundred years ago because of their religious preference.[215] Look at ISIS today. They are slaughtering thousands upon thousands of non-Muslims in the Middle East and worldwide.

The ongoing fallacy in the West and often espoused not only by political figures and by various Christian churches is that somehow peace can be made with the Muslim hordes and a truce can be negotiated. Nothing could be further from the truth. The Muslim movement has not changed its goals in the entire 1,400 years of existence: conquer the rest of the world and make all "infidels" Muslim and subject to Sharia law. It amazes me to hear so many use the term "moderate Muslims," who supposedly do not believe in the Muslim philosophy already described. Folks, the "moderate Muslim" does not exist and never has. There are only two types of Muslims: active and passive. Much play has been made about the Sunni and Shiite sects of Muslims. The bottom line is that they are both adherents to Mohammad and the Muslim theology. They may

---

[215] "The Massacre of the Armenians, 1915." Eyewitness to History. 2008. http://www.eyewitnesstohistory.com/armenianmassacre.htm.

hate each other, but that hatred is nothing compared to their hatred of "infidels" worldwide. For those of you that would like to read more about the history of the Muslim Movement, I recommend highly the book *The Sword of the Prophet* by Serge Trifkovic. The author has traced the movement to its origins and details specifically not only the atrocities committed by the Muslims over the past 1,400 years but how they are based and encouraged by their holy book, the Koran.

In the final analysis, peace between the Muslim world and our world will never happen. The issue is black and white. Either their world will conquer ours or we will. With this in mind, while we will continue the fight worldwide, I will speak specifically now about the Muslim peoples living in our country.

After 9/11 the USA made a grievous error in how we declared war against the Muslim movement. President Bush tied the war specifically to terrorist groups and nations that harbored terrorists. However, he was in reality not plain enough. The USA is at war with the entire Muslim movement and the peoples adhering to this movement. If you all remember our list of nations that are NOF, many of these adhere to or are controlled by the Muslims. There are no innocents with regards to the Muslims. Any regards otherwise leave our nation open to attack. Witness the horrors of the Iraq War and Afghanistan. The Muslims use not only themselves, but women and children to do their dastardly deeds. They all are indoctrinated from birth and happily strap on bombs and the like to kill "infidels." I have addressed the war outside the USA in detail; now it is time to address the Muslims living in our country.

I have already stated that immigration is to be halted indefinitely from all parts of the world. With the Muslim migrants, not only is entry into our county no longer acceptable, it will never be acceptable in the future. All Muslims who are not citizens of the

USA will be deported within the next six months. The Muslim peoples here will be given ninety days to voluntarily deport themselves back to their nations of origin. After that, they will be involuntarily deported. They will be allowed to liquidate any personal items, such as house and vehicles, before deportation and take the proceeds with them.

Furthermore, any Muslims who are found to be supportive of terrorist groups or have been found to be terrorists themselves shall be subject to trial by military tribunals, and if convicted, imprisoned, or if found to be active terrorists, will be executed. Any mosque in the USA that is found to harbor any terrorists or support terrorist organizations shall immediately be seized and the building razed to the ground. In addition, I am ordering an immediate suspension of any new mosques being built in the USA because of terrorist ties. Any Muslim clergy found to be supportive or have ties to terrorist organizations shall immediately be tried by military tribunal as a terrorist and at the very least deported immediately.

Much has been made of American citizens who have joined Muslim terrorist organizations voluntarily. All such citizens will forfeit immediately any citizenship in the USA. If said individuals are found in combat, they shall be killed as any other enemy. If captured, they shall also be tried by military tribunals and executed for treason. In addition, any families of said terrorists, if found to support their family members in such activities, shall immediately be tried as accessories to terrorist activities and imprisoned were applicable.

Folks, I make no bones about these peoples. They are a cancer in our midst and like all cancers must be eradicated. The allegiance of all Muslims is never to the USA but to Mecca. A recent poll of Muslims in the USA, both citizens and noncitizens, showed over 80 percent want Sharia law and not constitutional law. [216] This is insanity at the very least. To allow migrants into our country who want to destroy our country must stop immediately. Provisions will be made, as in the Muslim countries for non-Muslims, for Muslim citizens of the USA to renounce their adherence to the Muslim theocracy and Sharia law. Said citizens must again swear on our Bible, and not the Koran, allegiance to the USA. As such they may remain in the USA. However, they and their families will be monitored on a regular basis for adherence to our laws.

Lastly, no person of Muslim theology may be employed by any government agency whatsoever and may not serve in any armed forces of the USA. Any Muslims who are so employed now will be immediately terminated and given proper severance pay. No person of Muslim background will be eligible for any security clearance in any private or public industry. Any company with Muslim employees who has dealings with the federal government shall have their contracts suspended until the situation is rectified.

My fellow Americans, we are still at war and will be so for the foreseeable future. We must be vigilant and never let our guard down again. The last event we need as a nation is another 9/11. God bless you all, and

"GOD BLESS AMERICA."

---

[216] Rayne, Sierra. "Massive worldwide support for sharia law among global Muslim community." American Thinker. December 8, 2015. http://www.americanthinker.com/blog/2015/12/massive_worldwide_support_f or_sharia_law_among_global_muslim_community.html.

SECTION 9

AMERICAN VALUES

Day 88: "One Nation under God"

Good morning, America. God's blessing this important week! Today we continue our journey back to sanity with discussions over the next few days on American values, what made us a God-fearing nation, and how far we have digressed as a people, as Christians, and as a nation. As a faithful man, I long ago learned that if you reject God either overtly or covertly, God does not take revenge, He just lets you go your own way, increasingly lost and alienated. This is the pathway we as a people and as a nation have taken for the last fifty years. We had built a truly great nation, the most industrious and powerful in the world, and we have thrown it all away in the name of what? Progressivism, socialism, political correctness, liberalism?

This week we will examine the mainstays of our nation, our foundation as a Christian nation—not a Jewish nation, not a Muslim nation, not a secular nation, but a Christian nation. We will examine the fundamentals of life, what it is to be a male, what it is to be a female, what are our roles for family, for ourselves, and for our country. I will be hosting a conference soon for representatives of the top ten Christian churches in the USA, including the Jewish religion. During this conference we will be addressing many of these issues and how to again make our Christian faith the bedrock of our society. Lastly, we will examine a true gift from God, the work ethic, and how we have abused this ethic and how to reestablish this essential part of our nature as God-fearing humans. All in all, a lot to cover in these speeches. We covered some aspects of American values when we analyzed American culture, which forms from values. As usual, copies of all my speeches are on the White House website, WH2017.org. Feel free to peruse and write your comments on any topic that is pertinent to you, your family, your church, or your work.

In prior talks we have used the historical arena as a basis for discussion and to give us perspective on our current state of affairs. Here too we will use that perspective. From the earliest founding of our country, the pilgrims onward, Christianity in all forms formed the basis for our colonies, to the Declaration of Independence, and our Constitution. It is no accident that our public officials, including the president, swear an oath of office on the Christian Bible. Even on the Supreme Court building are the Ten Commandments. Sad to say with current Supreme Court rulings, either the justices have forgotten what the Ten Commandments say, or even worse, that the Ten Commandments exist. Because I think the Ten Commandments are essential to our future as a nation, I am issuing an executive order that a plaque of the Ten Commandments be placed in each federal government office in the USA and in all our embassies. I urge state and local governments to do the same. Lastly, all public schools should have a plaque of the Ten Commandments. Before I move on, I would recommend a short book by a well-known scholar, Dennis Prager, entitled *The Ten Commandments*. It is very readable for oneself and even instructional for one's family.

As the United States grew as a nation and expanded from "sea to shining sea," our Christian churches expanded also. Our initial colleges and universities were established as Christian institutions—Harvard, Notre Dame, Yale . . . Christian clergy were honored as instrumental in keeping our great nation on track. The reverend Billy Graham was an icon in the twentieth century and a confidant for numerous presidents. Bishop Sheen had one of the most successful TV shows nationally in the 1950s and 1960s. On Sunday mornings both TV and radio were devoted to Christian services.

When one went out on a Sunday, it was not uncommon to see church parking lots full of cars for Sunday services. In our public schools, prayer was not a four-letter word but used very frequently. Before sports activities it was not uncommon to spend a moment in prayer before the game. The Pledge of Allegiance with the insertion "under God" was freely said most days in school.

We as a nation were very proud to be Christian, be that Catholic, Baptist, Lutheran, Episcopalian, or whatever. There are thousands of Christian churches in the USA, all supporting the Bible and following the teachings of Christ.

This Christianity has formed the basis of our value system. We have always been a giving nation; in times of any crisis in the world, the USA is the first to help the misfortunate. After WWII we literally rebuilt the world including even our enemies, helping all to uplift themselves and recover. The Christian missionaries worldwide in the past hundred years have come mainly from the USA. All in all, a lot to be proud of, folks.

However, something happened in the last fifty years of our existence. Maybe it was the material wealth, maybe it was the lack of humbleness before our God, maybe it was pride—which, as the Bible states, "cometh before the fall." The reasons are many; the effects are also many and mostly bad. The Bible, especially the Old Testament, is replete with stories of how the Jewish peoples lost their way before God and became lost for many hundreds of years. History repeats itself, folks, and repeats itself. The seeds of destruction probably were sown many years before, and like infections that linger waiting for the host to weaken internally, become more and more powerful and invasive until the host gets too ill to resist. The progressive and secular movements have been at war with Christianity for hundreds of years and have progressed significantly in the last fifty years of our nation's history. Much has been written about the decline of other civilizations—the Roman Empire, for example—and if we as a people do not stop the spread of this infection, secularism, we too will be written about in the past tense.

Someone once said, "It is not God who is dead, it is the Christian churches." There is much truth to this statement. Starting with the civil rights insanity, where churches became activists and soon forgot their precepts—forgetting their roles in our society—political correctness seeped readily into all the Christian churches, even so into my Catholic church. Vatican II produced both huge and horrible changes to the church, the most horrible of which was the theory of relativism, or the lack of absolute truth, God's truth. Homosexuals were allowed to become priests, opening the doors to sexual abuse in the church, the likes that had not been seen before. The church did away with the Latin Mass, a mainstay of our religion for over a thousand years. Not a ripple from the laity. In 1973 the Supreme Court made that insane and totally irrational decision on *Roe v. Wade*, which allowed the mass murder of babies inside the womb. The decision was especially obscene since it focused not on a life but on the right to privacy, a concept not even mentioned in the Constitution. Again all the churches were silent, not wanting to risk their positions in the US for the sake of God. Tens of millions of babies aborted over the last forty-plus years attest to the abomination of the USA. The fifth commandment, "Thou shall not murder," was abandoned in the USA with the rest of the Ten Commandments. Convenience outweighs humanity. How can we as a Christian nation call upon God when we kill our babies wholesale? Recently, we compounded that error by destroying the other bedrock of our faith, the sacrament of marriage. Allowing an abominable behavior, homosexuality, expressly forbidden in the Bible by God, to have the same rights and privileges as heterosexuality continues the pathway to hell and oblivion. Folks, we are either a Christian nation or we are an abomination; we either follow our God or follow the devil; we are either pro-life or pro-death; we either seek heaven with God or hell with the devil. All this is black and white. There are no compromises in these regards. We as a nation have tried the secular conformist route for the past fifty years, and look where it has lead us. Frankly, our pathway is the title of an old rock-and-roll song by the band AC/DC, "Highway to Hell."

Nations can survive much—war, pestilence, famine, disease, natural disasters. However, no nation can survive the debacle and the aftermath of mass killing of its babies, the destruction of its families, and the abandonment of God. These are the reasons for my campaign to be your president. I do not claim to be a superman, just someone who wants to save our nation, our traditions, and our God fearing.

That is all for today; much more will be said in the following days. I promise you all, you will not be bored. Have a great day!

"GOD BLESS AMERICA."

DAY 89: MEETING WITH THE RELIGIOUS CLERGY

It is 9 a.m. in the ——— room in the White House. The long dining table is filled with representatives of the top ten Christian churches in the USA, plus a representative of the Jewish faith. Each major Christian religion has two representatives: Catholic, Lutheran, Episcopalian, Baptist, Mormon, Methodist, Pentecostal, Church of Christ, Protestant, and Jehovah's Witness. Breakfast is being served before the meeting commences. This mini conference has been in the works for some time. The WH finally coordinated the participants for today's meeting. The vice president has been seated and is conversing with various members of the clergy present. There is a knock on the door and the president enters. He greets all the representatives and everyone sits down.

"Thank you all for coming today," he begins. "I realize that all our schedules are quite hectic, but I assure you your time or mine will not be wasted. Before we begin, will one of you present do an invocation to God to bless this meeting?"

A member of the —— church stands up. "Dear God, bless this gathering of those that follow Your pathway. May we all be guided by Your light to show the world what it means to be a Christian. Amen!"

"Thank you," says the president. He continues, "You have all been listening to my daily speeches concerning many aspects of life in the USA over the past ninety days. One of my persistent themes is, of course, the belief that our country is and always has been a Christian nation, a nation that follows Christian values and beliefs. We who are Christians have been under assault for the past fifty years by the secular and progressive forces within and outside of our nation. Look at our churches—are they full? Look at the people attending. Where are the young families? Where are the young men and women?

"This is why I have called you here today, so that the Christian churches can begin to fight back against the tyranny and the forces of evil that have taken hold of our nation. I know we all have different Christian beliefs and divergent dogmas on Christianity. Those beliefs are your beliefs and are not the purpose of this conference. The purpose of this conference, and what I hope will be just the first of many conferences that we as representatives of Christian people will have in the WH, will be to address the attacks on our faith and to develop a unified front to defend our Christian principles and faith. My hope is that with each conference that you all attend as representatives of the leading Christian churches here in the USA, we can arrive at joint resolutions that we can present to the world at large. These resolutions ideally should center on universal Christian concepts that we all can agree upon. I realize that there are many differences in matters of faith in this room, but we all have the same foundation and the same start, namely, our belief in God and His role in our lives. Before I go any further, I wish to address our Jewish representatives. My comments do not reflect any disparagement on your beliefs. We all in this room acknowledge our Judeo-Christian origins. Our Bible is intimately related to your Torah and is proclaimed daily throughout the world. We here are all brothers in faith and belief in the one true God.

"Growing up in the US, my father was in the military and we traveled much throughout the USA. Wherever we went, no matter how small the town, there was always a Christian church present. It was a very comforting aspect of growing up in our great nation; it showed to me at least that our God was everywhere and that no matter what far reaches of the nation one was in, God was always present. In my inaugural address, I mentioned the priorities in life, God being the first priority. That proclamation still rings true to me.

"There are two aspects of Christian faith that I feel need to be addressed and broadened. In all our churches we readily address our personal relationship with God and how to enhance that personal relationship in our daily lives. That should always be the focus of our faith. However, as you all are aware, the Judeo-Christian heritage is being assaulted everywhere in the world today, not just in the media sense, but even more diabolically in the physical sense. People of faith everywhere are being slaughtered; our churches and synagogues are being razed to the ground. The death toll mounts and the world stands idly by and just watches. There was a time in the past when we actively fought evil and the devil. Now, I think, is again the time for all of us to stand up, united, and become active in the fight. We need to have the same furiousness as the forces of evil and not sit idly by. The progressives and the secular forces are tenacious in their propaganda against the Christian faith. They have infected our schools, our private institutions, our public institutions, our media. We are demonized as being irrelevant, that God is dead, and that a new world order is in place.

"Folks, nothing could be further from the truth. This has been used before and has always been false. It is more infectious now since no counterbalance has been given for decades. Today starts the 'push back.' Today is when we the faithful say, 'NO MORE!' I wish to thank personally the Baptist church for its stand on same-sex marriage after the Supreme Court debacle. We need more of that on a continuing basis.

"We also need to encourage our parishioners to become active in their schools, their churches, their workplaces, their social clubs. They all need to speak out and defend their faith. The laity should know that their churches will support them in these endeavors and especially let them know that they are not alone.

"Reverends and rabbis, we in the West have been fighting the Muslim movement for over fourteen hundred years. Why are they perceived as 'strong' in their faith and we are perceived as 'weak'? Because for over fourteen hundred years their clerics have been calling their faithful to action and continue to do so. Their peoples are extremely active not only with their personal daily prayers to Allah, but also their call to arms. If we are to defeat this evil—and I truly believe that this movement is horribly evil—we need to foster the same activism. Nothing less will win this war against the forces of the devil.

"Now to the main purpose of this conference. There are innumerable themes that we can look for in a united front. I will propose that the first of such resolutions should simply be the resolution reaffirming and upholding the Ten Commandments as God's central guiding force for all Christians and, actually, for the world. I would trust we all in this room can agree on that resolution. The Ten Commandments should proudly be displayed in our churches and synagogues, in our schools, and in our private and public institutions. This insanity into which the US has fallen that the Ten Commandments cannot be displayed in public is an obscenity and needs to be stopped. There will be a hue and cry from the secularists and the progressives, but if we stand firm, we will prevail. The Ten Commandments were given to us by God for all peoples as a guiding light on how we should conduct our lives. The Ten Commandments form the basis for our Declaration of Independence,[217] our Constitution,[218] our framework of governing laws. It needs to be formally recognized as such and defended by all who believe in God.

"A draft of the resolution is in the folder on each of your desks. I will leave you now to discuss the resolution and hopefully finalize the wording. My VP will remain to help direct the discussion. May God be with you all! Together we will restore our Judeo-Christian heritage and help take back our country from the dark forces of evil that roam our land. God bless you all."

On that note, the president leaves the room.

"GOD BLESS AMERICA."

---

[217] "Facts about Declaration of Independence." Help Save America. Accessed June 23, 2016. http://www.helpsaveamerica.com/declaration-independence.htm.
[218] "The Ten Commandments." Kjos Ministries. Accessed June 23, 2016. http://www.crossroad.to/Quotes/law/10_commandments-did_you_know.htm.

Day 90: Future of American Families

Good morning, my fellow Americans. Today we continue our dialogue into the frameworks of our American society and how they have been eroded over the last fifty years. We will start with the bedrock of our society and indeed the bedrock of all societies, the family. The definition of "family" in this discussion is simple — a husband, a wife, and children. Family does not include animals, same-sex partners, multiple partners, live-in partners, gender misidentification, and the like. In short, the family is biblical in nature and purpose. When God told Abraham, "Be fruitful and multiply," this is what He had in mind.

Our family heritage has been under ferocious attack since the "golden" 1960s. This decade was not "golden," but it did herald the onslaught of progressive carnage that has almost destroyed us as a people. Those of you who are older may remember the innocence of the 1950s. The USA was a different place then — churches were full, dads worked, and the moms stayed at home and raised the children. The economy was vibrant, inflation was nonexistent, and the necessities of life were affordable. Imagine a time where a nice car cost three thousand dollars and the average home cost five to ten thousand dollars. The wages were much lower than now, but the dollar bought so much more. Cars were left unlocked; people knew their neighbors. Schools said the Pledge of Allegiance. Christmas was an honored time. Movies with biblical themes — *Moses, The Robe, Exodus* — were big hits in the theaters.

All the above came crashing down during the decade of the '60s. Many blame the Vietnam War, and it did contribute to the ensuing chaos. However, the progressive agenda of societal destruction moved way beyond the war problems. As I mentioned before, much of the turmoil was professionally instigated by agitators sponsored in many respects by the communist regimes with whom we were fighting and still are. What better way to destroy the will of your opponent that to destroy his societal framework? What better way to destroy the family than through its children? Limit the children through abortion and contraceptives, destroy their minds through progressive education, and lastly limit the influence of the Christian churches in the family's daily lives. All these were long-term goals, but how rapidly we have come from the innocent '50s to the new millennia.

The progressive agenda has been incremental but has accomplished much in the last fifty years. Again the idea is to start with small steps, each building on the other, so that soon the whole scene changes. Propagandize the family into needing more material goods and not being able to afford, say, the bigger house or the second car. Add on the diabolical part of science, that of artificial contraception, and suddenly women can limit the size of their families. They can start to work outside the home. Start organizations such as NOW (the National Organization for Women). Harp on about women being second-class citizens. Denigrate their role in the family as demeaning and subservient. Proclaim the sexual revolution both in and out of marriage. With the "pill," women can be as sexually active as they like without any consequences. If married, they can start putting off having children. Instead of three to four children per household, downsize to two or three, then downsize further to one or two. Suddenly, instead of children, countless families are having pets instead—first one dog or cat, then multitudes. Walk in the park on any day these days, and you will see couples walking strollers. One would think that it is a child in the stroller, but you would be wrong. Now the vast majority have their dog(s) in the stroller. As I mentioned before, there are four times as many pets in the USA as children. Where once there were retail stores catering to children's needs, now those stores have been converted to gigantic *pet* stores. Insanity!

The current statistics on the family in America are horrifying. Over 70 percent of black households do not have a father present;[219] 56 percent of Hispanic households do not have a father;[220] 43 percent of white households do not have a father.[221] The divorce rate in the USA hovers around 50 percent,[222] and even more horrifying is that many of our young adults are delaying getting married and an increasing number are deciding to remain single indefinitely. The excuses to remain single are varied, but the bottom line is that increasing numbers of young adults do not see the relevancy of marriage, of children, of religion. They are encouraged by the media to enjoy life; in effect, to not grow up and accept responsibilities. Witness the latest trend in young adults living with their parents well into their late twenties. I am reminded of my own youth. I left home at seventeen to attend college and, outside of spending some summers at my parents' house, have been responsible for my own affairs since then. The thought of

---

[219] NewsOne staff. "72 Percent Of Black Kids Raised By Single Parent, 25% Overall In U.S." NewsOne. 2011. http://newsone.com/1195075/children-single-parents-u-s-american/.

[220] Anderson, Kirsten. "The number of US children living in single-parent homes has nearly doubled in 50 years: Census date." Lifesite News. January 4, 2013. https://www.lifesitenews.com/news/the-number-of-children-living-in-single-parent-homes-has-nearly-doubled-in.

[221] ACT Rochester. "Single-Parent Families." Center for Governmental Research, Inc. Accessed June 23, 2016. http://www.actrochester.org/children-youth/family-support/single-parent-families/single-parent-families-by-race-ethnicit.

[222] Wong, Brittany. "The Truth About The Divorce Rate Is Surprisingly Optimistic." *Huffington Post*. December 2, 2014. http://www.huffingtonpost.com/2014/12/02/divorce-rate-declining-_n_6256956.html.

living semipermanently with my parents is totally foreign to my nature.

The question now before us, my fellow Americans, is how to reverse this horrible trend and reestablish the family unit in America. I have discussed the relevancy of the family and how reversing the same-sex agenda, the free-love agenda, and the pro-death agenda of abortion will do much to ease the pressure on marriage. The bottom line is that in our own family life, in our schools, in our workplaces, in our churches, in our social environments, we all have to start regarding the necessity of family in our nation and in our future as a nation. The birth rate worldwide has been dropping precipitously over the last forty years. Many countries now have a national birth rate of under 2, which is not even reproducing itself.[223] In the USA it is 2.1, but that figure is misleading since it is biased because of the numbers of migrants and their increased fertility.[224] In Europe, the birth rate in the EU is less than 1.5.[225] In Asia, it is even lower. Many nations have been using the migrants to bolster the birth rate, forgetting that these migrants often do not assimilate into the basic culture and, in effect, bring their own culture into the nation. Witness the USA and our migrant problem. The Hispanics are not assimilating; as a matter of fact, they are increasingly keeping their original culture and even their language. Polls are showing that Spanish

---

[223] "Demographics of the European Union." *Wikipedia*. Accessed June 23, 2016. https://en.wikipedia.org/wiki/Demographics_of_the_European_Union.
[224] Howe, Neil. "U.S. Birthrate Falls – Again." *Forbes*. January 28, 2015. http://www.forbes.com/sites/neilhowe/2015/01/28/u-s-birthrate-falls-again/#194cabf3fdd9.
[225] "Demographics of the European Union." *Wikipedia*. Accessed June 23, 2016. https://en.wikipedia.org/wiki/Demographics_of_the_European_Union.

will be the prime spoken language in the USA by the year 2050.[226] Insanity! This must not happen!

In prior speeches, we have addressed some aspects of this decay. I personally believe that an essential component of reversing this trend is to become a God-fearing and revering nation again. Our churches need to come back to the forefront and start stressing the value of family and children. There should be in all churches special Sundays set aside to praise those parishioners who have large families with three, four, five, or more children. Churches need to become more intimately involved in decreasing the rates of divorce in the USA. Churches need to stress the immense necessity, sanctity, and relevancy of marriage not only for the church, but for our nation and mostly for the people involved. Every study sociologically shows that the state of marriage is one of the most stabilizing aspects of society and that the benefits—theologically, medically, economically, and sociologically—are invaluable in the stabilization of the individuals involved and our nation.[227]

While I do not believe that answers to the family lie with government, there are some avenues open to us that may help the situation. I will be proposing to Congress in my tax bill that married couples—and I do stress married—be given tax credits for each of their children instead of a tax deduction. One child equals $1,000 credit, two children $2,000, three children $3,000, four children $5,000, and increasing numbers of children will be at $1,500 tax credit each. Those married couples who do not have enough taxes

---

[226] Burgen, Stephen. "US now has more Spanish speakers than Spain – only Mexico has more." *The Guardian.* June 29, 2015. https://www.theguardian.com/us-news/2015/jun/29/us-second-biggest-spanish-speaking-country.

[227] "Marriage Is Our Freedom." YouTube video, 11:35. Posted July 29, 2015 by Alliance Defending Freedom. https://www.adflegal.org/issues/marriage/marriage-is-our-future.

payable can go back up to five years to offset any taxes due. Also, those married couples who are homeschooling their children will be eligible for a tax credit on par with the above already-stated tax credits. Virtually all studies on homeschooling have shown the immense advantages of such an education, far outstripping those gained in attending regular school.[228] I want to encourage moms everywhere to homeschool their children whenever possible. Your children need you much more than a bigger house, or another car, or another vacation.

I would encourage companies that can establish flexible work schedules for fathers and mothers so as to accommodate more family time to explore such avenues. With technological advances in the computer world and internet, much can be done to enhance family time. In regards to the internet, I would stress to all families that technology cannot substitute for family time. I seriously believe that the internet is an adult tool and all children under the age of eighteen should be restricted and not allowed to use the Net. When almost 45 percent of internet usage has to do with pornography,[229] it is time to rein in its usage. Add to the vast allure of Facebook, Twitter, and other social media among the young, the internet is vastly misused. It is the duty of parents to rein in their children both at home and outside of the home. A cell phone for a child should only be a cell phone; no other features should be allowed. The computer also should be limited, restricting access to

---

[228] Powell, Laura. "Homeschooling Statistics: What Research Reveals About Homeschooling." Bright Hub Education. May 15, 2014.
http://www.brighthubeducation.com/homeschool-methodologies/87123-what-do-the-statistics-say-about-homeschooling/.

[229] "Internet pornography by the numbers; a significant threat to society." Webroot. Accessed June 23, 2016.
http://www.webroot.com/us/en/home/resources/tips/digital-family-life/internet-pornography-by-the-numbers.

insane features named above. Activities such as "sexting" are a parent's responsibility to control.

With that I shall close for today. We have much work to do, America, to bring us back to sanity. To those parents with children, cherish them, guide them, and do not be afraid to say "NO!" They are our future. Tomorrow is Sunday, a time to relax and pray at the church of your choice. Until next week,

"GOD BLESS AMERICA."

DAY 91: REST

Our Father, Who art in heaven, hallowed be Thy name, Thy kingdom come, Thy will be done on earth as it is in heaven. Give us this day our daily bread and forgive us our trespasses as we forgive those who trespass against us. Lead us not into temptation but deliver us from evil. Amen.

DAY 92: WOMEN'S ROLES IN AMERICA

Today, folks, we continue our look at the bedrocks of our society and how each piece of bedrock is being systematically destroyed and dissolved before our eyes. Yesterday we focused on the family and children and their decline in our society over the last fifty years. What is the family, though? It is a man and a woman bound in matrimony and desirous to have children for their future generations.

The progressives knew that to destroy the family, one had to destroy the elements of that family, and like cracks in the basement of a house, the family would slowly dissolve over time. I debated on which side of the equation I should start, either man's roles or a woman's roles. I have decided to start with the woman's role. The answer to why is easy to explain. While I treat both men and women as equals, it is the woman who can procreate, it is the woman who carries the seeds for future generations, it is the woman who will be the deciding factor as to whether any society survives or dissolves. Back in the tribal days it was always the women who survived so that they could bear children for the conquering tribe. So it is today also. The decrease in many nations of the world and their declining birth rates is, of course, that women are not having children. China, because of its perceived population surge, limited forcibly the birth rate of couples to one child per family. Since the Chinese culture has always valued male progeny, the female babies were inexorably killed after birth or aborted before birth. Fast-forward forty years. Now millions of Chinese men do not have Chinese women to start a family. Many travel to other lands to find a wife, but unfortunately, very few women want to live in China. Many wealthy Chinese men pay Chinese ladies living in other lands to have their babies. The Chinese government has had to relent and provide incentives to couples to have female babies. Trouble is, the situation will take many generations to reverse.

Here in the USA, the female was targeted from the beginning as the focal point in the dissolution of the family and ultimately our society. First, as mentioned before, the pill was invented. Initially touted as a way to control menstrual difficulties, it became readily apparent that the pill was highly effective in controlling pregnancy. Women could take the pill throughout their reproductive life and thereby control the amount of children produced.

Once the biology problem was solved, it was shored up by the abortive rights issue proclaimed by the Supreme Court in *Roe v. Wade*. Now, if there were any "accidents," the women had "privacy" rights to abort the baby in their womb. Murder was now legalized in the USA. Sad to say, the Christian churches that could have stopped this evil were silent or had a tepid response. It has been said if the two top churches at that time, the Catholic and the Baptist, had united and refused to allow their parishioners to practice birth control and abortion, *Roe v. Wade* would probably have been overturned.[230] This did not happen, and over the past forty years, as we all know, over 50 million babies have been aborted in the USA, and over 15 million have been aborted to Catholic mothers.[231] The murder continues to this day; over 1 million babies each year are still aborted.[232] Even more tragic is that over 3 million couples in the USA cannot have children and are consistently looking to adopt.[233] Folks, a nation that kills its young will not survive as a nation.

Sad to say, as a population the women in America have bought into this insanity and think that it is their right to either have or abort a child in their womb. More and more women have become infertile because of the abortive processes, and many women have multiple abortions without any thoughts of the consequences. If there are any regrets, the abortion is treated as a tragedy instead of what it is—murder.

Meanwhile, women were harangued as second-class citizens and encouraged to become "independent"; careers in the workplace were touted as the new norm for women. Roles of being a wife and mother were and still are disparaged in all segments of society, in

[230] Mohler, Albert R. "Roe v. Wade anniversary: How abortion became an evangelical issue." On Faith. January 22, 2013. http://www.faithstreet.com/onfaith/2013/01/22/roe-v-wade-anniversary-how-abortion-became-an-evangelical-issue/11238.
[231] "U.S. Abortion Statistics." Abort73. May 25, 2016. http://www.abort73.com/abortion_facts/us_abortion_statistics/.
[232] "Number of Abortions – Abortion Counters." US Abortion Clock. Accessed June 23, 2016. http://www.numberofabortions.com/.
[233] Riler, Keith. "Thirty-Six Couples Wait for Every One Baby Who Is Adopted." Life News. July 9, 2012. http://www.lifenews.com/2012/07/09/thirty-six-couples-wait-for-every-one-baby-who-is-adopted/.

our schools, in our media, in our work environments, in our public institutions, and in our courts. Quotas became the norm; such and such a percentage of women had to be in the workplace. As more and more women entered the workplace, the family suffered. Divorces became increasingly evident and more and more women refused the family and desired other goals in life. Women were encouraged to explore their sexual nature both in and out of marriage. Alternative lifestyles were encouraged. The fight became even more hideous as the progressives targeted the male population for being the root problem in society. Of course, specifically, it was the white male that was the problem.

In the last twenty years, the ramifications in our society are becoming more apparent each day. Less and less people are getting married. There are now more single adults in our society than married, and those that are married are increasingly secular. Look at our churches—you will see some couples with children, but not many. You will see more single women with children, but no fathers present. Of course, you will see increasingly older generations in churches. Not good signs for a society at all. It is even worse in Europe. I was in England, where there are many grand cathedrals. I went to a mass in a giant cathedral in London. The church could hold many thousands of people. There were barely one hundred people in the church. The mosques were full, though!

The heart of this discussion, ladies, is that the future is up to you. After fifty years of "liberation," do you feel any better about yourself? Is it a joy not to have children, not to have a husband, not to have a family? Does the career and independence make up for home and hearth? Why are so many adult women on antidepressant medication? Why are most doctors' visits from women? Why are there so many fertility issues among women? Why are so many women barren? Why are so many bright, beautiful women single and choose to remain single? One of my most favorite female writers, who shall remain anonymous, is beautiful and immensely talented but has remained single all her adult life and is without children. Sadly, she is past the age to have children. My sisters are in the same boat; both chose to be single and without husbands and without children. They are all past childbearing age and, I suspect, are very lonely people.

I call on the women in America to wake up and realize the destruction that has been wrought on your behalf. God designed you for a purpose, and that purpose is not in the workplace, not in the military, not in sports, not in the media. God designed you to "be fruitful and multiply." Your role is also your responsibility. The churches cannot change your direction; the government cannot give you children or purpose, and the media serves only to denigrate you further. Only you can change the direction you and society are heading. I remember an old Simon and Garfunkel song. One of the lines was, "Do you sleep alone when others sleep in pairs?"

Lastly, ladies, examine your roles with the men in society. No matter what the media touts, men are not your enemy. Jesus Christ said it well two thousand years ago: "From the beginning, God made them male and female. It is for this that men and women shall marry." Your tasks are doubly hard, ladies. Not only must you relearn what it is to be a woman, but then you must also teach the men, for they have forgotten also. Your purpose will need to be God-inspired and will need to be profound. Help organize the churches in this fight, fight for traditional schools, fight the media, and let your voices be heard!

I shall close now. Tomorrow we will examine the roles of men in our society. Until then,

"GOD BLESS AMERICA."

DAY 93: MEN'S ROLES IN AMERICA

Good day, America. Our talk today continues and will examine the other essence of our society, the man's role in building and sustaining our nation. Up until the 1960s, the roles of men in our society were unquestioned. The men led our military, our branches of government, our workplace, our schools, and our medical fields. Women would seem to have been relegated to lower roles in society. What was ignored was that there are natural roles for men and women in any society and that these roles are not meant to be higher or lower, but different. The military, for example, is ideally suited for the male physique, not for the female physique. The muscle mass alone points to the male body. The military also is an aggressive force, a protecting force, and not necessarily a building force. That is not a role for women. However, in this age of totally feminine equality, anatomy and physics have little to do in role playing. The progressives have forced virtually every endeavor in which men formerly were the only participants to introduce women into the field. Suddenly women were everywhere, from the military, to sports, to firefighting, to police work. The environment had to be changed to include women, and if they were not included, the courts forced the issue. Of course, given the difference in physiques, accommodation had to be made for the women. In other words, standards were lowered. [234] In the forty years of including women in the above fields, the experiments have totally failed. The military is a shell of its former self. Women are promoted instead of men because of their sex, not their

---

[234] Wiser, Daniel. "U.S. General: Military Will Face 'Great Pressure' to Lower Standards for Women in Combat Roles." *The Washington Free Beacon*. January 12, 2016. http://freebeacon.com/issues/military-face-pressure-lower-standards-women-combat/.

qualifications. [235] Combat conditions deteriorate rapidly when women are present. [236] Sexual tensions abound not only in the military, but in all the above endeavors listed. Sexual conflict becomes the norm. Heaven forbid if someone complains about the female presence; one could be fired or at the very least ridiculed from their positions. In the workplace it is no longer "sexual harassment," it is an "offensive" environment.

Of course, it is the male that is accused of inappropriate behavior. Innocence is no longer presumed; the opposite is presumed. All levels of the men in our society are subject to abuse. Witness Supreme Court Justice Clarence Thomas, almost hounded out of office for a presumed affair with Anita Hill. No evidence was produced, just verbiage, but because a woman spoke, her testimony meant more than the word of Justice Thomas.[237] In the last election, Herman Caine was hounded out of the race because of vague testimony of "inappropriate" behavior with several women happening fifteen to twenty years prior. No evidence was produced, just hearsay, but it was enough to derail his campaign. Similarly, the smear campaign against Bill Cosby, the noted actor, was about sexual harassment on numerous occasions. Each supposed harassment occurred over many years ago, sometimes decades past; all testimony, of course, hearsay, with no evidence produced. Given the state of hedonism in Hollywood, any sexual admissions do not often ring true.

---

[235] "Military Quotas, Preferences." Adversity.Net. Accessed June 23, 2012. http://www.adversity.net/military.htm.

[236] Corombos, Greg. "Lady Marine: Huge Mistake To Put Women Into Combat." WND. May 21, 2016. http://www.wnd.com/2016/05/lady-marine-huge-mistake-to-put-women-into-combat/#!.

[237] Taylor, Stuart Jr. "The Hollywood Hit-Job on Justice Clarence Thomas." *Wall Street Journal*. April 17, 2016. http://www.wsj.com/articles/the-hollywood-hit-job-on-justice-clarence-thomas-1460930701.

Rape has become the common basis in which to harass any male, especially single white males. You would think that all our colleges are cesspools of depravity and that women are being preyed upon and that the vast amount of rapes are not even reported. Yet it was on these campuses that the well-known documentary *Girls Gone Wild*—actually a series of films—was filmed from campuses around the USA. Our schools, our whole education system, now serves to denigrate and demean males from kindergarten on.[238] Is it no wonder that the American male has become so defensive as to be a shell of his former self? Is it no wonder that single, eligible, young male adults prefer to be single and not married? Men increasingly seek refuge from the storm and find little. Even the churches do not recognize the problem and offer little help to their single male parishioners. No mention is made on any Sunday when women come into church with their children, but there is no father present. Sad! I remember in my youth asking that my church sponsor more young adults, men and women, for social gatherings. Unfortunately, all my suggestions were ignored.

What have we as a people wrought for ourselves with this diabolical denigration of our male population? Homosexuality continues to grow as more men question their sexuality. Gender-identification questions abound with the male population. The "metro male" has become commonplace, a PC, sycophantic, nonsexual male who is afraid of his own shadow. Males and also females now commonplace disfigure themselves with full-body tattoos and metal piercings on most parts of the body. Think about this, folks: why does someone disfigure themselves willingly? It points to a basic hatred of oneself, externally and internally. Our whole society has to take responsibility for this killing of the male

---

[238] Annie. "Bias Against Boys?" *PhD In Parenting.* July 12, 2008. http://www.phdinparenting.com/blog/2008/7/12/bias-against-boys.html.

spirit. The media portrays men as either "rapists" or the other end of the scale, as stupid, incompetent people not much removed from Neanderthal species. All "modern" movies never portray the family role for men; they never portray men as fathers, as husbands, as responsible adults.

Folks, the onslaught is taking its toll. Men are retreating into themselves, retreating from their active roles in society. Colleges are increasingly female,[239] and the military actively advertises for the female, the homosexual, the transgender.[240] One study showed that adult males have a decreasing presence in all churches.[241] Catholic males, young singles especially, represent only 23 percent presence in the church.[242] The most common reason—the lack of acceptance and relevancy for the young male. Males are less and less likely to get married, and those who do, do not want to have children. Pets have become the new norm. Men have forgotten what it is to be a father, a husband, a spouse. Toys become increasingly prevalent. The expression "child in a man's body" is very relevant these days.

I am one of the fortunate males who grew up in a traditional household with a father and mother, both very comfortable in their inherent roles and both wanting to perpetuate those roles for their

---

[239] Borzelleca, Daniel. "The Male-Female Ratio in College." *Forbes*. February 16, 2012. http://www.forbes.com/sites/ccap/2012/02/16/the-male-female-ratio-in-college/#10ccc8951525.

[240] Wyant, Carissa. "Who's Joining the US Military? Poor, Women and Minorities Targeted." Mint Press News. December 18, 2012. http://www.mintpressnews.com/whos-joining-the-us-military-poor-women-and-minorities-targeted/43418/.

[241] Grossman, Cathy Lynn. "At nation's churches, guys are few in the pews." *USA Today*. July 25, 2008. http://usatoday30.usatoday.com/news/religion/2008-07-23-males-church_N.htm.

[242] Christoff, Matthew James. "The Case for a Mass Conversion of Men." Catholic World Report. April 6, 2015. http://www.catholicworldreport.com/Blog/3795/the_case_for_a_mass_conversion_of_men.aspx.

children. My father worked two jobs to provide for his family. While he was not a perfect father and husband, there was never any doubt what it was to be a man. Honor, duty, country, church, and family were the essences of his life. Working many days and hours to support his family, there were never any complaints about the lack of material wealth or the lack of opportunity. He worked and saved his entire life. Every day he read the Bible and often made notes for himself. He was an avid tinkerer; he loved machines and engines. He taught himself to repair TVs, and in the evening hours we would find him with his various brands of TVs, getting them to work. Once they worked, he usually gave them away. He was never a businessman. So many of my values and standards in life and, yes, my religious beliefs have evolved from his influence. There were many arguments, and sometimes heated ones, but not a day goes by that I do not miss the "old man." He is with God; of that I am sure.

While it takes much time to build a society, it takes little time to tear one down, and we as a nation have been actively tearing down our foundations. The government has been a prime culprit in this "denigration" of males and our roles in this society. Much of my legislation and tasks have been centered on the reversal of much of this so-called social legislation and civil rights legislation. Much of my duties now and in the rest of my term will be to constantly limit the size and influence of our government, especially our courts. They have been responsible for much of the destruction that our society has experienced.

Where do we go from here, my fellow Americans? That which is being destroyed can be rebuilt! But it will take much work on all our parts. Being a faithful person, I think the churches must lead the way in much of our society in reaffirming the roles of man, woman, and the family. Rebuilding our churches will rebuild our society. As I have been mentioning in prior days, both men and women have fallen prey to the devil of progressivism. It is time to stand up to the forces of evil and recount the truth of whom and what we are. If you are a male, be proud of your sex; you are a *man*. You are not gay, you are not metro, you are not transgender. Be who you are, created by God to be who you are. Be proud of your strengths and, yes, your frailties. You have commanded armies, countries, huge corporations, medicine, and the public domain. You are the originator of countless inventions to enhance humanity. Look at the Nobel prizes over the last hundred years—you have won almost all of them. It is your genius that built America, built our railroads, piloted our planes, won our wars, and shed your blood for our nation. Be respectful, but also demand respect. Reject the rabble on the left that denigrate you and your sex. Honor women for who they are, bearing the future of our nation and the world. Do not succumb, however, to the ridicule and diatribe from any source, even the women. Know that they need your strength, your wisdom, your "maleness." You need their femininity, their succor, their love, and their support. Together you once again can form family units with children and belief in God and save our nation.

With that, I shall close for today.

"GOD BLESS AMERICA."

Day 94: The White Dilemma

Good morning, America. Today's topic continues on the road of "politically incorrect" by addressing the founding race of our country, the white Caucasian race and its continued denigration by the progressive left. Much has been made in the public institutions, media, schools, and government of "white privilege." This euphemism adopted by the progressive left is the rallying cry on all that is wrong with our nation and the people that founded and grew our country. Heck, they even made a "documentary" on white privilege recently, narrated, of course, by an illegal.[243] This ongoing war against the Caucasian race is very political these days and has been the basis for much of the social upheaval in the USA since the 1960s. The black rioting then set the stage for a collective guilt of being white and therefore privileged among all peoples. This white privilege also became the basis for much of the social legislation that has been promulgated in the USA for the past forty years. The quota system, the anti-discrimination laws, the new immigration laws, all have their aims on denigrating the Caucasian race and demeaning our nation as "racist."

School curricula were changed. Our children now are taught that we are a "racist" nation, founded by racists, and that Caucasians were responsible for the minority ills in our nation.[244] Compounded by the horrific Kennedy Immigration bill in 1965, countless millions of third-world nationalities were given preference in getting into our country. European nationalities, who were the basis of our immigration policies for over two hundred years, were forcibly excluded. Instead of European migrants of Polish, German, British, French, and Italian descent being allowed into our country, every third-world nationality gets ahead of the line, along with their extended families. The rules of the "best and the brightest" were thrown out the door. Our nation has been flooded during the past forty years with the illiterate, the

---

[243] Zimmerman, Amy. "'White People': MTV Takes On White Privilege." The Daily Beast. July 20, 2015.
http://www.thedailybeast.com/articles/2015/07/20/white-people-mtv-takes-on-white-privilege.html.
[244] Resmovlts, Joy. "American Schools Are STILL Racist, Government Report Finds." *Huffington Post*. March 21, 2014.
http://www.huffingtonpost.com/2014/03/21/schools-discrimination_n_5002954.html.

uncultured, the sick, the criminal, the lowlifes of the world, all in the name of "diversity."

I mentioned a while back that in the 1960s the white population of the USA was 170 million, or about 80 percent of the US total population. In the past forty years our population has grown to 320 million. The white population is still 170 million, thanks to the migration policies and, of course, the abortion tsunami, killing over 50 million babies in the last forty years, 90 percent of them being white babies.[245] The extra 150 million population of the USA are from third-world countries. Folks, we have changed the racial makeup of the USA to point of irreversibility. We are in danger of becoming a third-world country ourselves. These millions of migrants, many of whom are illegal, do not assimilate into our culture, our language, our way of life. I ask you all, do you want English to be the second language of the USA? Currently nearly 70 million people in the USA do not speak English.[246] Do you, if you are of European ancestry, want to be relegated as a minority? Is the USA to remain true to its heritage as a God-fearing, Christian, European-ancestry nation or an amalgamation of whatever and all not well to the good?

For forty years we have become a collection basket of not the best of any nation but the worst of the lot. Every other nation in the world has high standards of whom they allow into the country. Canada, for example, had extremely strict guidelines on who can not only enter but stay in Canada; wealth, health, social status, and education are all standards for getting into Canada. Canada makes itself clear: no riffraff allowed. I would recommend an excellent

---

[245] "U.S. Abortion Statistics." Abort73. May 25, 2016. http://www.abort73.com/abortion_facts/us_abortion_statistics/.

[246] Barron, Lisa. "Census: Non-English Speakers in U.S. Nearly Triple in 30 Years." Newsmax. August 7, 2013. http://www.newsmax.com/US/english-language-speakers-report/2013/08/07/id/519251/.

book by the infamous author Ann Coulter, *Adios, America*. As usual, Ms. Coulter has ripped the facade off the immigration problem and exposed the progressive agenda for what it has become, a radical transformation of the USA into something nobody will want or recognize.

I have talked about my European heritage before. All my grandparents came through Ellis Island and made their mark in the USA. As a second-generation American, my allegiance is to the USA. I am not Polish American, just American. I speak English, not Polish. While I acknowledge my ancestry, America is what defines me, not Poland. I pledge allegiance to the American flag, not the Polish. I think it is time for people of European ancestry whose forefathers came to America in the last 250 years to stand up and fight for the makeup of our country. This country is not Mexico, not Pakistan, not China, not Japan, not South America, not Africa, and our population should not emulate those nations. If people want another nation, let them migrate to that nation and go back to that culture. I am proud to be an American, and I have no desire to be in any other culture.

Part of the problem, folks, is that we have forgotten our heritage and need to remember our heritage—our forefathers who created this great nation and the ancestors who have died for our country.

Let us take a few moments and look at some of the contributions our white forefathers have given to this country:

Who wrote and signed the Declaration of Independence? White males.

Who wrote the Constitution? White males.

Who wrote *The Federalist Papers*? White males.

The first forty-three presidents were . . .? White males.

In WWII the USA had 405,000 casualties; 99.4 percent were white males.[247]

During the Civil War, fought to free the slaves, 350,000 casualties were sustained; almost 100 percent of them white males.[248]

Who had probably the most prodigious mind ever? Einstein, a white male.

Who invented the Polio vaccine? Salk, white male.

The most famous generals for the USA? Washington, Jackson, Grant, Lee, Pershing, MacArthur, Eisenhower, Patton, Bradley, LeMay, Nimitz—all white males.

The greatest American inventors—Whitney, Colt, Winchester, Browning, the Wright brothers, Edison, Tesla, Bell, Frank Lloyd Wright—white males. These inventors have given America guns, ships, petroleum, glass containers, cars, trains, electric power, the telephone, the telegraph, the toilet, and, most important, toilet paper. The list is again endless.

Penicillin, the greatest antibiotic ever—discovered by Fleming, a white male.

The greatest entrepreneurs—Ford, Rockefeller, Carnegie, Mellon, Vanderbilt, J. P. Morgan, Gates, Buffet—all white males.

Look at the Nobel prizes awarded the past hundred years. The vast amount of the recipients (95 percent) white males.[249]

---

[247] "By the Numbers: The US Military." The National WWII Museum of New Orleans. Accessed June 23, 2016. http://www.nationalww2museum.org/learn/education/for-students/ww2-history/ww2-by-the-numbers/us-military.html.

[248] "Civil War Soldiers: Information and Articles About Soldiers from the Civil War." History Net. Accessed June 23, 2016. http://www.historynet.com/civil-war-soldiers.

[249] Duggan, Oliver and Peter Spence. "How the Nobel Prize Has Favoured White Western Men for More Than 100 Years." American Renaissance. New Century Foundation. October 8, 2014. http://www.amren.com/news/2014/10/how-the-nobel-prize-has-favoured-white-western-men-for-more-than-100-years/.

The above is just a smattering of the contributions the Caucasian race, and most specifically the Caucasian male, has made to the USA growth and development. If we add the European white, and most specifically again, white males, the list becomes even larger. Virtually all advancement of the sciences for the last thousand years have been started, invented, and promulgated by the Caucasian males. No other race in the history of mankind had contributed more to the well-being and advancement of the whole human race.

The recital of the above is necessary to remind us, America, who made this country great. Yes, there have been minority contributions, but they pale by comparison. The life we have these days in the USA was created by white men accomplishing extraordinary deeds. This is our heritage, an American heritage, not a Mexican, not a Chinese, not a Latin American, not an African, not a Japanese heritage, but an American heritage. If we do not wake up, America, that heritage will be cast aside, and the follow-up will be ugly.

Tomorrow, we will continue our profile on America with the topic of work. Until then,

"GOD BLESS AMERICA."

SECTION 10

WHERE DO WE GO FROM HERE?

Day 95: The Christian Work Ethic

Good morning, America. As the new week develops and those of us that are working look forward to being productive, we will celebrate that truly Christian ethic, that is, the nobility and dignity of an activity given to us by God, which not only defines us, but if truly followed keeps us on the path to our Creator—the work ethic, or WE. I have recently read a wonderful book by Michelle Malkin called *Who Built That*. She recounts the stories of a number of entrepreneurs in our nation who changed the course of millions of lives and represent some of the best minds in our society. It is worthy to note that the book is about men, industrious men, whose inventions and products still bear their names a hundred years after their deaths, which still are used even to this day. Scott tissue, Libbey glass, Westinghouse Electric, Hires Root Beer—the list goes on and on.

I use this illustration because another one of the diabolical effects of the progressive movement over the last sixty years is the destruction of the work ethic. The progressive model of incrementalism is alive and well and eating away at the America you and I grew up in. I started working at the age of ten. I discovered that returning glass bottles to the store earned me money. So after school I put a pillow in my cart and went up and down the street and fields looking for glass bottles—soft drinks, beer bottles, whatever. I could earn up to five cents a bottle. I did not think it was demeaning work, only that for the first time in my life I had money and I was earning money every day. My piggy bank became full rather rapidly and so I bought another, then another. I was living with my aunt and uncle at the time; they thought my endeavors were degrading, and what would their neighbors think seeing me walking the streets looking for bottles?

I basically ignored them and went out every day, earning money by honest labor. Thankfully, when my dad found out about my venture, he encouraged my initiative and made sure that I saved most of my earnings for schooling. I still remember the thrill at the age of ten, having my own money, being able to buy something without asking permission. I started a ledger on my earnings and every Sunday remembered to put my tithe into the church offering.

That small beginning led to my next venture, my paper route, which supported me throughout high school. I built up a sizeable base for newspaper delivery, but it was a taxing venture. There were no holidays, and papers had to be delivered every day, seven days a week. In addition to delivering I had to collect my monies. I quickly learned about cash flow, revenues and expenses, and how to make a profit. I had to pay the newspaper company each week for the papers delivered. If I did not collect enough to pay for the papers, I had to go to the bank and get my savings in order to pay my bills. This I never had to do, since on Saturdays and at nights I was diligent in going to my customers to collect monies due. I also learned the meaning of service, since I would get tips for good and dependable paper delivery. High school was the time for studying and work, but no frivolity. No sports, no social life were in my life. On days when school was closed for snow, I went around shoveling driveways and sidewalks for extra money. My family was poor then; many times my mother had to borrow money from me to pay or buy something essential. The monies were always paid back, but it did teach me the value of having money to support myself. My free time, if any, was spent in the woods, hunting and fishing and exploring. I bought my first shotgun with my earnings, my first rifle with my earnings, my first fishing pole, my first hunting boots. Back then one could buy surplus arms through the magazine. By the time high school had ended I had amassed a sizeable amount of firearms. They were all locked in my closet and my parents knew about the firearms, but I was always a responsible person.

College was also a time for working. While many students had their parents paying for their schooling, I paid my way through college with savings, part-time work, and borrowing.

Two interesting stories about my college days—when I was getting my advanced degree, I ran out of my savings. A friend convinced me to go down and apply for food stamps. I went down to the welfare office in Phoenix. Standing in a long line, I remember looking at all the other people, all destitute, all relying on government largesse even then. After about a half hour, I said to myself, "This is not me!" I went back to campus, went to the human resources department (which ran a part-time employment listing for college students), found a part-time job doing accounting for a mortuary, and was hired the next day. I stayed on the job until I graduated.

The other interesting story was when I graduated. The country was in a recession then, and jobs were not commonplace. Again I had choices. I read a newspaper article about the Alaskan Pipeline and that jobs were plentiful in Alaska. I bought an old PU truck, and my brother and I drove up the Alaskan Highway (1,200 miles) to Anchorage, Alaska. I found a job within a week and stayed there for almost six years working and saving.

The point of these stories, America, is not to regale you with my hardships in life; we all have a certain amount of hardship. The beauty of the work ethic is that those who love to work always know that there are jobs to be had, if you are industrious enough. It may not be the job you are trained for, it may not be the job you want or desire, but it is work and if it puts food on the table and a roof over your head, it is an honest day's work. The trouble is in America today, government largesse is everywhere. Depending on the state you are in, any unemployed person can receive up to $40,000 in goods and goodies from the government.[250] That amount of money is a tremendous disincentive to go out and get a job. It becomes a situation of "Why should I work? I get all this from the government." As with all government largesse, the effects are always to the detriment of the individual by hampering better pathways in life. Minimum wage is another abomination. There is not one company that does not promote from within. One may start at the bottom rung, but if you have a WE, promotion comes rapidly and with promotion comes a better standard in life. McDonald's, Home Depot, Lowe's, and Costco are all multinational corporations that promote heavily from within.

Folks, the "entitlement" policies of the federal government over the past eighty years has eroded the work ethic tremendously. Starting with FDR and his Social Security, the idea of "retirement" and living the good life without worries has become the mantra over the last years. When FDR and Congress passed SS, there were forty workers to support each SS recipient; currently there are fewer than three.[251] Soon it will be even less. Where will the entitlement money come from? Americans, instead of saving for their children and grandchildren, the "golden years" became the goal. Everywhere one looks, the media, the government, they no longer stress the greatness of work but 401K plans, SEP IRA, Roth

---

[250] Swoyer, Alex. "Food Stamp Use at All Time High Despite Eight Year Low Unemployment Rate." *Breitbart*. March 2, 2016. http://www.breitbart.com/big-government/2016/03/02/19-million-more-americans-on-food-stamps-despite-low-unemployment-rate/.

[251] "Ratio of Social Security Covered Workers to Beneficiaries Calendar Years 1940-2013." Social Security Administration. Accessed June 23, 2016. https://www.ssa.gov/history/ratios.html.

IRA, whatever. Americans have been very covertly inculcated into thinking of "work is a chore; retirement will be my golden time." Insidious at best, the mentality of all Americans thus has been steadily changed to embrace the "entitlement" mantra: SS, Medicare, and pension plans are all entitlements from the government, making masses of our population dependent on the government for their security and financial well-being. Any politician who even mentions decreases in any government entitlement, especially for the retired, will immediately be shouted down and vilified. Even if there is only one worker to support the entitled, they will demand the support. Look at what has happened in Greece—fewer workers with more and more entitled; the system is broken, but the entitled do not care. They want their "goodies."

FDR's programs were increased dramatically during the wild 1960s with the implementation of more entitlement programs: Medicare, welfare, food stamps, disability insurance, housing assistance, federal mortgage programs. The list seems endless. But the main effects still stand—more and more Americans have lost the work ethic and are beholden to the government. Fast-forward to the new millennia; 93 million Americans permanently out of work and on the dole,[252] 25 million Americans on some sort of "disability,"[253] 50 million Americans on welfare.[254] In FDR's time

---

[252] Jones, Susan. "Record 94,610,000 Americans Not in Labor Force; Participation Rate Lowest in 38 Years." CNS News. October 2, 2015. http://www.cnsnews.com/news/article/susan-jones/record-94610000-americans-not-labor-force-participation-rate-lowest-38.

[253] Hargreaves, Steve. "Disability claims skyrocket: Here's why." CNN Money. April 11, 2013. http://money.cnn.com/2013/04/11/news/economy/disability-payments/.

[254] Jacobson, Louis. "Are there more welfare recipients in the U.S. than full-time workers?" Punditfact. January 28, 2015. http://www.politifact.com/punditfact/statements/2015/jan/28/terry-jeffrey/are-there-more-welfare-recipients-us-full-time-wor/.

the life expectancy was seventy, today it is over eighty-five and rising.[255] More and more Americans will have twenty to thirty or more years of entitlements. Where is the money coming from?

I have mentioned in prior talks steps we will be taking to decrease the entitlement programs. The solution to the work ethic though needs to start with the family, folks. Tomorrow we will continue our discussion on how we can change our society back to the vibrant work-oriented and God-oriented society we once were. Until tomorrow,

"GOD BLESS AMERICA."

DAY 96: REBUILDING THE WORK ETHIC IN AMERICA

Good morning, America. I hope you are fired up today, for I am. The WE is a topic that is dear to me and to our nation. How to reinstall the WE into our society is a complex topic, but we shall get some ideas across to you all. As I mentioned through these lectures, the family is the foundation of our society. Children have to be shown and embrace the WE from an early age. Those of you who have children, if you give them an allowance, tie it into some work—cleaning their rooms, doing chores, reading books, mowing the lawn, whatever. Make them aware that money is to be earned, not gratis. If a child earns a dollar, make sure that on Sundays, 10 percent is given to the church. Some of their allowance should be saved for future purchases. If they want something they need to save for that something. Children learn fast that effort will mean rewards, namely money. I knew from an early age that I needed to

---

[255] Copeland, Larry. "Life expectancy in the USA hits a record high." *USA Today*. October 9, 2014.
http://www.usatoday.com/story/news/nation/2014/10/08/us-life-expectancy-hits-record-high/16874039/.

save for college; that was part of my "growing up" period. Children also learn the entrepreneurial spirit very early on. Many children start enterprises when young and very often are successful at those enterprises. I can use myself as an example.

Parents also need to instruct their children on the basics of living in the world: finances, work, debt, taxes, and the like. Children also need to be aware that college is not for everyone. Many have successful careers without college. Bill Gates, the richest man in the world, never went beyond one year in college. As a matter of fact, most of the billionaires in the world who earned their billions do not have college degrees. I credit the Mormon church for their missionary work enabling their young adults after high school to do two years of missionary work in various parts of the world. Not only do these young adults mature quickly, they many times learn a second language and learn a skill in those two years.

The military remains one of the best vocational learning institutions around. Two to four years in the military matures all who go that route. Not only do these young adults learn skills, save money, and are prepared to enter the work force well ahead of any college student, they are mature beyond their years. There have been many studies showing that young adults who go to alternate learning areas mature much more rapidly than the college route.[256] Besides, after four years learning a skill set, they are also more marketable than any college graduate. Fifty years ago college was not for everyone; as a matter of fact, most graduating high school did not go to college. The progressive mantra over the last fifty years has put forth the falsehood that college is the only way to prosperity. Balderdash! Most of the inventors did not go to college;

---

[256] Gordon, Jillian. "Why I'm telling some of my students not to go to college." PBS Newshour. April 15, 2015. http://www.pbs.org/newshour/updates/im-telling-students-go-college/.

most successful entrepreneurs did not go to college. College unfortunately teaches one to be a "worker bee" and not an independent person. The McDonald's corporation, for example, has their own management course to promote from within. Graduates end up running a franchise and are well-paid for their services. Many end up owning their own franchises and becoming quite wealthy. The additional benefit is monetary—while gaining the skills, they are paid as they learn and do not incur the debt the college graduates take on.

One last note on college, parents. I knew from the onset that if I went to college I would need to pay my own way. My parents were too poor to help pay my college. It is insanity for the massive numbers of middle-income families to incur tens of thousands of dollars of debt to send their children to college. College is not a rite of passage to adulthood and should not be treated as such. At the most, parents should pay for tuition and books only; all other expenses should be borne by the student. If the child does not get good grades the first year, all support is forfeited.

Trade schools should be enlarged for the young adults in high school. Skills should be taught in these schools that will enable young men and women to function in the real world. Teenagers in high school should be encouraged to find some type of part-time work as soon as possible. Many companies are always looking for extra help and are willing to start a teenager on the right pathway. Parents need to prioritize life's pathways for their children. Instead of focusing on esoteric activities like sports and music lessons, focus on the real-world possibilities. I know this is anathema to many parents who see their child as the next Van Cliburn or Wilt Chamberlin or the next Pete Rose. Folks, these are dream cases and not applicable to the world at large.

There was a time not long ago, America, when our work ethic made us king of the world. "Made in the USA" was a symbol of pride. This sign was present in many retail outlets—Walmart, for example. Look at items manufactured in the USA up until the 1960s. The workmanship was remarkable, whether it was furniture, cars, weapons, appliances, whatever. Breakage was never a problem. I remember well the TV ad showing the Maytag repairman, sitting in his shop with nothing to do because Maytag appliances never broke down. Not so in these days! Now everything has to have a warranty to cover the item not being made well. Detroit was the most famous city in the USA up until the 1960s. Our vehicles were the best in the world. Today Detroit is a decaying wasteland, a bitter testimony to our loss of the work ethic and a symbol of what was and now is not.

America, we have to awaken and take back our heritage. Our government will not do it for us, sad to say; even our churches nor our schools will help. All journeys start with small steps. Encourage your children along the right pathways, to be inquisitive, to be looking at the world and what they can do to improve their lot or their world. I am reminded of a fisherman I met in California. He loved to catch large bass in Lake Castaic. He made his own lure, a very large lure, twelve to fifteen inches long. He painted it to imitate a trout and started to catch very large bass, fifteen to twenty pounds. People wanted to buy his lures. So he patented his design and started a small factory making these lures. Fast-forward, his lure sells like wildfire and is the lure that caught the world-record bass in California. The fisherman is very successful and employs a number of people to help build his lures. A hobby turns into a very lucrative business. His main complaint is that he does not have enough time to go fishing!

Invention, folks. We as Americans always have had the spirit of invention in all walks of industry. We need to invigorate that spirit again. When we encourage our children and ourselves to see other possibilities, we start the process of invention all over again. It does not matter how many times we try to invent something, most maybe will never see the light of day, but once in a while something will click and endless possibilities result. The human mind, body, and sport were created by God for endless possibilities, since we were all "created in His image." The mind is a most powerful tool. Someone once said, "If you can imagine it, it can be accomplished." We need to start again, America, to renew the spirit!

Lastly, I would encourage all those who are in the second half of their lives. Do not quit! If you retire from one career, start another. Stay active, and invest your time and talents into being productive. Learn a new trade, enhance your skills. The world is open to possibilities. The more you continue to embrace the work ethic, the more fulfilled you will remain. The possibilities are endless. When I was in medical school, a retired couple lived next to me. The man was very good with his hands. He and his wife would go out each weekend and buy furniture in disrepair. He would take the items home and repair and refinish the items. He then would sell them at his garage sale. He made a decent living and enjoyed his work. Many times people would bring their furniture to him gratis and he would repair and refinish the items and resell them. Again, entrepreneurs making the world a better place and earning a profit besides. Challenge yourself, folks. See how well you can live without using the SS. Put that money away in a bank. The longer you can earn a living, the longer you are productive, the better our country will be and, most importantly, the happier and healthier you will be.

Until tomorrow, folks.

"GOD BLESS AMERICA."

DAY 97: NASA REVIVAL

Good morning, America. Today I will continue on rekindling the spirit of America and our heritage. I am reminded back in the 1960s, with all its turmoil and upheavals, the spirit of possibilities still prevailed in America. An American president sounded the clarion, JFK, and pushed us to points beyond our imagination. To those who were not alive then, JFK represented the best and the worst of America and her people. I will not dwell on the bad side, for to me the one goal he inspired for America went beyond our borders, beyond our earth, into the realms of science fiction. He challenged America to land a man on the moon before the decade was out. NASA was a nascent organization then. We were just entering into the outer space realm; to go to the moon and return seemed like a feat beyond the capacities of any nation.

This was America, though, the time for the "best and the brightest." While chaos reigned in our streets and society was coming apart, the path to the moon never wavered. Rockets were developed, and suddenly we were circling the earth; more and more missions in space came about. Missions were designated— *Mercury, Gemini,* and finally the *Apollo* missions. It seemed like a few days and the mission to the moon with the three astronauts was a go. For a little while, the nations of the world collectively held their breath. So many things could have gone wrong. We had mission after mission fail, but on this day, July 20, 1969, while the world watched, man landed on the moon. The films were mighty— Neil Armstrong stepping off the shuttle onto the moon and saying those famous words, "One small step for man, one giant leap for mankind." All would never be the same after that day. Other *Apollo* missions proceeded, some ending in tragedy, some near tragedy, but on that day in 1969 we as a nation had shown the world what possibilities were and what man can do with the gifts God has given us.

Unfortunately, along with so much of our inner resolve as a "can-do" nation, the space program over the years steadily degenerated into a shuttle service. With the explosion on the *Challenger* and the loss of the seven astronauts, it seemed the will to explore and go beyond evaporated. It is ironic that it was during this time frame that science fiction exploded in the media of America. The *Star Trek* movies were instant hits. TV's *Star Trek: The Next Generation* also was an audience favorite, and *Star Wars* continued the fantasy. The stars continued to beckon, but the means were not there. This coincided with the massive increase in our "entitlement" government, and the monies were diverted to those efforts. Finally, NASA was eviscerated into a shuttle service to the space station, private enterprise started building rockets, and NASA became a mouthpiece for the Muslim Brotherhood? [257] Insanity!

While I do not claim the oratory of JFK, I can still use his example to reignite this imaginative aspect of American spirit. NASA will emerge from its ashes like the phoenix bird and reclaim its rightful mission as the instrument of space exploration. I am calling for two very special missions for NASA. The first mission will be to establish a permanent moon base in five years by the year 2022. This moon base will be expanded into a lunar city within ten years and then hopefully into a number of lunar cities. Folks, the moon has untold potential, not only for exploration but also as a station for future space missions into our solar system and beyond. The

---

[257] "Obama cuts US space program, orders NASA to work with Muslim countries." *Creeping Sharia*. February 17, 2010. https://creepingsharia.wordpress.com/2010/02/17/obama-cuts-us-space-program-orders-nasa-to-work-with-muslim-countries/.

moon will be colonized in our lifetime. As our ancestors explored the Wild West in the 1700s and 1800s, so we shall explore the moon and harvest its unknown bounty. The scientific discoveries awaiting us can only be imagined. Just using the moon as a base for a new telescope far beyond the Hubble telescope will open vast reaches of our universe. I will be proposing a $50 billion budget each year to enable this program. While *Star Trek* was a fantasy, the moon base will be a reality very soon.

And that is just the start, my fellow Americans. The second mission for NASA will be even more monumental and ambitious. Once the moon base is established, we will use that platform to launch our mission to the planet Mars. Our goal will be to land men on Mars in ten years by the year 2027 and even more ambitiously establish a base on Mars by the year 2032. These endeavors may also seem in the realm of fantasy, but we as a nation, inspired by God, have always taken the "impossible path" and made it possible. Such will be our task now. These missions will be fraught with risk, as were our earlier missions in the 1970s and into the 1980s, but mankind grows by taking risks, by exploring, by always looking beyond. We have much going for us. America has always lead the way in new ventures and will do so now. Technological knowledge has exploded since the days of the *Apollo* missions, and we will use that knowledge to start the exploration of our solar system. Mars is extremely close to our planet in makeup. Who knows what riches await us there and what opportunities to expand our knowledge of the universe.

These missions will move our nation beyond what we have become. Each night when you look at the stars, the moon, the planets, let your imagination run wild. It is conceivable that your children or grandchildren will be walking on another planet, be exploring space, be piloting a spacecraft, or possibly colonizing another planet. The fantasy will become real, folks. It will take much work and dedication for every one of us as a nation, as a people, and as an American society. These missions are uniquely American. I know of no other country on earth that has the God-inspired faith; mental, emotional, and economic strength; or the "can-do" spirit to accomplish these tasks. Pray to God for our success and we will prevail. God bless you all, and

"GOD BLESS AMERICA."

DAY 98: REST

Our Father, Who art in heaven, hallowed be Thy name, Thy kingdom come, Thy will be done on earth as it is in heaven. Give us this day our daily bread and forgive us our trespasses as we forgive those who trespass against us. Lead us not into temptation but deliver us from evil. Amen.

DAY 99: ALMOST THERE

"Two roads diverged in a yellow wood, and I took the one less traveled by . . ." —Robert Frost

Good morning, America. Today and tomorrow mark the completion of my first hundred days in office. While it marks the end of my initial promises to you, the American citizenry, it is really the beginning of our journey back to reality, back to the promises of our forefathers, back to the Constitution, back to our families, back to the "can-do" American spirit that built this nation, and most importantly, back to our churches and God.

WHERE DO WE GO FROM HERE?

During these next two days I will try and sum up the more salient points of our discussions these past three months. All my speeches are on our website, WH2017.org, for you all to review and also make comments. There is also a wealth of backup data with links from our website where you can research your favorite topics both good, bad, and otherwise. As I have stated on numerous occasions these past months, I would urge all American citizens— I am not really interested in hearing the opinions of noncitizens— to contact your government officials, your church leaders, friends, and family. Encourage them to vocalize their opinions also. Bombard the website of the federal, state, and local officials with your comments, opinions, and action items. It is only through you, the people, that we can retake and restore our great nation.

As we sum up today and tomorrow the progress and barriers to our agenda to reform America, I will also bring you up to date on those relevant topics that the media has been hiding from the American public, mainly because the topics do not fit the progressive agenda.

With this in mind let us start with the grand action that the states have been wrestling with the past three months and before, the Constitutional Convention. I am happy to announce as of now twenty-five state legislatures have ratified the approval of the convention process and will be sending delegates as soon as a quorum of states is reached. As we talked about, thirty-four states need to ratify through their state legislatures the convention resolution. Once that number is reached, the convention is a go, and the site can be chosen ASAP and the date for the convention can be set. Given the huge momentum for this convention, it is highly likely that within the next three months, the quorum will be reached and the convention will be held this fall. I would again urge those of you who have not read Mark Levin's book, *The Liberty Amendments*, to purchase a copy and acquaint yourself with the amendments he proposed. You can review my speeches over the first thirty days in which I added my own second Bill of Rights amendments as well as highlighting Mr. Levin's suggestions. Folks, I need to reiterate, these amendments are not cast in stone. They will be debated as others will be debated at the convention. Whatever amendments the delegates decide upon will be sent to the states for final ratification.

Again, the beauty of this process, my fellow Americans, is that Washington has no say in the convention process, not Congress, not the president, not the Supreme Court, not anyone in the judicial branch, either state or federal. This convention will truly be the convention of the American people, not the government. You will be getting bombarded by the powers that be who will cajole, threaten, and beg you to oppose this convention. They will state that this will be the end of the USA. All *lies*, my fellow Americans. It will be the beginning of the end of the progressive agenda and Big Government that has infected our country these past sixty years. The convention will the "shot heard around the world" and will herald the return to the USA that once was and has almost been obliterated.

I, and this administration, await eagerly the day that the quorum is reached. Those of you living in states that have not passed the legislative approval, I would urge you all to contact your state representatives and demand their support for this convention. The progressive representatives will, of course, hem and haw to stop the vote. But if you, the American people, keep up the pressure, the convention will prevail. The day the quorum is reached will mark our second Independence Day and mark the day we took back our country. The day is coming, America. Pray for our country!

The next topic I would like to discuss is also vitally important to the welfare, security, and future of our country, namely, the securing of our borders and the removal of the illegals who have infiltrated our country over the last twenty to thirty years. I am happy to announce that our southern borders—Texas, New Mexico, Arizona, and California—are virtually secure. Over a thousand miles of border fencing is in place. The marine base at Camp Pendleton has been reinforced by a division of marines, who are patrolling the California-Mexico border on a daily basis. The army base at Sierra Vista, Arizona, Fort Huachuca, has also been reinforced with another division of army personnel. The Arizona border along with the California border were especially porous. Both borders have been effectively secured. In both places there have been a number of battles between the US military and illegal "terrorists," much to the detriment of the "illegal" forces. Fort Bliss, Texas, has also been reinforced with a division of US military who are actively patrolling the New Mexico and parts of the Texas borders. Juarez, the Mexican border town across from Fort Bliss, which had become a large murder city and a haven for the cartel, has been cleaned up with our forces and with cooperation with the Mexican government. Once again, citizens of both countries can enjoy and feel safe in border towns. Lastly, Fort Alamo in San Antonio, Texas, is under construction and already houses almost a division of US military forces living in temporary quarters.

All in all, my fellow Americans, four forts have been reinforced with four divisions of US military, armed and extremely dangerous, not to mention the air force, drones, and other ancillary services.

The results have been impressive, folks. Many tons of illegal drugs have been confiscated. Thousands of armaments of various types, from pistols to automatic weapons, to anti-tank weapons, to various types of IED devices, have been confiscated. Hundreds of illegals have been killed in battles against our forces, some of them very extensive battles. The "terrorists" are learning quickly that to deal with our military means death. As I stated long ago, capture is not an objective of our military in these battles. Our objective is the obliteration of the enemy, in plain words, killing and keep killing them until they cease to be a danger to our border and country. For those who actually get captured, military tribunals have been working around the clock to try, convict, and sentence the "terrorists."

We have been conducting air raids and ground raids across the border with the cooperation of the Mexican government, who have acknowledged that they needed our help in securing their side of the border. We have found and eliminated over a hundred tunnels in the above four states. We have sealed all tunnels found, and enemy personnel that were found in the tunnels were sealed in them.

Besides the terrorists' infiltration, the mass amount of illegal infiltration has also been effectively halted. Four staging areas have been established in all four southern states where the illegals are held before deportation. We have been able to deport most illegals within forty-eight hours. In addition, construction is commencing very rapidly on prison facilities next to military bases for housing illegal felons and terrorists. These prisons will be permanent. As I had stated before, illegals guilty of multiple deportations will be spending a large amount of their lives in prison.

Lastly, I issued an executive order addressing the outflow of funds from the US to other countries by illegals. To date, over a billion dollars has been collected from various sources. In addition, the fines to business entities for knowingly hiring illegals has also borne fruit. Millions of dollars in fines have been charged and are in the process of collection. Businesses are getting the message that to hire illegals is going to be very expensive.

The State Department had been diligent in curbing the various visa programs that have corrupted our economy. Student visas have been curtailed and will be virtually nonexistent by the end of the year. HBA1 visas have also been curtailed and will be eliminated by the end of the year. Temporary visas for visitation to the USA are being enforced now. All aliens overstaying their visas will be immediately jailed and deported. If guilty of any felony, such illegals will be tried as terrorists.

When I came into office, over 30 million jobs were held by noncitizens in the USA. I am happy to announce that that figure is down by 30 percent, opening up tens of millions of jobs nationwide for US citizens. Everywhere, changes are being felt. English is becoming more and more pronounced. One can actually use the telephone to call up a business and hear an English recording. Many retail advertisers are returning to English-only advertisements. Look in the classified ads, and there are decreasing numbers of ads wanting bilingual employees. The "sanctuary" cities are very visibly reviewing their policies now that federal funds have been curtailed. California, our "sanctuary" state, is, of course, whining the loudest about the new federal policies. As I stated before, the choice is simple: America or not America. Policies that do not upgrade our nation are being steadily curtailed.

It has not been easy, America. There have been many court battles so far, even injunctions against the use of forces against the terrorists. I have been threatened with impeachment. To all I say, stand in line. This country will be secured, that is my oath of office. Tomorrow, my fellow Americans, we will focus on other momentous aspects of these hundred days. Until then,

"GOD BLESS AMERICA."

DAY 100: HERE AT LAST

"And that has made all the difference." —Robert Frost

Good morning, my fellow Americans, and it is a glorious morning. It is hard to believe but today is the hundredth day of a new beginning for America. It is spring here in Washington, a clear, beautiful, sunny day and a great day to be alive in this great nation of ours. It seems like yesterday that I was giving my inaugural address to you. I remember well that day, the millions of faces—some smiling, some scowling, some sad, some happy. I hope that today, after listening to me talk about the changes in America, that there are many more happy and expectant faces than before. As you can tell from the bags of mail behind me, many of you have awakened to the possibilities of a better America and many of you are energized again. Together we can make a difference.

While this is the hundredth day, it is only the beginning of our pathway back to sanity and back to old-fashioned values. So many of us have been inundated with the progressive mantra that those values do not exist anymore. This a "new age." I am here and have been here these past three-plus months to tell the secularists not only "no," but *"hell no"*—pardon my language. Someone once said, "Extremism in the pursuit of virtue is not a sin!" To that I say amen! There has been much progress in the past three months, some of which I relayed to you all yesterday. Today I will continue with more good news for our country and more bad news for the enemies of our nation. We, America, are winning back our country, and the leftists are losing control.

First of all, the economy is showing many signs of more vibrant economic growth patterns. You may have noticed that the employment figures are completely different from when I took office. The Bureau of Labor Statistics had for many years skewed the figures so that the numbers became essentially meaningless. The new statistics more adequately reflect what has been going on in our country for the past three months. We have also published a revision going back eight years to reflect a more realistic picture of the unemployment figures over the past decade. As many of you already knew but could not prove, our government has consistently unreported employment in America. This has changed and we will start to reflect what is going on in America and not some fictitious statistics that are totally irrelevant. While the revised numbers paint a totally different picture of the past and the present and caused a great shock to all the pundits that lived in fantasy world, you will now notice definite trends to a more vibrant economy and a healthier employment picture.

Moving on, as I mentioned in my inaugural address, the key element in reinvigorating our economy is to energize the lifeblood of our economy, and that is energy. For too long the progressives have been hell-bent in destroying this lifeblood in the name of whatever. They have proposed all sorts of energy alternatives, even to the point of using crops and algae to produce oil. However, all have fallen by the wayside since the costs of production are astronomical. I remember two years ago when the prior administration forced the military to buy oil and gas made from algae. The cost was $150 a gallon, fifty times what we were paying at the pump.[258] INSANITY!

Think of this, folks: if it takes only twenty dollars to fill your gas tank and not fifty dollars, are you better off? Think also of what you can do with that extra thirty dollars a week. If your utilities cost

---

[258] Markay, Lachlan. "Report: Pentagon Paid $150 Per Gallon for Green Jet Fuel." *The Washington Free Beacon.* May 7, 2014. http://freebeacon.com/national-security/report-pentagon-paid-150-per-gallon-for-green-jet-fuel/.

fifty dollars a month instead of one hundred dollars a month, are you better off? Look at any product in the stores. What is the most egregious part of the cost of that product? Transportation. What is the prime element in transportation costs? Energy to move the product. Cheap energy is one of the greatest booms to any economy, especially to the third-world countries. Soon we will be the prime exporter of energy around the world and all will benefit.

I am pleased to announce the Keystone Pipeline has finally been approved and construction has already begun. This construction will create over thirty thousand new jobs and will create a needed boost in the economy of many states. On a related topic, Congress has passed and I have signed legislation authorizing the first water pipeline from the Mississippi River in Missouri to the West Coast, namely California. This pipeline will serve many needs, not the least of which is providing adequate water to meet the needs of California and other states in the West affected by drought conditions over the last ten years. California's huge agriculture base will benefit greatly by a steady, consistent source of water for many generations. The Mississippi River Complex has always suffered with a surfeit of water, and floods have always been a constant problem in the past. This pipeline will do much to alleviate flood conditions in the Mississippi River region. This pipeline will be financed by federal dollars and built by private enterprise. The fees from the water supplied by the pipeline will first be used to pay off the debt of the pipeline. Thereafter the pipeline will be sold to private enterprise, and the monies received will be used to pay down our national debt. Lastly, I have also signed legislation authorizing the construction of two major desalinization plants to be built in Southern and middle California. These two desaliniza- tion plants, when completed in three years, will supply hundreds of millions of gallons of water daily to both private and commercial interests, namely agriculture. Again, as with the pipeline, the fees for obtaining the water from the desalinization plants will be used to pay down the cost of construction. Afterward, the "refineries" will be sold to private enterprise. One last thought on these plants, the byproducts from this process will include a multitude of various minerals and salts, which have much commercial potential. On our website we have a page listing the various minerals, salts and such, the plants will be producing for commercial application. The gold extracts alone will increase our national reserves substantially.

Four oil and natural gas refineries are in the final approval stages from the Department of Energy. Construction should start within the next six months. Along those lines the natural gas pipeline in Alaska is in the final stages of approval. Once Congress approves the construction, Alaska will establish itself as the major oil and gas producer in the world. The economic stimulus to Alaska and the Pacific Northwest will be immense.

Last but not least, three nuclear power plants in N——, M——, and M—— are in the final approval stages. Hopefully within six months the approval process will be complete and construction of these plants will be started. In ten other states application for construction of a nuclear power plant has been filed. These plants will be a boon to the states involved as well as providing an additional source of clean and consistent energy for generations to come. As I stated earlier, our goal is to have at least one nuclear power plant in each state, supplying vital power needs for the residents of that state.

Folks, the projects mentioned above are just the start to providing millions of jobs for Americans, and those jobs will have enormous effects on the other various parts of our economy, from agriculture to housing, to transportation, to manufacturing. This office has already been in contact with a number of corporations who over the past thirty years have had their manufacturing done overseas. Many have expressed optimism on returning their manufacturing facilities back to the USA. Over the next six months I hope to announce these companies in detail. Once again, "Made in America" will be a standard for products across the board. Hopefully that slogan will also be a symbol of quality in our goods.

The next major area that has been addressed is, of course, our bloated federal government. You all have seen the current federal government budget, which is still being argued in Congress. The progressives are howling about the cuts across the board, mainly in their "social" programs. Howl as they must, I would encourage all of you to contact your state representatives in the federal government and voice your opinion for the balanced budget. Your voices will carry the day and help decide the future of our country.

This office is not just about balancing the federal budget. The examination of each of the cabinet agencies has begun and changes have already been started. The EPA, for example, is being drastically reduced. A review of their enormous amount of regulatory power is being conducted as we speak. All regulations pertaining to climate control are being discarded. As a matter of fact, every cabinet post that has involvement in the climate-control debacle is in the process of discarding all such regulations. The savings to our economy will amount to trillions over the next four years. All cabinet posts are being analyzed in depth as to their involvement in this climate control. Needless to say, all federal personnel involved with any aspect of climate control will be furloughed within thirty days. Speaking of decreases in federal personnel, almost 5 percent of federal workers in all branches of government have been furloughed. Many will think this is harsh, but as I mentioned over the last three months, many cabinet functions will now be handled by state and local governments. I would assume that many federal employees will be now be working for the state instead of the federal government.

Folks, this process of decreasing the federal leviathan will take years to fully implement. We have been on the federal government dole for so long many do or cannot imagine a world where the American people are in charge again and not the federal bureaucrats. The world will be changed, one step at a time. Along these lines I have had conferences with both houses of Congress to discuss these issues and pathways to a more vibrant nation. My relationship with Congress is not friendship, folks, and never will be. It is adversarial at best. Congress has its own agenda, but with God's help and patriots in both houses, we can arrive at legislation that will move America forward and not backward to third-world status. Representatives in Congress, as you all have observed, are finally having to work instead of using taxpayers' funds for vacations, reelections, and the like.

The next area, foreign affairs, is also having worldwide ramifications. The State Department is being reorganized as we speak to handle the new "Masters Doctrine" policies. The "spheres of influence" that have been proposed is being very well-received by our friends and, of course, not so well by our "not our friends." Treaties are being devised, and hopefully by the end of this year, some will have been presented to the Senate for approval. The nations on the NOF list are all in the process of reviewing their relations with the USA. All foreign aid to these nations has stopped. Some commitments are being continued on a pay-as-you-go basis and will be terminated by the end of the year. NOF countries have been notified of the removal of our embassies from their respective countries.

Our commitments in the Middle East are under review. Our backing of Israel has been reaffirmed and is unconditional. ISIS and other terrorist organizations are served notice that we will not be lenient in our dealings with these groups. They are vermin and will be extinguished as vermin. War is coming to them and war will be hell. They will not know the day or the hour, but they will feel our wrath. Other minor terrorists such as the Sudanese pirates will also be exterminated and their bases destroyed. Any attack on our embassies will be an attack on the USA and treated as such. Along those lines, all remaining US embassies are being reinforced with marines who are equipped to do battle with any group attacking our embassies. Support military forces are being deployed around the world with emphasis on supporting any embassy that may come under attack. Benghazi will not be repeated under my watch! We will not ask for permission from any world organization to retaliate in force. The Iranian agreement has been nullified, sanctions have been reimposed, and any evidence of nuclear enhancement for war purposes will be dealt with immediately.

Speaking of world organizations, the United Nations organization has formally been given notice to vacate the New York premises by the end of the year. Our membership in the UN will be terminated as of July 4, 2017, our Independence Day. All contributions except for medical necessities have already been terminated. Our "dues" to the UN will cease on July 4. Needless to say, the various mostly third-world countries who are on the NOF list are howling about the end of their "foreign aid." To them all I say is that it is time to grow up and be responsible for your own destinies. If you cannot, there are major countries on the NOF list — Russia, China, Iran, and Cuba — who have the resources to come to your aid. Good luck!

An essential part of the Masters Doctrine is, of course, our military and defense capabilities. I have met with the JCOS and discussed the ramification of the Masters Doctrine with them. As you have read, there have been a number of high-level generals and such who have resigned or retired over the past three months. Most, frankly, as has been reported in the media, were adherents to the progressive view of America and the military. I wish them all Godspeed! On the positive front, enlistments in the military are up by almost 15 percent from the last four years. While the role of females in the military has been drastically reduced, they are being steadily replaced by the young, educated men in our country eager to serve and make our country safe. The military benefits for enlistment have been enhanced especially along the lines of further education. I have always maintained that the military is an ideal way for a high school graduate or even college graduate to get needed job skills, save money, and mature in a way that benefits them, their families, and our nation.

Congress will be presented in the very near future the spending legislation for the revised defense budget. The figures will all be adjusted upward in terms of military personnel, ships, planes, equipment, and the like. As I mentioned, entitlements are being lowered, and defense spending is increasing. On our website is a breakdown of our military status during the Reagan years in the 1980s. Those are our immediate goals. This buildup will take some time. I am an optimistic person; I want to achieve those goals by the end of my term in office. We won WWII in four years; we can save our military in the same time.

You all may have noticed radical changes in our airport security. The transition from the TSA to the military police is almost complete. There will be less hassles for the American citizenry and more hassles for any potential enemies trying to infiltrate our country. Our military police have been actively borrowing valid inspection techniques from other countries, especially Israel, and are implementing those techniques in our airport security. Folks, we will be profiling more high-level suspects trying to enter our country and less American citizenry. Any suspicious personnel will immediately be turned away and not allowed access to our nation. Any suspected terrorist will immediately be detained and imprisoned if deemed necessary. The ninety-year-old American widow is not high on our suspect list and should never be. People from the Middle East and people from Muslim countries will be high on our suspect list. Our State Department will be examining much more closely visa applications for people coming from NOF nations. Most, frankly, will be turned down.

This last month our attention has shifted to cultural and personal issues for America. Most of these topics have been highly sensitive to the American citizenry, as witnessed by the flood of e-mail and letters pouring into the White House. The issues have been monumental, and while all are controversial, folks, you do not solve problems by running away, or ignoring them, or kicking the ball down the road and hoping that later generations will find answers. The solution and courses of action for the three minority groups—Latinos, Indians, and the blacks—are in many ways not pleasant to the people involved. Here again, "the buck stops here," as President Truman stated long ago. The Latino question is very simple in my eyes: if you are a citizen, you have the rights of a citizen; if you are not, you have no rights and will be deported back to where you came from. The illegal question, as I mentioned yesterday, is rapidly coming under control. What the progressives said could not be done is being done and we are rapidly taking back our country. Of the estimated 30 million illegals in the US, 30 percent have been deported or self-deported. Our goal within the next year is to have 90 percent of all illegals out of the USA and pushing for almost 100 percent within the following six months.

The Indian problem is actually being resolved even more rapidly. The Indian tribes have been very responsive to greater independence—financially, socially, and culturally—and hopefully by the time all federal aid is ended for the Indian tribes, self-sufficiency will not be a dream but reality. The casinos have been an outstanding source of revenue for the tribes as well as the increase in agriculture and manufacturing revenues. The Indian tribes have been applying for many of the applications for nuclear power plants in the various states. Construction of these power plants and the subsequent electrical power generation will be an immense economic boost for the Indian nations and America.

The "black" dilemma is, of course, very highly charged and emotional. I am encouraged, though, after the dust settled with my speech, that coherent minds actually started having dialogues along the lines this office presented. While initially the ideas promulgated were deemed highly inappropriate, they are getting more and more support from the black community. The Indian tribes have had over a hundred years to get used to the idea of separate but equal; the black population will need time also. Our solutions, while regarded as totally "racial" find merit among all population groups. Black leaders have called my administration totally "racist" but here again, any solution to this cultural problem will automatically be termed "racist" if presented by anyone other than a black. I always find it curious that so many on the left will name-call but never offer any viable solutions to the race issue, except of course to chastise the white race and demand more handouts. Of the three main historical eras in dealing with this race issue—slavery, segregation, and civil rights—while totally vilified, this was perhaps the most beneficial, economically, socially, and culturally. While "separate but equal" may not be the final solution, done with thought, it should lead to better race relations in the US.

The personal issues that were discussed have brought an amount of hellfire, usually from the self-interest groups who have controlled the agendas for so many years. These groups do not care about America, our values, our culture, or our heritage. They only want to tear down and destroy. Going back to values, such as God, family, roles of men and women in society, the work ethic, and valuing children again as the future of our nation, all will take time. It took fifty years to tear down much of what we had so many centuries worked to achieve, it will take many generations to rebuild. How do we, how does any nation rebuild? One step at a time. As mentioned so often in these past three months, we need to find God again and get right with the Lord. To anyone who has read the Bible, both Old and New Testaments, God did not reject the Jewish people, they rejected Him. The price they have paid in the last two thousand years is horrific.

After God, family issues are the paramount item on the personal side. I am happy to announce that Planned Parenthood, or PP, has been totally defunded from any federal monies. Also, the Justice Department has filed legal action against the heads of PP on various issues; among them, hopefully, murder will be added. Legal action has already begun in all states against doctors affiliated with PP in the illegal aspects of committing abortions and the distribution of the fetal remains. Some of the more egregious issues should result in the doctors losing their licenses and hopefully facing felony charges regarding their abortive practices.

Folks, PP did not arise out of thin air. We as a nation denied our heritage and especially our children and allowed the travesty of abortion to thrive in a supposedly "God-oriented" society. The values, or lack thereof, are finally being addressed across America, in our churches, our social gatherings, and our schools. Part of the answers, after God, is for both men and women needing to reevaluate their roles for themselves, their families, their children, and our society, our American culture. I do not wish to repeat my earlier speeches, but both sexes require the courage to evaluate who and what roles they are meant to play. For example, along those lines, men have to learn again what it is to be a "man" and not a pseudo male. Tattoos, piercings, vulgarity, and femininity do not make a man. The virtues of integrity, honesty, honor, duty, pride, and a work ethic are what make a man a man and a productive member of society. One of the greatest roles for a man is under the classification of "father." Men have to relearn what it is to be a father and be the head of a family. One does not learn that in a bar, smoking pot, or being a profligate person with no responsibility. One learns that by growing up and doing the right thing at the right time. Hopefully remembering the lessons from their fathers, or if not, learning about great men in the past. Remember, men, no matter what the women say, they want men to be men, not a pseudo male, not a gay male, not a male who has his "feminine" side.

Women, especially, need to find themselves. Society has contributed to the loss of womanhood in America and unless women find the right answers, we are doomed as a society. Here again it is gratifying to see many Christian churches again espousing family values, children, and the work ethic. This will be a long road. Generations of women have grown and forgotten what God and, yes, biology decreed for them. To bring forth life into this world is perhaps God's greatest gift to women and humankind. There is no other goal in life that can come close to the significance of children.

All in all, my fellow Americans, it has been a tumultuous three months. Our nation is confronting many issues on all fronts, local, state, and federal. More importantly, the fires of change are happening in our homes, our schools, our work settings, and our churches. I am proud of all of you Americans who are voicing your opinions in the media and in the social settings. Yes, many on the left, the glorious progressives, have been and will continue to howl about the "dastardly deeds" being done. The conservative side has been called every name in the book. The fight to take back our country is growing every day and with the fight, our country is finding its heritage again. Oh, by the way, another piece of good news—the Justice Department is preparing indictments against a number of former congressional representatives for malfeasance when in office. Already millions of dollars have been repaid by various congressional personnel who were overly indulgent in their spending of the taxpayers' monies.

Where do we go from here? Well, folks, as you can surmise, the work is just beginning. Congress is inundated with probably four years of legislation generated in the last hundred days. The representatives of Congress at times seem as if in a daze, but that is good. You, the people, need to keep up the pressure. Organize small groups, visit your representatives in Washington, force them to commit to a new restored America, force them to adhere to the principles that founded our country and not some "politically correct" agenda devised by people who hate America and will always hate America. More importantly, remind your representatives that if they do not follow the correct paths to restoring America, they will be very firmly voted out of office. Americans, you do not need to fear your politicians, they need to fear *you*.

This office will continue the battle for God and country. So many positive aspects are arising on the horizon, just a few of which were addressed yesterday and today. I look forward to announcing the Constitutional Convention hopefully this fall. That convention will be the voice of the people being heard at last. The war against Satan and the progressive left will continue, possibly beyond our lifetimes. The battle between good and evil has been ongoing since the beginning of time. For us, to restore what was will be a great victory and achievement. I close now to continue the tasks you elected me to do. With God's help and your encouragement, this administration will continue the great work. So to all of you, God's blessing and GOD BLESS AMERICA! Together, we can change the world!

THE END . . . or maybe just the beginning

Our Father, Who art in heaven, Hallowed be Thy Name, Thy Kingdom come, Thy Will be done on earth as it is in heaven. Give us this day our daily bread and forgive us our trespasses as we forgive those who Trespass against us. Lead us not into temptation but deliver us from evil. Amen.

APPENDIX

A. Biblical Quotes on the Sanctity of Marriage

- "Marriage should be honored by all, and the marriage bed kept pure, for God will judge the adulterer and all the sexually immoral" (Hebrews 13:4–7, NIV).

- "But at the beginning of creation, God 'made them male and female.' For this reason, a man will leave his father and mother and be united to his wife, and the two will become one flesh. So they no longer will be two but one flesh. Therefore, what God has joined together, let no one separate" (Mark 10:6–9, NIV).

- "Then the Lord God made a woman from the rib He had taken out of the man, and He brought her to the man. The man said, 'This is bone of my bone and flesh of my flesh, she shall be called "woman" for she was taken out of man.' That is why a man leaves his father and mother and is united to his wife, and they become one flesh" (Genesis 2:22–24, NIV).

- "He who finds a wife finds what is good and receives favor from the Lord" (Proverbs 18:22, NIV).

- "Houses and wealth are inherited from parents, but a prudent wife is from the LORD" (Proverbs 19:14, NIV).

- "A wife of noble character who can find? She is worth far more than rubies" (Proverbs 31:10, NIV).

- "But since sexual immorality is occurring, each man should have sexual relations with his own wife and each woman with her own husband. The husband should fulfill his marital duty to his wife, and likewise the wife to her husband. The wife does not have authority over her own body but yields to her husband. In the same way, the husband does not have authority over his own body but yields it to his wife" (1 Corinthians 7:2–4, NIV).

- "Wives, submit yourselves to your husbands, as is fitting in the Lord. Husbands, love your wives and do not be harsh with them" (Colossians 3:18–19, NIV).

B. Biblical Quotes on Homosexuality

- "So God created man in His own Image, in the image of God He Created him; male and female He created them" (Genesis 1:27, ESV).
- "You shall not lie with a male as with a woman; it is an abomination" (Leviticus 18:22, ESV).
- "If a man lies with a male as with a woman, both of them have committed an abomination" (Leviticus 20:13, ESV).
- "Or do you not know that the unrighteous will not inherit the kingdom of God? Do not be deceived: neither the sexually immoral, nor idolaters, nor adulterers, not men who practice homosexuality nor thieves, nor the greedy, nor drunkards, nor revilers, nor swindlers will inherit the kingdom of God. And such were some of you" (1 Corinthians 6:9–11, ESV).
- "But because of the temptation to sexual immorality, each man should have his own wife and each woman her own husband" (1 Corinthians 7:2, ESV).
- "For this reason God gave them up to dishonorable passions. For their women exchanged natural relations for those that are contrary to nature; and the men likewise gave up natural relations with women and were consumed with passion for one another; men committing shameless acts with men and receiving in themselves the due penalty for their error. And since they did not see fit to acknowledge God, God gave them up to the debased mind to do what ought not to be done" (Romans 1:26–28, ESV).
- "The sexually immoral, men who practice homosexuality, enslavers, liars, perjurers, and whatever else is contrary to sound doctrine . . ." (Timothy 1:10, ESV).
- "Just as Sodom and Gomorrah and the surrounding cities, which likewise indulged in sexual immorality and pursued unnatural desire, serve as an example by undergoing a punishment of eternal fire" (Jude 1:7, ESV).

C. Civil Rights Legislation in the Past Fifty Years

- Civil Rights Act of 1957 (PL 85–315)
  - Created the six-member Commission on Civil Rights and established the Civil Rights Division in the US Department of Justice. Authorized the US Attorney General to seek court injunctions against deprivation and obstruction of voting rights by state officials. Passed by the 85th Congress (1957–1959) as HR 6127.
- Civil Rights Act of 1960 (PL 86–449)
  - Expanded the enforcement powers of the Civil Rights Act of 1957 and introduced criminal penalties for obstructing the implementation of federal court orders. Extended the Civil Rights Commission for two years. Required that voting and registration records for federal elections be preserved. Passed by the 86th Congress (1959–1961) as HR 8601.
- Civil Rights Act of 1964 (PL 88–352)
  - Prohibited discrimination in public accommodations, facilities, and schools. Outlawed discrimination in federally funded projects. Created the Equal Employment Opportunity Commission to monitor employment discrimination in public and private sectors. Provided additional capacities to enforce voting rights. Extended the Civil Rights Commission for four years. Passed by the 88th Congress (1963–1965) as HR 7152.
- Voting Rights Act of 1965 (PL 89–110)
  - Suspended the use of literacy tests and voter disqualification devices for five years. Authorized the use of federal examiners to supervise voter registration in states that used tests or in which less than half the voting-eligible residents registered or voted. Directed the US Attorney General to institute proceedings against use of poll taxes. Provided criminal penalties for individuals who violated the act. Passed by the 89th Congress (1965–1967) as S 1564.
- Civil Rights Act of 1968 (Fair Housing Act) (PL 90–284)
  - Prohibited discrimination in the sale or rental of approximately 80 percent of the housing in the US. Prohibited state governments and Native-American tribal governments from violating the constitutional rights of Native Americans. Passed by the 90th Congress (1967–1969) as HR 2518.

- Voting Rights Act Amendments of 1970 (PL 91–255)
  - Extended the provisions of the Voting Rights Act of 1965 for five years. Made the act applicable to areas where less than 50 percent of the eligible voting age population was registered as of November 1968. Passed by the 91st Congress (1969–1971) as HR 4249.
- Voting Rights Act Amendments of 1975 (PL 94–73)
  - Extended the provisions of the Voting Rights Act of 1965 for seven years. Established coverage for other minority groups including Native Americans, Hispanic Americans, and Asian Americans. Permanently banned literacy tests. Passed by the 94th Congress (1975–1977) as HR 6219.
- Voting Rights Act Amendments of 1982 (PL 97–205)
  - Extended for twenty-five years the provisions of the Voting Rights Act of 1965. Allowed jurisdictions that could provide evidence of maintaining a clean voting rights record for at least ten years, to avoid preclearance coverage (the requirement of federal approval of any change to local or state voting laws). Provided for aid and instruction to disabled or illiterate voters. Provided for bilingual election materials in jurisdictions with large minority populations. Passed by the 97th Congress (1981–1983) as HR 3112.
- Civil Rights Restoration Act of 1987 (PL 100–259)
  - Established that antidiscrimination laws are applicable to an entire organization if any part of the organization receives federal funds. Passed by the 100th Congress (1987–1989) as S 557.
- Fair Housing Act Amendments of 1988 (PL 100–430)
  - Strengthened the powers of enforcement granted to the Housing and Urban Development Department in the 1968 Fair Housing Act. Passed by the 100th Congress (1987–1989) as HR 1158.
- Civil Rights Act of 1991 (PL 102–166)
  - Reversed nine US Supreme Court decisions (rendered between 1986 and 1991) that had raised the bar for workers who alleged job discrimination. Provided for plaintiffs to receive monetary damages in cases of harassment or discrimination based on sex, religion, or disability. Passed by the 102nd Congress (1991–1993) as S 1745.

APPENDIX

- Voting Rights Act of 2006 (PL 109–478)
  - o Extended the provisions of the Voting Rights Act of 1965 for twenty-five years. Extended the bilingual election requirements through August 5, 2032. Directed the US Comptroller General to study and report to Congress on the implementation, effectiveness, and efficiency of bilingual voting materials requirements. Passed by the 109th Congress (2005–2007) as HR 9.

D. Patriotic Songs

"You're a Grand Old Flag"

> You're a grand old flag,
> You're a high flying flag
> And forever in peace may you wave.
> You're the emblem of
> The land I love.
> The home of the free and the brave.
> Ev'ry heart beats true
> 'neath the Red, White, and Blue,
> Where there's never a boast or brag.
> Should auld acquaintance be forgot,
> Keep your eye on the grand old flag.

"God Bless America"

> God Bless America, land that I love
> Stand beside her and guide her
> Through the night with the light from above
> From the mountains to the prairies
> To the oceans white with foam
> God bless America, my home sweet home
> From the mountains to the prairies
> To the oceans white with foam
> God bless America, my home sweet home
> God bless America, my home sweet home

"America the Beautiful"

> Oh, beautiful for spacious skies,
> For amber waves of grain,
> For purple mountain majesties
> Above the fruited plain!
> America! America! God shed His grace on thee,
> And crown they good with brotherhood
> From sea to shining sea!
> beautiful for pilgrim feet,
> Who stern impassion'd stress
> A thoroughfare for freedom beat
> Across the wilderness!
> America! America! God mend thine ev'ry flaw,

Confirm thy soul in self-control,
Thy liberty in law!
beautiful for heroes proved in liberating strife,
Who more than self their country loved,
And mercy more than life!
America! America! May God thy gold refine
Till all success be nobleness,
And ev'ry gain divine!
beautiful for patriot dream
That sees beyond the years
Thine alabaster cities gleam,
Undimmed by human tears!
America! America! God shed His grace on thee,
And crown thy good with brotherhood
From sea to shining sea!

"The Star-Spangled Banner"
Oh, say can you see by the dawn's early light
What so proudly we halled at the twilight's last gleaming?
Whose broad stripes and bright stars through the perilous
fight,
O'er the ramparts we watched were so gallantly streaming?
And the rocket's red glare, the bombs bursting in air,
Gave proof through the night that our flag was still there.
Oh, say does that star-spangled banner yet wave
O'er the land of the free and the home of the brave?

FOR MORE INFORMATION:

www.WH2017.org